Monetary Policy and Economic Activity in West Germany

Monetary Policy and Economic Activity in West Germany

compiled by

S. F. Frowen A. S. Courakis M. H. Miller

A HALSTED PRESS BOOK

John Wiley & Sons
New York

First published by Surrey University Press
450 Edgware Road, London W2 1EG

Published in the U.S.A.
by Halsted Press, a Division
of John Wiley & Sons Inc.
New York

First published 1977

Library of Congress Cataloging in Publication Data
Main entry under title:

Monetary Policy and Economic Activity in West Germany.
  "A Halsted Press book."
  Bibliography: p. 251
  Includes index.
  1. Monetary policy—Germany, West—Addresses, essays,
lectures. 2. Germany, West—Economic conditions—
Addresses, essays, lectures. I. Frowen, Stephen.
II. Courakis, A. S.   III. Miller, Marcus H.
HG999.5.M67 1977   332.4'943   77–2403
ISBN 0–470–99131–3

Printed in Great Britain by Butler & Tanner, Ltd
Frome and London

Contents

List of Contributors

ARESTIS, Philip, Thames Polytechnic

BEENSTOCK, Michael, H.M. Treasury

BULL, Peter A., Bank of England

COURAKIS, Anthony S., Brasenose College, University of Oxford

FISHER, Gordon R., Queen's University, Kingston

FROWEN, Stephen F., University of Surrey

GAAB, Werner, University of Mannheim

HENNINGS, Klaus H., University of Hanover

KÖNIG, Heinz, University of Mannheim

LÄUFER, Nikolaus K. A., University of Constance

McMAHON Patrick C., University of Birmingham

MILLER, Marcus H., University of Manchester

NEUMANN, Manfred J. M., Free University of Berlin

PARKIN, Michael J., University of Western Ontario

SCHLESINGER, Helmut, Member of the Directorate, Deutsche Bundesbank

SCHLIEPER, Ulrich, University of Göttingen

SIEBKE, Juergen, University of Essen

WILLMS, Manfred, University of Kiel

WOLTERS, Jürgen, University of Mannheim

Editors' Introduction

In common with other Western economies in the post-war period the Federal Republic of Germany has pursued the goals of high and steady growth, price stability, and full employment. From the late 1950s till the recent world depression starting in 1974, real GNP in West Germany rose at an average rate of 5% per annum, industrial production by 6% per annum, unemployment was lower than in any Western economy and so indeed was the rate of increase in prices, while performance in the foreign sector resulted in considerable appreciation in the external value of the Deutsche Mark. Of course experience varied considerably over this period. Indeed, as the table and charts below reveal, fluctuations in demand and production, as marked in amplitude as those recorded since 1974, were not unknown. But such fluctuations seem to have been dealt with in ways that avoided the creation of imbalances that beset some other economies such as the U.K. and Holland[1].

How much credit for this is due to policy is not easily determined. Certainly policy has on occasions much to answer for the magnitude of the deviations recorded. However, the high priority accorded to the objective of price stability and, until recently, the relative unimportance of fiscal policy as a tool for demand management, must be noted as characteristics that distinguish West Germany from other industrialized countries. Furthermore the independence afforded to the central monetary authority implied a degree of freedom in the monetary sphere conducive to the pursuit of their objectives, while constraints imposed on central, regional and local government budgetary actions, since 1967, have contributed in this direction.

Despite the importance accorded to monetary policy in the Federal Republic and the success it is widely believed to have had, the evidence provided by empirical studies on the behaviour of the authorities and on the responses of the economy to monetary factors, is nowhere available in convenient form. A volume that provides an insight into the conduct of policy and the responses of economic units thus seemed not only worthwhile, but necessary.

In examining various aspects of German experience, the volume begins with a review, by *Helmut Schlesinger*, of some recent developments in West German monetary policy. Focusing on the shift of policy in the spring of

A*

Table 1. *Key indicators: an international comparison*

	1960	1	2	3	4	5	6	7	8	9	1970	1	2	3	4	5
Industrial production (percentage change)																
Belgium	7·5	5·5	6·0	7·5	7·0	2·0	2·0	1·5	5·5	10·0	3·0	3·0	6·0	6·5	3·5	—10·0
F.R.G.	11·5	6·0	4·5	3·5	8·5	5·5	1·5	—2·0	12·0	13·0	6·0	6·0	4·0	7·0	—1·0	—7·0
France	9·5	5·5	6·0	4·5	7·5	1·5	7·0	2·5	5·0	10·5	5·5	6·0	5·5	7·0	2·5	—7·0
Italy	15·5	11·0	9·5	9·0	1·0	4·5	11·5	8·5	6·5	4·0	6·5	—2·5	3·0	10·0	4·5	—10·0
Netherlands	10	3·5	5·5	5·5	10·0	5·5	6·0	5·0	9·0	11·0	8·5	6·0	4·5	6·5	2·5	—5·0
U.K.	7·0	0·5	1·0	4·0	7·0	3·0	2·0	0·0	5·5	3·5	0·5	0·0	2·5	8·0	—3·0	—4·5
U.S.	3·0	1·0	8·0	5·0	6·5	8·5	9·0	1·0	7·0	4·5	—3·5	0·0	8·0	9·0	—0·5	—9·0
Unemployment ratio (in per cent of total employees)																
Belgium	4·4	3·4	2·6	2·1	1·7	1·9	2·2	2·9	3·5	2·9	2·4	2·3	2·8	2·9	3·3	5·5
F.R.G.	1·3	0·9	0·7	0·9	0·8	0·7	0·7	2·1	1·5	0·8	0·7	0·8	1·1	1·3	2·7	4·9
France	1·0	0·8	0·7	0·7	0·7	0·9	0·9	1·3	1·6	1·4	1·6	2·0	2·2	2·2	2·7	4·6
Italy	4·3	3·7	3·2	2·5	2·7	3·6	3·9	3·5	3·5	3·4	3·1	3·2	3·7	3·5	2·9	3·3
Netherlands	1·5	1·0	0·9	0·9	0·8	0·9	1·2	2·4	2·2	1·7	1·4	1·8	2·9	2·9	3·5	5·0
U.K.	1·5	1·3	1·8	2·2	1·6	1·3	1·4	2·2	2·3	2·3	2·5	3·3	3·6	2·6	2·5	3·9
U.S.	5·5	6·7	5·5	5·7	5·2	4·5	3·8	3·8	3·6	3·5	4·9	5·9	5·6	4·9	5·6	8·5
Hourly earnings in industry (percentage change)																
Belgium	4·0	3·5	7·5	8·5	11·0	9·5	10·5	7·0	5·0	7·0	12·5	12·0	14·5	16·5	21·0	20·0
F.R.G.	10·0	11·0	12·0	7·0	8·5	9·5	7·5	4·0	4·5	9·0	13·5	11·0	9·0	10·5	10·0	8·0
France	8·0	10·0	9·5	9·0	7·0	6·5	6·0	7·0	10·5	9·0	12·0	12·0	12·0	13·5	19·0	20·5
Italy	3·0	4·0	8·0	10·5	14·5	8·5	3·0	4·0	3·5	6·5	18·0	10·5	8·5	20·5	25·0	27·5
Netherlands	9·0	6·5	9·0	8·0	16·0	10·0	10·0	6·5	7·5	9·5	11·0	11·5	12·5	13·0	17·5	13·5
U.K.	7·5	7·0	4·5	4·0	6·5	8·5	8·0	4·0	7·5	8·0	14·0	13·5	12·0	12·0	20·0	27·0
U.S.	3·0	2·5	3·0	3·0	3·0	3·0	4·0	4·0	6·5	6·0	5·5	6·5	6·5	7·0	8·0	9·0
Cost of living (percentage change)																
Belgium	0·5	1·0	1·5	2·0	4·0	4·0	4·0	3·0	2·5	4·0	4·0	4·5	5·5	7·0	12·5	13·0
F.R.G.	1·5	2·5	3·0	3·0	2·5	3·5	3·5	1·5	1·5	2·0	3·5	5·5	5·5	7·0	7·0	6·0
France	3·5	3·5	5·0	5·0	3·5	2·5	2·5	2·5	4·5	6·5	5·0	5·5	6·0	7·5	13·5	11·5
Italy	2·5	2·0	4·5	7·5	6·0	4·5	2·5	3·0	1·5	1·5	5·0	5·0	5·5	10·5	19·5	17·0
Netherlands	2·5	1·0	2·5	4·0	5·5	4·0	6·0	3·5	4·0	7·5	3·5	7·5	8·0	8·0	9·5	10·0
U.K.	1·0	3·5	4·5	2·0	3·5	4·5	4·0	2·5	4·5	5·5	6·5	9·5	7·0	9·0	16·0	24·0
U.S.	1·5	1·0	3·0	1·0	1·5	1·5	3·0	3·0	4·0	5·5	6·0	4·5	3·5	6·0	11·0	9·0

Source: De Nederlandsche Bank N.V., Annual Reports

x

Chart 1. *Indicators of industrial activity*: demand*

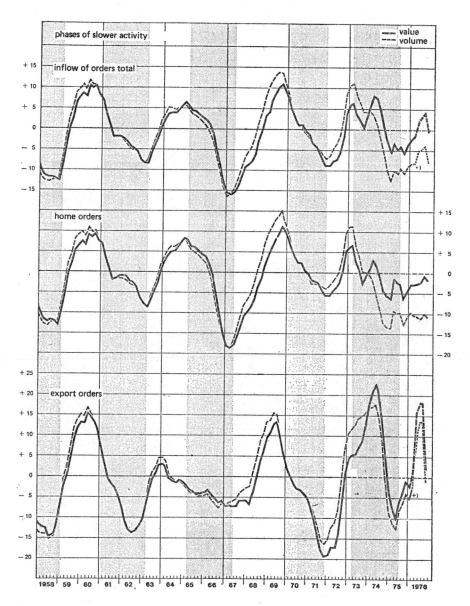

phases of slower activity

value
volume

inflow of orders total

home orders

export orders

1958 59 60 61 62 63 64 65 66 67 68 69 70 71 72 73 74 75 1976

* Percentage deviation from trend of two monthly seasonally adjusted data—moving 3-period averages.
Source: Statistical Supplement to the Monthly Reports of the Deutsche Bundesbank.

Chart 2. *Indicators of industrial activity: production, costs and prices**

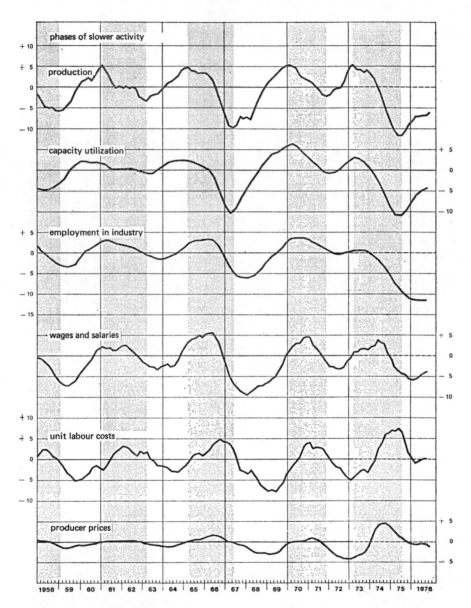

* Percentage deviation from trend of two monthly seasonally adjusted data—
moving 3-period averages.
Source: Statistical Supplement to the Monthly Reports of the Deutsche Bundesbank.

1973 (from emphasis on bank holdings of free liquid reserves to the stock of Central Bank money as the indicator of monetary policy) he outlines the main features of Central Bank policy and of policy instruments in the new environment and concludes that, given appropriate insulation from external disturbances, these instruments are sufficient to ensure monetary control.

For a longer period (1960–76), an attempt towards a unified account is presented, in the second chapter, of policy objectives, of the conception through which policy operates, and of the instruments of policy upon which the authorities have relied and continue to rely. Bank free liquidity as the main focus for policy for most of the period under review is emphasized, while the conceptual bases of the definition of Central Bank money are questioned. Despite these criticisms the stock of Central Bank money, for the period 1960–76, is shown to bear a relationship to real income and the price level in accord with Bundesbank claims, a feature that contrasts sharply with estimates derived for other monetary aggregates. On the other hand, in contrast to the popular view that, since the turn of the decade, free liquid reserves have ceased to provide reliable information regarding future developments, it is argued that the free liquid reserves to deposits ratio continues to comprise a leading indicator no less reliable than that on which the free liquid reserves doctrine was founded. It is suggested, however, that free liquid reserves and the stock of Central Bank money should not be regarded as alternatives since their relative behaviour embodies information that neither of them in isolation nor any other single variable index secures.

An appraisal of alternative indicators, and in particular of the monetary base, narrow and broad money, bank credit, free liquid reserves and the calculated credit maximum, is presented by *Manfred Willms*. In the Brunner-Meltzer tradition[2], he describes the need for indicators on the basis of which past and current policy actions can be interpreted, the criteria for choosing between possible alternative indicators and the relative merits of the above indicators in the context of the West German Monetary System. On *a priori* grounds, Professor Willms concludes that the money stock narrowly defined ought to be regarded as the 'best' indicator. However, some qualifications to this analysis are raised by *Peter Bull* and, contrary to *a priori* conceptions, the empirical findings suggest that no unequivocal verdict as to the best policy indicator for Germany can be given.

Also following Brunner and Meltzer[3] *Manfred Neumann* examines the main determinants of the money supply process in the Federal Republic of Germany. To this end the credit market theory of the money supply is employed as the framework within which to order the information pertinent to the behaviour of the authorities, the banks and the public. Manfred Neumann then provides an exhaustive examination of the behaviour of the various determinants of the money stock both for the period 1959–72 as a whole, and for various subperiods. In so doing he relies on two variants of the general framework employed namely, the *adjusted multiplier approach*, (where bank borrowing from the Bundesbank, acquisition of short-term foreign assets by banks and the demand of foreigners for German deposit liabilities appear in ratio form in the multiplier) and the *extended multiplier approach* (where these three items appear as source components of the monetary base). The results reveal the superiority of the extended base and also point to the conclusion that the Bundesbank can control the monetary base by appropriate variation in such components of the base as are under its direct control. Furthermore, estimates of simple money supply functions suggest that control of the base ensures control of the money supply narrowly defined.

As pointed out in the comment on Neumann's chapter, however, an argument can be made for yet another definition of the monetary base. Granted the Bundesbank's conception of policy over the period under review the relevant monetary base, it is claimed, should comprise not only high-powered money but also bank holdings of other assets included in banks' free liquid reserves. In the circumstances, it is argued, the regularities observed between the extended monetary base and the money stock are a manifestation of the endogenous nature of the former, while a recommendation to control the stock of high-powered money must derive from evidence that during the period examined there has been a stable relationship between the money stock and this 'super extended monetary base'.

A relationship between the money stock and the 'super extended monetary base' was, subsequent to this comment, derived by *Stephen Frowen* and *Philip Arestis* in their study of demand and supply of money functions. The results suggest a predictable relationship between the narrow money stock and the monetary base so defined. The money supply is also found to depend significantly on the discount rate and on the money market rate on three-month loans. In the case of demand for money functions the results, from both single equation estimates and from a three equation model employed in attempting to avoid simultaneous equation bias, confirm earlier findings to the effect that the demand for money is a function of income and interest rates, with the short rate being relatively more important than the long rate.

The basic model employed by Frowen and Arestis to describe the demand for money is that of Feige, and Laidler and Parkin[4]. As pointed out in the comment to the Frowen and Arestis paper, this approach had not satisfactorily determined the source of lags in the demand for money in the case of the U.K. Furthermore attention is drawn to the implications of including prices as an independent variable in the demand for money function, a course of action followed by Frowen and Arestis in one variant of their model, and to the omission of some measure of wealth from that function.

Some eighty years ago Irving Fisher argued that when inflation is anticipated nominal interest rates would rise in response to such expectations. This view, also expressed by Alfred Marshall in his evidence before the Gold and Silver Commission of 1886[5], was rejected by Keynes on the grounds that, since bonds and money are both assets denominated in money terms, neither of them can be a hedge against inflation and hence neither can their relative value change as a result of a belief that prices would rise[6]. Examining the empirical evidence regarding the Fisher effect *Juergen Siebke* presents some estimates of the impact of past changes in the price level on the nominal long-term rate in the Federal Republic of Germany. In line with the findings of similar research undertaken for the United States, Holland and other countries[7], the results suggest a positive and significant effect of inflation on the long-term rate of interest while also emphasizing the importance of other factors. However, the precise framework of analysis adopted is challenged by *Michael Parkin* who questions the implications of certain assumptions made by Siebke, drawing attention to some econometric problems, and suggesting the need for further study on formation of expectations.

In the following chapter *Heinz König*, *Werner Gaab* and *Jürgen Wolters* present their nineteen equation structural econometric model of the financial sector of the Federal Republic. The paper begins with a brief description of the structural equations and definition of the variables and a discussion of certain theoretical propositions pertinent to financial model building. In the latter context the importance of certain *a priori* constraints is, in line with the Tobin–Brainard analysis[8], emphasized while attention is drawn to certain practical limitations in imposing all prior desirable constraints. To test the validity of their model the authors perform deterministic and stochastic simulations over the sample period, using actual values of lagged endogenous variables.

The absence of a real sector to complement this financial model, its limitations and the pitfalls to which such a partial analysis may give rise are pursued in the comment by *Gordon Fisher*. He draws attention to the problem inherent in the use of permanent income as a *proxy for wealth*, to the restrictions imposed on the researchers' ability to capture certain aspects of behaviour, to the desirability of *imposing and testing behavioural* restrictions, and to the absence of anticipations regarding expected inflation and exchange rates from the model (issues taken up in other chapters in this volume).

Although fiscal policy was, as mentioned earlier, a means much less relied upon for aggregate demand management than monetary policy, measurement of the efficacy of monetary policy must take account of variations in the stance of fiscal policy. *Nikolaus Läufer* uses a variant of the Andersen–

Jordan procedure to examine the responses of aggregate demand, as measured by nominal GNP, to fiscal and monetary stimuli. Unlike studies for the U.S. and previous studies for Germany[9], a variable designed to measure the impact of 'foreign impulses' (which are obviously of much greater importance for the Federal Republic than for the U.S.), is introduced in addition to monetary and fiscal variables. Läufer experiments with a variety of lags and concludes that, in the absence of more precise information about the lag space to be considered, the Andersen and Jordan framework fails to yield firm conclusions with regard to Germany. Indeed if lags are assumed to be no longer than two and a half years the effects of fiscal policy appear to be equally strong and at the same time faster and more predictable than those of monetary policy. Yet this conclusion is called into doubt by *Klaus Hennings* who points to the possible misspecification of the equations presented by Läufer, and as an example reviews the evidence relating to the relationship between exports and GNP, while also reminding the reader of the need to specify explicitly the structural model from which the equations are derived.

Another aspect of the foreign sector, namely capital flows, is the subject of *Michael Beenstock's* paper. On the assumption that international capital movements depend on uncertainty about future exchange rates and the investors' aversion to risk, a model of capital movement is developed and estimates are derived for the covered interest elasticity of short-term arbitrage flows and the response of the supply of forward cover. Surprisingly, his estimates suggest low values for these parameters, and he concludes that the West German monetary authorities should therefore be deemed as enjoying considerable independence in setting short-term interest rates. Estimates for long-term capital flows, on the other hand, reveal high capital mobility. It is argued in the comment to Beenstock's paper that this contrast ought to be attributed to the inadequacy of the model employed when measuring the response of highly mobile short-term capital moving at virtually zero uncovered differentials in response to the availability of cover at forward rates determined by uncovered interest differentials. Furthermore, attention is drawn to the consistency of previous estimates for short-term capital flows, derived by Porter[10], with what Beenstock finds in respect of long-term capital.

The impact of aggregate demand on the Balance of Payments is examined by *Ulrich Schlieper* and *Patrick McMahon*. After a theoretical discussion of the role of 'spillover' effects they present some preliminary estimates for both the Federal Republic and the United Kingdom. They find that in both countries the multiplier is smaller in boom than in recession periods. However, for Germany the results for boom periods are rather poor, a feature that may, it is suggested, relate to the fact that in such periods this economy was operating at full capacity, so that output is more likely to be determined by capacity constraints rather than aggregate demand pressures. They also report the outcome of pooling the data and using dummy variables to improve the estimates of these multipliers.

Most of the papers in this volume were originally presented to the Surrey Conference on West German Monetary Developments arranged jointly by Stephen Frowen of the Department of Economics, University of Surrey, and the Money Study Group with the support of the Goethe Institute, London. All papers were invited by Stephen Frowen who also offered useful suggestions in the editing of this volume. Finally thanks are due to Ian Bond for compiling the subject index.

Anthony S. Courakis
Marcus H. Miller

Footnotes

1. See for example, Bacon, R & Eltis, W., *Britain's Economic Problem: Too Few Producers*, Macmillan, 1976; and den Dunnen, E., 'Dutch Ecomomic and Monetary Problems in the Seventies', in Courakis, A. S. (ed.), *Inflation, Depression and Economic Policy in the West: Lessons from the 1970's*, Basil Blackwell, 1977.
2. Brunner, K. & Meltzer, A. H., 'The Meaning of Monetary Indicators', in Horwich, G. (ed.), *Monetary Process and Policy: A Symposium*, Irwin, 1967; Brunner, K. & Meltzer, A. H., 'The Nature of the Policy Problem', in Brunner, K. (ed.), *Targets and Indicators of Monetary Policy*, Chandler, 1969; and Saving, T. R., 'Monetary Policy: Targets and Indicators', *Journal of Political Economy*, **75**, Supplement, Aug., 1967, pp. 446–56.
3. See Brunner, K. & Meltzer, A. H., 'Liquidity Traps for Money, Credit and Interest Rates', *Journal of Political Economy*, **76**, 1968; also Brunner, K. & Meltzer, A. H., 'A Credit Market Theory of the Money Supply', in *Essays in Honour of Marco Fanno*, Padova, 1966, pp. 151–76.
4. Feige, E. L., 'Expectations and Adjustments in the Monetary Sector', *American Economic Review*, **57**, Papers and Proceedings, May, 1967, pp. 462–73; Laidler, D. & Parkin, J. M., 'The Demand for Money in the United Kingdom, 1955–1967: Preliminary Estimates', *The Manchester School*, Vol. 38, Sept., 1970, pp. 187–208, reprinted in revised form in Johnson, H. G. and Associates (ed.), *Readings in British Monetary Economics*, Clarendon Press, 1972.
5. See Sir Roy Harrod's discussion of M. Friedman's 'Monetary Theory of Nominal Income', in Clayton, G., Gilbert, J. C. & Sedgwick, R. (ed.), *Monetary Theory and Policy in the 1970's*, Oxford University Press, 1971.
6. See Keynes, J. M., *General Theory of Employment, Interest and Money*, Macmillan, 1936, pp. 136 *et seq.*
7. See, for example, Yohe, W. P. & Karnosky, A. S., 'Interest Rates and Price Level Changes 1952–1969, *St Louis Review*, Dec., 1969, pp. 18–38; Gibson, W. E., 'Interest Rates and Inflationary Expectations: New Evidence', *American Economic Review*, Dec., 1972, pp. 854–65; Fase, M. M. G., 'Bond Yields and Expected Inflation: A Quantitative Analysis of Dutch Experience', *Economic and Quarterly Review*, Amsterdam–Rotterdam Bank, N.V., Sept., 1972; Fase, M. M. G. & van Nieuwerk, M., 'Anticipated Inflation and Interest Rates in an Open Economy: A Study of the Gibson Paradox for the Netherlands', in Masera, F., Fazio, A. and Padoa-Schioppa, T. (eds.), *Econometric Research in European Central Banks*, Banca d'Italia, 1975.

8. See Tobin, J. & Brainard, W., 'Pitfall in Financial Model Building', *American Economic Review*, **58**, Papers and Proceedings, May, 1968.

9. See, for example, Keran, M. W., 'Monetary and Fiscal Influence on Economic Activity: The Foreign Experience', *St Louis Review*, Feb., 1970, and 'Selecting a Monetary Indicator: Evidence for the U.S. and other Developed Countries', *St Louis Review*, Sept., 1970.

10. Porter, M. G., 'Capital Flows as an Offset to Monetary Policy: The German Experience', *International Monetary Fund Staff Papers*, 1972.

1

Recent Developments in West German Monetary Policy

HELMUT SCHLESINGER

Policy Changes of March, 1973

The rediscovery of money and revival of interest in monetary theory has given stimulus for further thought on practical monetary policy also. But monetary policy is not made in the vacuum of econometric models with their manifold premises and monetary analysis to be useful must include in its calculations the traditional structures and behaviour patterns of its target groups. If the Central Bank finds that there are sustained changes in the institutional peculiarities on which its decisions have hitherto been based, it is obliged to rethink its previous ideas as well and to adapt itself to the changed position if it is not to lose control over monetary expansion. Efficient monetary policy must not stick to traditional positions; it must be sensitive to the changing 'environmental conditions'.

The policy pursued by the Bundesbank since March, 1973, is a good example of how a change in the external framework and in behaviour patterns influences monetary policy. Until a few years ago the Bundesbank's credit policy decisions were principally oriented towards the 'free liquid reserves' of the banks. This term covers those of the banks' liquid assets which can be converted to Central Bank money at any time, that is to say, those assets which the Bundesbank is obliged to purchase at any time and without limitation, such as money market paper, bills of exchange up to the limit of the rediscount quotas, and—until the fixed rates of exchange in relation to most currencies were suspended—short-term liquid external assets. By selling those assets which were eligible at the Central Bank, the banks were able to obtain at any time the money they needed in order to fulfil their payment obligations towards other banks, or to replenish their balances at the Bundesbank for meeting the minimum reserve requirements.

The free liquid reserves in the sense thus defined were a reliable indicator for the Bundesbank as long as the banks wished to maintain them for reasons of contingent liquidity provision. Indeed, for many years the banks reacted to fluctuations in their liquidity ratio—that is to say the proportion of their liquid assets to total deposits—by changing their lending policy. The greater the liquidity ratio was, the more credit could be given, and vice versa. In any case the Bundesbank could rely on the banks not to go below a certain minimum amount of free liquid reserves. By varying the liquidity ratio the Bundesbank was therefore able to control the credit granted by the banks, and thus the money stock, in so far as it was not disturbed by foreign exchange inflows—as so often happened.

In the last few years, however, there has been a marked change in the way in which the banks have handled their liquidity position. From the operational point of view the free liquid reserves were regarded less and less as serving the purpose of contingent liquidity provision. With the increasing efficacy and further development of the national and international money markets the banks no longer relied so strongly on support at the Bundesbank, but tried to secure their solvency by means of a network of interbank money market relationships, outside the scope of the Central Bank. From the standpoint of any individual bank this procedure is absolutely correct because, from the operational point of view, it is immaterial whether excess expenditure can be covered by having recourse to the Central Bank or to other banks, as long as the individual bank has made sufficient provision for any withdrawals of funds that might be made.

For the Bundesbank, however, the basic superfluity of free liquid reserves from the banks' point of view meant that it could no longer control the credit granted by banks by changing the liquidity ratio. The banks regarded the free liquid reserves more and more as a source of finance for the growth of their balance sheets, and not as a quantity which must be maintained unconditionally. Logically, the Bundesbank therefore had to do away with the free liquid reserves or at least reduce them practically to zero if it was to regain mastery over credit expansion. This was done in March, 1973, and since then the Bundesbank has been following a credit policy course of keeping the liquidity ratio close to zero.

The elimination of the free liquid reserves was made possible by a further important change in the basic conditions of Central Bank policy. In previous years the Bundesbank had been plagued at ever shorter intervals by waves of speculation against which monetary policy was powerless. Influxes of foreign exchange from abroad reached such proportions that any systematic credit restriction, which would actually have been appropriate for the economic situation involving accelerating price increases, could be undermined from abroad. On one single day—1 March, 1973—the Bundesbank was obliged to purchase dollars to the record amount of DM 7·5 billion. Of course, by skimming off the liquidity which had accrued to them the banks were prevented from stepping up their lending with the aid of foreign money and thus from adding further fuel to the excess demand which existed already. But to the extent that foreign funds flowed to domestic non-banks—whether by way of financial credits raised abroad by German enterprises, or through merchandise transactions and changes in the terms of payment—the Bundesbank had to tolerate the resultant primary expansion of the money stock. Its measures could be directed solely against secondary effects of influxes of liquid funds to the banking sector.

Thus it came about that the monetary mantle in the Federal Republic of Germany grew greater and greater, without the growth of real national product anywhere near keeping pace. But this situation changed all of a sudden when in March, 1973, the Federal Government decided to let the rate against the dollar float, thereby releasing the Bundesbank from its obligation to create any amount of Central Bank money as soon as the dollar had reached the lower intervention point. Practically overnight the Bundesbank regained its room for manœuvre in credit policy, and used this advantage immediately to embark on a severely restrictive policy. Without running the risk of its policy being undermined by renewed foreign exchange influxes, the Bundesbank could draw the consequences from the banks' changed liquidity behaviour which were long over-due. By means of a drastic increase in minimum reserve ratios and rigorous restrictions on refinancing facilities it reduced the banks' free liquid reserves to virtually zero.

The New Indicator of Monetary Policy

Since the spring of 1973 the free liquid reserves have therefore forfeited their value as an indicator of Central Bank policy. If they are nevertheless still observed in our analyses, this is principally to prevent from the very start their renewed resurgence, or at least to keep it under control. As long as there is any assurance of rediscounts for certain money market paper and commercial bills in connection with the rediscount quotas, the Central Bank must keep an eye on the movement of these eligible assets. The free liquid reserves were not done away with as an institution, they were simply reduced to practically zero. From the analytical point of view they are primarily a *pro memoria* item which indicates whether—against the Bundesbank's will— banks are acquiring an expansion potential which might hamper the pursuit of monetary policy aims. They are no longer any measure of the expansive or restrictive effect of monetary policy.

The movement of Central Bank money supply has now become the main indicator of the effects of Central Bank policy, because the banks cannot expand their overall volume of business unless the Bundesbank makes the necessary Central Bank money available to them. A rising volume of deposits leads of necessity first to the maintenance of larger minimum reserves on the banks' Central Bank accounts, and second to a growth in currency, since the cash withdrawal quota will scarcely show a corresponding change at short notice. Now that the banks' free liquid reserves are exhausted, they can only obtain the funds for an increase in minimum reserves and currency from the Bundesbank, and then, indeed, only when the latter considers it necessary, and only on its own conditions.

Thus the Central Bank money supply is both a reflection of and a condition for the monetary trend. The faster Central Bank money grows, the more the money stock increases, and vice versa. If, therefore, the Bundesbank puts up with large additions to the Central Bank money supply and satisfies the banks' requirements of funds at moderate conditions, its monetary policy has a highly expansive effect. Its policy is restrictive, on the other hand, if it en- deavours to throttle the expansion of the Central Bank money supply and satisfies the banks' expansion-induced requirements only at rates of interest which have a deterrent effect for the future. The success of monetary policy can therefore be measured directly by the movement in the Central Bank money supply. When the growth in the Central Bank money supply is large, the Bundesbank finances a corresponding rise in the banks' volume of busi- ness and thereby of the money stock; if, on the other hand, it holds only little Central Bank money available, the banks' volume of business, too, can only increase slowly.

Contrary to the monetary base concept of monetary literature, the Bundes- bank does *not* include the banks' surplus balances and the minimum reserve on external liabilities in its definition of the Central Bank money supply, but confines itself to currency and the minimum reserve on domestic liabilities. The purpose of this narrow definition is to identify that portion of Central Bank liabilities which is internally related to domestic monetary expansion. The Central Bank money supply so defined is thus no longer at the disposal of the banks. Surplus balances, that is to say, the banks' overall Central Bank balances less the required minimum reserve, on the other hand, belong to the free liquid reserves, though they are as a rule only very small because the banks seldom allow their non-interest-bearing balances at the Bundesbank to exceed the absolutely essential amount. They have not yet been absorbed by the monetary trend, but represent a part of the expansion potential which the banks could use for financing a further expansion in lending. The minimum reserve on external liabilities is left outside the Bundesbank's definition, just as by our criteria M_1 and M_2 also comprise only the money holdings of domestic non-banks.

Time-lags in the Process of Money Creation

But the shift from the free liquid reserves towards the Central Bank money supply as the main indicator of monetary policy does not mean that the Bundesbank can now simply restrict itself to autonomously fixing the Central Bank money supply and leaving it to the banks and their customers to adapt themselves accordingly. Such a notion of the Central Bank's possibilities of action is based on a lack of appreciation of the time-dimension in the process of money creation.

The growth in bank balance sheets, and therefore in deposits, is in the first instance based on the individual decisions of the banks and their customers. The more liquid the banks would like to be, the less credit will they extend and the smaller is the overall growth of deposits. Conversely, total deposits go up more quickly the more the banks apply their liquid assets to lending. The banks' individual preferences for liquidity determine the composition of the assets in the banks' balance sheets, and when the optimum is departed from they lead to shifts between liquid and non-liquid assets.

For the individual bank, assessment of its liquidity position depends on the Central Bank money being made available to it. However requirements of Central Bank money do not come first in the process of expansion in bank balance sheets. Central Bank money is not needed until the banks' decisions on lending have been made and have led to an increase in the volume of deposits. When this time arrives, however, the trend can no longer be reversed, because the banks have already committed themselves. They now have to finance the increasing withdrawals of cash to the debit of their Central Bank accounts, and in addition to that fulfil their minimum reserve obligations which increase with the deposits made in the banking system.

This problem is not only due to the fact that in the Federal Republic of Germany, as in other countries, the minimum reserve has to be maintained with a time-lag, although this enlarges the lag between the banks' business decisions and the Central Bank money being required. The minimum reserve to be maintained in a calendar month is calculated on the basis of the liabilities position on the 23rd and last day of the preceding month and on the 7th and 15th of the current month. At the beginning of each month, therefore, half of the minimum reserve demanded in that month is already immutably fixed. So once the banks' volume of business has expanded due to the individual operational decisions, a fixed requirement of Central Bank money results which then can no longer be influenced by the banks and with which the Central Bank is confronted.

Now the decisive question facing any intended policy of direct Central Bank money control is how the Central Bank is to behave with regard to this fixed and now irreversible demand for Central Bank money. If the Central Bank wished to pursue unflinchingly the target figure it has chosen, the rate of interest for the day-to-day money might possibly rise extremely high, and yet it would still be impossible for the banks to fulfil the minimum reserve requirement, because even the highest interest rates cannot enlarge the available Central Bank money supply.

The Central Bank would therefore be making demands on the banks which, objectively, they could not fulfil, even if they exhausted all possibilities for doing so. The final result of rigidly maintaining a position once taken would be to endanger the efficacy of minimum reserves as an instrument of policy, since individual banks could scarcely be reproached with not fulfilling their minimum reserve obligations if such fulfilment had been made impossible for the banking system as a whole. A Central Bank with a sense of responsibility, wishing to prevent total collapse of the money market and also to ensure the efficiency of the instruments at its disposal, therefore has no choice but to cover the short-term inelastic demand for Central Bank money; the crux of the matter, however, is the conditions on which it does so. Taking everything into account, this is the only way in which the Central Bank can control the Central Bank money supply.

The fixing of the conditions for the availability of Central Bank money calls for adjustment processes at the banks, whose portfolio decisions between liquid and non-liquid assets determine the volume of deposits. The creation of Central Bank money by the Central Bank does in fact sanction an expansion which has already occurred and which can no longer be nullified by refusal to provide the money required. However, by the price charged for the Central Bank money required, the Central Bank can bring about changes in the banks' *future* business behaviour. The amount of Central Bank money made available to the banks is a measure of the magnitude of monetary expansion. If the Bundesbank does not consider the trend in Central Bank money to be reasonable with respect to the economic situation at any given time, it will have to alter its interest rates in such a way that when the banks have adapted themselves to the changed conditions, only as much Central Bank money will be demanded as is consistent with the Bundesbank's longer-term targets.

Policy Instruments in the New Environment

The changed basis of monetary policy makes it essential to reconsider the Bundesbank's individual instruments since they are not equally suited to cover Central Bank money requirements of the banks. Provided that the free liquid reserves were to be kept close to zero in future also, changes in the rediscount quotas or in the minimum reserve ratios, which are still the sharpest weapons in the Bundesbank's armoury, will be required only comparatively seldom, so far as the domestic sources of the movements of the monetary stock are concerned. Rediscount credits or a reduction in the minimum reserves then serve principally to cover the longer-term basic requirements for Central Bank money, which are connected with the trend towards expansion of bank balance sheets. Because they are designed to have long-run effects, they play no part in balancing liquidity in the short term. Both are indispensable, however, for compensating foreign exchange movements in the banking system. For skimming off influxes of foreign exchange and for releasing liquid funds for financing effluxes of foreign exchange, recourse will still have to be taken to the minimum reserves instrument and to the rediscount quotas.

Measured by the frequency of its application, open market policy has recently been forced right into the foreground. Because of its flexibility it is especially suitable for evening out the short-term liquidity fluctuations on the day-to-day money market, if large deficits or surpluses threaten the fulfilment of minimum reserve obligations. Under the regime of free liquid reserves sizable tensions could hardly arise on the money market, as the banks could obtain practically any amount of Central Bank money required by selling assets eligible at the Central Bank. Conversely, Central Bank money which was not needed for fulfilling minimum reserve obligations could as a rule be invested at any time in money market paper or by repayment of debt to the Central Bank. Unless the banks have fairly large holdings of free liquid reserves they have no possibility of effecting any adjustment on the money market; in this respect they remain dependent on Central Bank aid. With the interventions necessary on the money market it cannot be the aim of Bundesbank policy, however, to keep the money market rate as constant as possible. Use of the instruments of precise control should only prevent the money market rate from running too far upwards or downwards. Money market rates of zero and of over 20% are useless, as such violent fluctuations do not seem to be necessary for the success of monetary policy, since, even when changes in interest rates are small, the banks adapt themselves to the changed money market conditions. From the Bundesbank's standpoint it is sufficient for interest rates to settle down freely within a certain spread, which of course depends on the rate of inflation.

In the logical pursuit of its policy of keeping the liquidity ratio near to zero the Bundesbank was able to have little recourse to its 'traditional' open market transactions in balancing operations on the money market. In order not to let free liquid reserves be formed again, the Bundesbank had to reduce sales of Treasury bills and discountable Treasury bonds, which are regulated on the money market and can be returned to the Bundesbank at any time, and instead promote sales of so-called N paper, which the banks cannot exchange for Central Bank money before maturity, but must hold throughout its life. Just recently, Federal Government bonds serving to finance the budget have been issued as N paper. By shifting the emphasis towards Treasury securities which are not included in the Bundesbank's regulation of the money market and also have comparatively long periods to maturity ($1\frac{1}{2}$ to 2 years, for example) the Bundesbank wishes to keep the way open for a strict course of liquidity policy, without running the risk of having to create Central Bank money involuntarily through repurchase obligations attaching to market-regulated money market paper.

Such transactions are unsuitable for very short-term balancing operations on the money market; the Bundesbank was therefore obliged to develop new forms of open market policy. If the money market rate threatened to move downwards towards 0%, the Bundesbank sold Treasury bills with maturities of only 5 or 10 days to the banks in order to skim off at short term the Central Bank money which was superfluous in a minimum reserve period. Conversely, in times of great tension on the money market, the Bundesbank purchased commercial bills from the banks in open market transactions, which the banks were obliged to repurchase after 10 days. From the economic point of view these are transactions under repurchase agreement for 10 days, the purpose of which is to make it possible for the banks to fulfil their minimum reserve obligations.

Open market transactions by way of commercial bills under repurchase agreement proved insufficient, however, to ensure the necessary measure of orderly conditions on the day-to-day money market, because firstly they have a fixed maturity of 10 days, and secondly the banks did not always have sufficient bills available for sale to the Bundesbank. The Bundesbank therefore needed an instrument by means of which very large amounts could be mobilized at quite short notice and varied from day to day. Originally this was the role to be played by the Lombard credit, because it was designed only for the short-term bridging of a temporary need for liquidity. In the course of time, however, the banks resorted ever more frequently to this facility so that the Bundesbank was obliged to limit it quantitatively by the so-called Lombard mark, which was 20% of the respective rediscount quota. Like unutilized rediscount quotas, the free Lombard margin also counted towards free liquid reserves giving the banks unconditional access to Central Bank money.

With the realignment of Bundesbank policy, the banks' free refinancing lines were eliminated, automatic 'normal' Lombard credits under the Lombard mark were done away with and no substitute provided. Instead, some time later the Bundesbank introduced the so-called special Lombard credit, which—depending on requirements—is mobilized at quite short notice and, when transactions are terminated, can be made repayable the next day. The interest rate is determined anew for each single period during which special Lombard credit is granted; generally speaking it is considerably higher than the Bundesbank's normal Lombard rate. In contrast to former times there is no longer any automatic entitlement whatsoever to Lombard credit.

With its newly-developed instruments of precise control—i.e. very short-term open market transactions and special Lombard credit—the Bundesbank is now in a good position to influence events on the money market as it thinks fit, and thereby to set new points of reference for the banks' business policy and monetary expansion.

The Behaviour of the Monetary Aggregates

In the Federal Republic of Germany the year 1973 showed how drastically Central Bank policy can take effect if it is applied consistently and is not disturbed by an open flank on the foreign trade and payments side.

The first few months of that year were characterized by increasing cyclical tensions. The inflation of money supply went hand in hand with a rapid increase in overall demand. At the same time, production capacities were largely utilized to the full and the labour market was empty of reserves, so that there was little scope for economic growth, and the upward trend of prices threatened to accelerate. Monetary policy was to a large extent paralysed by heavy foreign exchange inflows; and inflationary forces could operate unhindered. But when in March the Federal Government decided to let the rate against the dollar float, the Bundesbank took immediate advantage of the freedom of action thus gained and adopted a severely restrictive course. As mentioned above, it reduced the free liquid reserves practically to zero and tightened the suppy of Central Bank money. The result was extreme rises in interest rates on the money market, which spread very quickly, first to time deposits at banks, and then to the entire interest rate structure of the economy.

In actual fact, the Bundesbank has always made as much Central Bank money available to the banks as these needed for the fulfilment of the minimum reserve requirement, but the banks were obliged to take considerable risks in respect of interest rates. The Bundesbank did not always intervene immediately on the money market, and generally it demanded a high rate of interest for additional Central Bank money. Contrary to normal experience, the maintenance of large liquid reserves was highly profitable in 1973, whereas the investment of liquid funds in credit transactions sometimes even resulted in loss in interest, because the banks' lending rates did not go up at the same speed as the deposit rates.

The high Central Bank interest rates definitely slowed down the supply of and the demand for credit and were reflected in a slower growth of the Central Bank money supply. From May until the end of the year the Central Bank money supply went up by an annual rate of only 5·6%, seasonally adjusted, after a rise of 13·1% in the first four months of 1973. The growth of the money stock held by domestic non-banks also showed a marked decline. M_1, especially, went up by only 2% in 1973, after a rise of 14% in 1972.

Supported by a strict anti-inflationary programme under the Federal Government's financial policy the Bundesbank succeeded in regaining control over monetary expansion in the course of 1973 and in largely eliminating the surplus money supply. If in spite of this the Bundesbank did not achieve ultimate success in stabilizing the level of prices, this was not because its policy lacked strength—monetary policy could hardly have been any more restrictive in 1973 than it was—but was due to the entirely new situation presented by the oil crisis. By the autumn the cyclical tensions had already slackened to such an extent that the rise in consumer prices was decelerating considerably. In view of the time lags with which monetary policy measures are reflected in the price trend, and in a startling position characterized by such intense inflationary pressure, the Bundesbank could hardly have achieved better results with its policy in so short a space of time.

From the sharp braking of monetary expansion in 1973 it can therefore be concluded that, if the economy is safeguarded against external influences, the instruments in the Bundesbank's armoury are sufficient to keep the monetary trend under control. Thanks to the scope granted by the Bundesbank Act, the bank is strong enough to influence the banks' business behaviour in the way it wishes. The Bundesbank is in a powerful position owing to the fact that the banks have a basic need for Central Bank money in order to extend their volume of business, and that once they have exhausted their free liquid reserves they can only obtain this Central Bank money from the Bundesbank on the latter's conditions, and then only if the Bundesbank considers it necessary. As long as these conditions are fulfilled there is no need for any other instruments such as credit ceilings or reserve requirements on the growth of bank assets. When the debate on an amendment to the Bundesbank Act was going on in 1972 there was no thought of the new instruments discussed being applied immediately. But Acts of Parliament are not revised every day, and the main idea was to take precautions against all eventualities.

The Costs and Benefits of Anti-inflationary Monetary Policy

As always in times of restrictive credit policy, the Bundesbank has since 1973 been confronted with the fact that its instruments act very sharply on the economy and affect its various branches in very different ways. As soon as

the Bundesbank's braking measures—which have only an overall effect—
begin to bite, structural problems are revealed which were hitherto hidden
under the veil of inflation. On this occasion it was the construction, motor
and textile industries which were particularly concerned. Unless they are
adequately capitalized, many smaller business enterprises also get into difficulties, when rates of interest climb as steeply as they did in 1973. Not the
least to suffer, of course, are private savers, especially the owners of fixed-
interest securities, because not only is the interest yield on their investments
consumed by the rate of inflation, but over and above that they have to put
up with a sharp fall in the value of their securities.

The Bundesbank is not unaware of the difficulties and hardships ensuing
from its restrictive credit policy. It particularly regrets the losses suffered by
those who save through buying securities, who have relied on the stability of
the currency and have often planned to safeguard their provisions against old
age by building up financial assets. Since Central Bank policy works solely
through the market, credit restrictions affect the 'just' and the 'unjust' equally.
The Bundesbank has no possibility, therefore, of pursuing a structural policy
and balancing out social hardships. Fundamentally, the Bundesbank can
only use instruments of monetary policy in an overall way, with a view to
doing justice to the needs of the economy as a whole. A differentiation between individual groups of the economy is a matter for general political
decision and belongs to the tasks of the Government and Parliament. The
Bundesbank would exceed its sphere of responsibility were it to take any part
in this political activity. Apart from that, by creating precedents with their
fateful consequences, it would gradually undermine the effectiveness of the
instruments at its disposal. Finally, and this would appear to be the main
reason, any purposive liquidity assistance would not be limited to the spheres
to which it should exclusively apply; it would mean rather a general release of
Central Bank money which would very rapidly spread throughout the whole
banking system. In this way the Bundesbank would again create expansion
potential at the banks and again place a considerable obstacle in the way of
the policy which it has just recently adopted.

Far from doing this, the Bundesbank in future will, in pursuance of its
legal obligations, rather do everything in its power to maintain price increases
within narrow limits, if not to eliminate them. It is assumed that the damage
caused by sustained and progressive inflation in the economy is much more
serious than the—presumably only temporary—stabilization losses in some
sectors of the economy. In the long run, the purposes of all groups of the
economy would be better served by stability of price levels—though it is, alas,
only relative stability—than by spurious inflationary prosperity, even if the
concomitant process of adjustment is found to be painful. Until now the
logical pursuance of restrictive monetary policy has at least resulted in

domestic consumer prices not rising by any means as steeply as feared at the end of 1973, in spite of the boom in raw material prices. Apart from this—to use a rather widespread metaphor—the Federal Republic of Germany is at present the slowest ship in the international inflation convoy. (Monetary expansion continued at such a moderate rate that the Bundesbank could accept a certain lowering of interest rates at the short-term end without the demand for credit being stimulated. This was responsible for a considerable easing of tension in the capital market as well, though the interest rate level remained sufficiently high to have a deterrent effect.)

Even if monetary policy occupies a key position in economic policy as a whole, the Bundesbank cannot restore the stability of the value of money by itself. In order to guarantee satisfactory future economic development, the Government's financial policy and the wage and salary policy of the employers and the trades unions must work in the same direction. Furthermore, monetary policy must not be allowed to be upset by external processes. Even after the floating of the exchange rate in relation to most currencies, the Bundesbank has a residual obligation to purchase foreign currency for the maintenance of fixed exchange rates within the European mini-snake. Thus from the end of March until the middle of May, 1974, the Bundesbank once more had to buy DM 5 billion of foreign exchange and therefore create Central Bank money against its own will, a course of action partly offset by a reduction of the banks' refinancing facilities by 25% with effect from 1 June, 1974. Nevertheless recent experience suggests that though it is difficult to bring down the rates of price increases it is not impossible. At any rate, there is a growing consensus of opinion in the Federal Republic of Germany that economic growth and stability of the value of money are not contradictory but are in fact complementary. Only healthy money can be the precondition for long-term satisfactory progress in the economy. The Bundesbank regards the attainment of this objective as its highest aim.

2

Monetary Thought and Stabilization Policy in the Federal Republic of Germany 1960-1976*

ANTHONY S. COURAKIS

Introduction

For the neoclassical economist, and hence for the monetarist also, any action can be interpreted as one of maximization of some objective function subject to constraints. Whether aimed at explaining the behaviour of the firm and the household (however these may be defined) or of the 'macro-economic decision-taking unit' the analysis pursues the choice between alternative states perceived by the decision taken as attainable.

For the policy maker an objective function in ultimate goal variables (conceived in terms of a scale of preference attaching to the variables and of perceived trade-offs between them) can in theory be described, and his use of instruments of policy interpreted as the deployment of his 'resources' in securing a maximum defined in terms and future values of the ultimate goal variables.

The function of the empiricist does, in this scheme of things, appear to be that of providing information about:

(*i*) the policy maker's objective function,
(*ii*) actual trade-offs between ultimate goal variables,
(*iii*) the impact of alternative instruments of policy in securing alternative states of the goal variables.

In the process we may perhaps discover that an indirect objective function can be defined that describes some unique maximand for expressing the aims of policy. But even in this (unlikely) eventuality it is essential to define the links between policy actions and this intermediate variable as well as between the latter and ultimate goal variables. From a conceptual standpoint this

requires a definition of the transmission mechanism. From an empirical standpoint it presupposes that our analysis embodies the response functions
characteristic of the period to which our observations relate and thus not only
the institutional environment (itself in part a manifestation of such responses)
but also the objective function, direct or indirect, that conditioned the actions
of the policy maker over the period from which our information derives.

The aim of this paper is to amplify the information contained in the rest
of this volume by providing an account of the decision taker's own interpretation of the spectrum of choices available to him.

The Decision-taking Unit

In the monetary sphere policy decisions rest entirely with the Deutsche
Bundesbank. Article 3 of the Bank Act provides that the Central Bank

. . . making use of its powers in the field of monetary policy conferred upon it under
this law shall regulate the volume of money circulation and the supply of credit
to the economy with the aim of safeguarding the currency and shall ensure appropriate payments through banks within the country as well as to and from foreign
countries. [1]

In this respect the Bundesbank is no different from most Central Banks.
Yet there is one important difference. For in its relationship to the Federal
Government the

Deutsche Bundesbank shall be obliged insofar as is consistent with its functions to
support the general economic policy of the Federal Government. But in the exercise
of the powers conferred on it under this act it shall be independent of instruction
from the Federal Government. [2]

Nor is this independence merely a matter of legal fiction. For though for
the latter part of the period under review there has been cooperation between
the Bank and the Government, for the first half of this period no such har-
mony existed. The possibility of conflict was not overlooked when defining
the powers of the Bank referred to above. Indeed various proposals for subordination of the Bank to the Government or reconciliation procedures were
tabled [3]. Given, however, the German experience with dependent Central
Banks and consequent fear of state-propelled inflation, subordination of the
Bank to the Government was deemed undesirable, while the impracticality
of setting up an arbitration body with a better grasp of the issues than the
two parties to the conflict implied that no reconciliation procedure could be
established. In the event the Federal Government's power is, to date, limited
to postponement of a decision by the Bank for up to two weeks. If agreement
has then still not been reached, the Bundesbank can pursue its chosen course
of action. In the final analysis therefore the Bank's decisions and actions
have been, and are being, based on its own interpretation of the duties

imposed on it by the Act, duties which are (fortunately, and despite the ultra-legalistic German structure) sufficiently inadequately defined to afford it considerable freedom in its view of objectives. Thus,

Even before the Stability and Growth Law (enacted in 1967) . . . the Bank always tried to perform its task in the sense of a policy embracing all economic aims.   [4]
     Safeguarding of currency (was interpreted as) . . . not only safeguarding *stability of the domestic price level* but also . . . *equilibrium in the balance of payments* and promotion of *employment* and *growth*.   [5]

Yet despite such continuity of objectives the two sub-periods, pre- and post-1967, are distinct in at least one respect. For whereas in the first sub-period pursuit of the objectives referred to above implied policies designed to offset not only the influence of purely exogenous factors but also the pro-cyclical responses of Federal and Länder Governments' policies, the 'conflict' as the Bank put it between *political aims* and *monetary stability* [6], in the second sub-period the constraints imposed on fiscal freedom ensured that the latter was at least not obviously destabilizing [7]. Provisions for greater coordination of Länder and Federal Government policies and for adjustments in Government expenditures through the creation of 'cyclical reserve funds' as well as for greater harmonization of monetary and budgetary policies were, in 1967, seen by the Bank 'to afford some relief, whereas formerly the efforts of credit policy . . . were hindered by the public authorities' failure to behave anticyclically and at times . . . actually thwarting monetary policy by their procyclical actions' [8]. And at least in recent years fiscal policy is accorded considerable weight in macroeconomic management [9].

Alas the task of identifying objective functions is not as simple as dividing the period into pre- and post-1967. For not only has the information regarding actual trade-offs between policy objectives altered considerably during this period, as, for example, reflection of 'new' and 'old' views of inflation-unemployment trade-offs reveals, but so also perhaps have preferences and certainly the constraints perceived as relevant to the choice of instruments of policy employed. The latter is particularly pronounced in, though by no means unique to, the sphere of simultaneous pursuit of internal and external balance where original convictions about 'free' movement of capital gradually give way to severe controls, and similarly sacrifice on the altar of exchange rate stability, prolonged in the vision of E.E.C. union, gives way to flexible exchange rates.

While, however, the task of identifying direct objective functions will appear to be one of horrendous magnitude and thus one from which even the purist may claim (brief?) respite, that such a function can in principle be identified as relevant to decisions at any particular point in time cannot be in dispute [10]. If then an indirect objective function in the variables describing the transmission from policy instruments to ultimate objectives

B

can be secured, we may perhaps enquire whether this function appears temporally more determinate than the direct one sought above.

Conception of the Process through which Policy Operates [11]

Any attempt to identify the conceptual framework guiding the policy of a Central Bank is inevitably fraught with difficulties that arise not only from multiplicity of objectives but also, and perhaps more uncomfortably, from the tendency of the authorities to rationalize such events as have taken place so as to present their policy under the best light and as consistent with the dominant school of thought. In this respect the Deutsche Bundesbank is no exception. Yet from amidst the mass of varied statements, sometimes expressed in terms of credit policy, sometimes in terms of interest rate policy, and more recently in terms of monetary aggregates, some loose but unifying framework can be identified.

As conceived by the Bundesbank, monetary policy operates by '*influencing the liquidity structure of the economy*' and thereby through changes in interest rates economic activity in general [12].

To this end the Bank has focused its attention on the potential for expansion available at any given moment with *bank liquidity* serving, until recently, as the main index of such tendencies. And while recently greater attention has been given to the behaviour of the *Stock of Central Bank Money* this should not be taken to suggest a fundamental change in the Bank's view of the policy process. Acknowledging the fact that the volume of deposits and credit is the product of interaction of the maximizing decisions of the banks and their customers, and as such conditioned by various economic incentives, the Central Bank accommodates the demands for Central Bank money made of it [13] while seeking to influence future behaviour by altering the terms on which such 'assistance' is made available.

This position, apparent also in Schlesinger's remarks [14], is aptly described in the following extract from the Bank's 1974 Annual Report.

A precondition for a steady course of monetary policy is that the Central Bank is not forced to conduct transactions and thus to provide Central Bank money, through which the banks gain too much scope for creating money themselves. In creating money the banks must remain dependent on the Central Bank contributing to monetary expansion by supplying Central Bank money. True, in the very short run the Central Bank has no choice but to meet the Central Bank money requirements associated with monetary expansions. But in the somewhat longer run it controls the pace of monetary expansion through the conditions on which it is prepared to satisfy the banks' demand for Central Bank money. [15]

In so far as the emphasis now placed on the Stock of Central Bank Money derives from greater willingness than previously to alter the terms on which banks are allowed to substitute interest-yielding liquid assets for non-interest-yielding ones [16] the Bank's policy may, if one so chooses to describe experience [17], be said to have changed from one in which the 'relevant monetary base' includes free liquid reserves to one where only that part of such reserves as is held in the form of Central Bank money is so included [18]. More appropriately however (see below) the change in emphasis may be said to relate to the replacement, as a means of expression of monetary developments, of an 'operating target' (free liquid reserves) situated in the early stages of control by an intermediate monetary target (the Central Bank Money Stock).

Central Bank Operations: Instruments of Policy

In view of the harassed experience of commercial banks in some countries, such as for example the U.K. and until recently the Netherlands [19], we may perhaps begin by referring to the fact that the Bundesbank *does not exercise any direct administrative control over the credit operations of the various banks*. It has no statutory powers to dictate or even indicate to the banks the percentage by which they are to expand or contract lending either in aggregate or to specific types of borrower. While, however, in earlier years the Bank had shown no interest in acquiring such power [20] a proposal that powers be incorporated in the Bundesbank Act enabling the Bank to lay down ceilings on credit expansion was tabled to the Federal Government in December, 1972. Recognizing the distortionary effects of such an instrument, it was reasoned that 'powers of this kind would only be desired and exercisable for a limited space of time' [21]. In general such an instrument was intended to apply 'only as a general measure and not selectively in the sense that the Bundesbank could differentiate according to the purpose of the loan. A possibility of differentiation in accordance with general considerations would only be necessary should certain banking groups or credits with particular maturities make differences in treatment indispensable in certain circumstances [22]. It will appear, however, that this proposal has not been pursued further. Indirectly of course it is within the Bank's power to regulate, for 'monetary' control purposes, the credit activities of banks by attaching certain conditions on the exercise of its loan facilities to credit banks. Yet since 1951 [23] the Bundesbank has never made use of this possibility for it has considered it preferable to operate by '*influencing the liquidity position of the banking system*' [24] and thereby interest rates, credit, the demand for money and aggregate expenditure.

The term *liquidity of the banking system* refers to banks' holdings of Central Bank money and other short-term assets that can be used to increase such holdings. Within this category the Bank has traditionally distinguished between non-cash assets, sometimes referred to as potential liquidity, and bank

Chart 2.1. Monetery policy and free liquid reserves

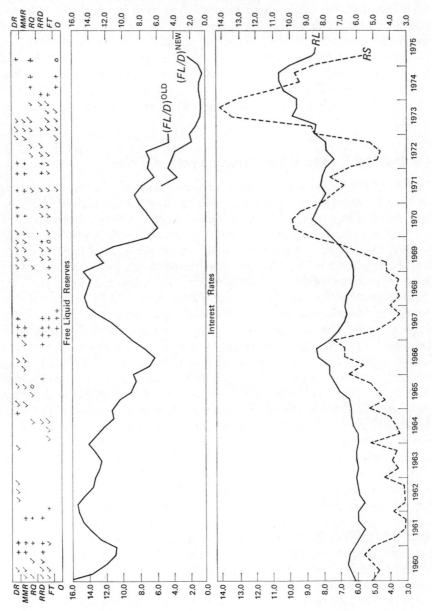

holdings of Central Bank money, *cash liquidity*. A more relevant distinction employed, however, is that between *immobilized liquidity* (i.e., assets frozen by compulsory reserve ratios) and *free liquid reserves* [25]. Chart 2.1, below, depicts the behaviour of the latter aggregate during the period under review.

In addition to concern with the absolute volume of bank liquidity, the sources of changes in such liquidity are examined (i.e., whether through changes in the public's demand for cash or credit, changes in net balances of non-banks—particularly public bodies—with the Bundesbank, and until recently changes in foreign exchange reserves of the Bank and in money market investments of banks abroad). The Bank has sought to discourage undesirable positions and tendencies. In so doing the following instruments are at its disposal:

(*i*)   Discount rate policy
(*ii*) Conditions for access to rediscount facilities
(*iii*) Open market operations
(*iv*) Minimum reserve ratios
(*v*)   Controls on capital movements

Chart 2.1 depicts the deployment of such instruments during the period under review while the rest of this section concentrates on descriptions of their characteristics.

Discount Rate Policy

Section 15 of the Bundesbank Act authorizes the Central Bank to fix 'such rates of interest and discount as are appropriate to the business undertaken' with the aim of influencing 'the amount of money in circulation and the volume of credit granted'. But although the Bundesbank can, therefore, apply different rates of discount for various classes of business its activities have focused on the one hand on the rate of interest at which it is prepared

---

Chart 2.1. Explanatory notes
DR   = Discount and Lombard Rates
MMR = Money Market Selling Rates
RQ   = Rediscount Quotas
RRD = Reserve Ratios on Domestic Liabilities
FT   = Measures on International Transactions
O   = Other measures
FL/D = Free Liquid Reserves to Deposits Ratio
OLD = Old definition
NEW = New definition
RL   = Rate on long-term government securities
RS   = 3 Month Money Market Rate
+   = expansionary measure
√   = contractionary measure

to discount eligible paper, and on the other at the rate at which it is prepared, when it is so prepared, to make advances on the security of such paper. The latter so-called 'Lombard rate' has in general stood at a fixed margin above the discount rate thereby playing a 'penal' role as Bank Rate does in some countries [26].

Changes in discount rate do affect money market rates. Furthermore, as in many other banking systems, changes in the rates paid and levied by banks are geared, albeit in recent years less tightly, to changes in the discount rate. Prior to 1967 rates on loans and on deposits were subject to maxima in relation to the discount rate [27], and although this practice has ceased the discount rate is thought to continue to provide an important guideline in the formation of bank deposit and lending rates [28]. Finally, changes in the discount rate affect the course of interest rates in the capital market in terms of induced (rather than direct) effects arising partly from the information contained in discount rate changes [29] as to the future course of Central Bank policy and partly by the effect that the change has on the liquidity position of banks and thereby on availability of credit.

Conditions for Access to Rediscount Credits

General aspects
The Bundesbank's rediscounting and similar business covers two types [30] of operations:

(a) Rediscounting operations
(b) Advances against certain types of security

The usual form taken by Bundesbank 'assistance' is the rediscounting of bills; by comparison the granting of advances against security comprises a less sizable, though from a policy standpoint no less significant, means of Central Bank assistance.

Rediscounting refers to transactions by the Bank in:

(i) Bills of exchange backed by three parties known to be solvent; the necessity for the third signature may be waived if the security of the bill of exchange is guaranteed in some other manner; the bills of exchange must mature within three months from date of purchase; they must be good trade bills.

(ii) Treasury bills issued by the Federal and Länder Governments or other public bodies and maturing within three months from date of purchase. Certain limits, however, as to the holding of such bills are imposed [31].

Advances against security [32] are, in principle, granted by the Bundesbank only for the purpose of easing, for short periods, unforeseen and temporary strains in a bank's liquidity position, or, exceptionally, when a bank has exhausted its *rediscount quota*. Such assistance is given against the security of:

(i) discountable bills (see 'rediscounting') for not more than 0·9 of their *nominal* value;

(ii) discountable Treasury bonds with less than one year to maturity, for not more than three quarters of their *nominal* value;

(iii) debentures and debt-register claims of public authorities, for not more than three quarters of their *quoted* value [33].

(iv) other fixed interest securities and debt-register claims appearing in the List of Securities Eligible at the Bundesbank as Security for Advances, for not more than three quarters of their *quoted* value.

Apart from determining the general qualitative requirements that bills must satisfy to be eligible for rediscount or advances against security, the Bundesbank may influence behaviour by

(*a*) stating which bills it will discount,

(*b*) laying down 'rules of good conduct' for the banks in their operations.

Under the former the Bank has frequently refused to discount bills relating to certain classes of business, thereby making specific types of business more difficult at least to the extent that the cost of credit to the *ultimate borrower* increases. From the standpoint of credit policy, however, 'rules of good conduct' (at least in certain periods in the past) it is claimed [34] have been of greater importance. These rules do not, as we have seen above, provide for ceilings on advances but rather relate to the structure of business, the soundness of credit granted or the provision of precautionary reserves. Although not explicitly binding, such requirements (General Business Conditions) have to be met by such credit institutions as need to have recourse to Bundesbank assistance. In addition to these, credit institutions are also subject to the conditions of the Law on the Credit System. Article 11 of this Law requires that such institutions have adequate liquid [35] portfolios. Non-observance of this basic requirement may lead to the application of sanctions by the Federal Supervisory Office, such as prohibition of dividend payments or further credit-granting and the refusal of rediscount or similar facilities at the Bundesbank. Although the Law itself does not set up any absolute standards for adequate capital resources and liquidity, it grants the Supervisory Office the power to draw up and issue, in agreement with the Bundesbank, basic ratios that are legally binding. These basic ratios (normally known as 'guiding ratios in regard to credits') are taken as criteria in judging whether the banks' capital resources and liquidity are adequate. The drawing up of the ratios, in which the Bundesbank plays a major part, provides it with an important regulatory instrument.

Rediscount quotas

Although all Central Banks employ strict criteria for the quality of bills eligible as a basis for 'last resort' credit and manipulate rediscount rates, the Bundesbank is among the very few that lay down strict criteria for the quantity of such credit as well.

Chart 2.2. Rediscount quotas and their utilization

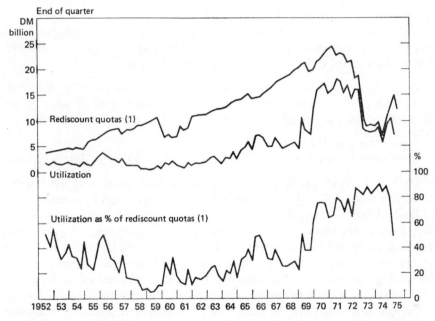

(1) From 8 February, 1973, to 28 February, 1974, and from 3 July, 1974, calculated on the basis of the utilization limits.
Source: Deutsche Bundesbank Monthly Report, June, 1975.

Rediscount quotas were first introduced in 1952 (and have been revised on occasions since). Chart 2.2 presents the behaviour of such quotas from 1952 to mid-1975. Every credit institution eligible for rediscounting facilities at the Bundesbank is allocated a quota which it may not exceed. In case of need a bank that has exhausted its rediscount quota, or the percentage of quota permissible at any particular moment [36], must resort to dearer advances against security (Lombard loans). The latter, however, are *normally* not available to it in unlimited quantities. They are granted only under certain conditions, must be repaid within 30 days, and should normally not exceed a specified percentage of the rediscount quotas [37]. The method used to calculate the size of rediscount quotas is based primarily on the 'liable funds' (i.e. capital including published reserves) of each bank; the method contains, however, sufficiently flexible elements to avoid too rigid an application of a quota system. The special positions of individual banks have, within certain limits, been taken into account in determining their quotas provided that such a course of action is compatible with monetary and credit policy [38].

As in the case of the instruments already discussed, rediscount quotas can only be evaluated in full appreciation of the Bundesbank's conception of the process of policy. Changes in quotas generate changes in the maximum amount of potential bank holdings of Central Bank money. In effect whether or not banks can increase such holdings through conversion of foreign short-term assets, their ability to do so has altered and, accordingly, given their objective functions, so have their desired level of deposits and volume of credit. Such a change need not of course imply a net reduction in the actual volume of credit granted or in bank deposit liabilities; but in conjunction with simultaneous rises in discount rates it does (particularly under free floating) most certainly imply a slower process of expansion than would otherwise be experienced.

Open Market Operations

Unlike the tale told of the use of this instrument in Anglo-Saxon countries, there appears to be a general consensus of opinion that at least until the early 1970s open market policy 'has not been of very great importance'. One reason for this, it is claimed [39], has been that public debt in Germany is lower than in most comparable industrial countries, particularly those in which debt policies play a major part (e.g. the U.K.) [40]. A second reason for this, earlier, relative unimportance of open market operations is that the scope for such transactions in amounts sufficient to regulate bank liquidity was limited by the fact that only a small proportion of long-term debt, particularly Federal debt, was in the form of negotiable bonds, the major part being made up of direct credits by banks and other financial institutions to the Federal Government. Thus 'material' for open market operations was lacking and had to be especially created [41]. (I return to this below.)

Open market policy such as existed therefore was said to aim at supporting rediscounting and similar business by bringing the credit banks 'in the Bank' and has been regarded as complementary to the rediscounting and other facilities previously mentioned. But while it is true that open market policy was, and continues to be, seen in the context of other policy aiming at effecting ease and tightness in the market, and it is proper that it should be so regarded, it is, I think, a misinterpretation of the role of open market operations to regard Bundesbank behaviour in this sphere as one dictated by the small volume of Government debt and such like.

Under Bundesbank Law, Section 21, the Bank may, for the purpose of regulating conditions 'in the money market', buy and sell in the open market 'at market prices':

(a) bills eligible for rediscount (see above);
(b) debentures and debt register claims issued by the Bund, Länder or one of the special funds;
(c) other bonds officially listed in the stock exchange.

As regards money market paper Bundesbank dealings comprise practically the whole of dealings in the market. Hence the ruling of transactions 'at market prices' imposes no constraints on the ability of the Bank to determine interest rates in this market, and more generally fix the terms on which it sells or buys money market paper. In particular 'the Bundesbank fixes buying and selling rates for this type of paper, varying them according to trends in the money market and the aims of *credit policy*. The rates at which money market paper is repurchased before maturity are not published but are fixed at a certain margin above the published selling rates. These margins may vary according to the state of the money market, the way in which the Bank wishes to influence the market and the type of security concerned; but the margins between selling and repurchase rates are narrow and have often remained unchanged for fairly long periods so that the rates at which the Bundesbank will repurchase—although somewhat higher—vary in accordance with selling prices' [42].

The stock of money market paper is determined by:

(a) the size and mode of financing the Government's borrowing requirement;
(b) conversion of 'equalization claims' into 'mobilization paper';
(c) provision of 'liquidity paper';
(d) 'storage agency bills';
(e) 'prime acceptances'.

With regard to (a) the Bank may request the Government to finance part of its borrowing requirement through the issue of securities that are not convertible into Central Bank money before maturity, thereby generating a less liquid position than would prevail under the alternative of financing the deficit through creation of readily convertible assets. Thus in 1974 the Federal Government issued almost one billion DM of short-term Treasury bonds, the purchase of which by the banks did not create any free liquidity as the securities concerned were so-called 'N' paper that cannot be sold to the Bank before maturity and hence cannot be converted into Central Bank money. This way of financing budget deficit requirements, unlike, for instance, the raising of cash advances at the Bundesbank, does not enhance the banks' potential for credit expansion.

In addition, the Bank may, in accordance with section 42 of the Bundesbank Act, request the Government, 'as the debtor of the equalization claims held by the Deutsche Bundesbank', to convert all (DM 8000 million) or part of this claim into Treasury bills or discountable Treasury bonds, referred to as 'mobilization paper'; these serve as tap stock for the purpose of open market policy. Another section of the Act, 42a, now provides that 'if mobilization paper has been put into circulation by the Deutsche Bundesbank up to the nominal amount of the equalization claim, the Federal Government should hand over to the Bank at request Treasury bills or discountable Treasury bonds, in denominations and on terms of the Bank's own choice (liquidity paper), up to a maximum amount of a further DM 8000 million'. As in the case of mobilization paper the issue of liquidity paper does not enable the Government to increase its own expenditure as the credit corresponding to the issue of such paper may '*only* be used to redeem liquidity paper at maturity or repurchased by the Bank prior to maturity'. Thus the stabilization programme laid down in the Federal Government's annual economic Report for 1973 provided for, among other measures, the 'issue of a loan in several tranches of up to DM 4000 million to skim off liquidity and purchasing power in the private sector; the funds thus obtained being frozen in a special account with the Bundesbank' [43].

Finally, 'storage agency bills' and 'prime acceptances' refer respectively to Government guaranteed promissory notes issued by the Import and Storage Agencies within the ceilings granted to them by banking syndicates and up to a limit agreed with the Bank, and bank acceptance 'of a special type' with less than 90 days to maturity. The Bank has undertaken the commitment of buying to the magnitude of DM 850 million and DM 1500 million respectively.

As mentioned above, the Bundesbank Law (Section 21) authorizes the Bank to engage also in transactions in other quoted paper it chooses. Thus in 1967 the Bundesbank declared its willingness to trade in medium-term paper with less than one year and a half to maturity of the Bund and Länder, the Federal Post Office and Federal Railways. In contrast, however, to the practice followed *vis-à-vis* Treasury bills, etc., with regard to transactions in medium-term paper the Bank acts as a price-taker deciding on what amounts to buy or sell, leaving it to the market to determine the equilibrium price and rate.

Thus on reflection it appears that the Bundesbank enjoys substantial freedom in its choice of open market paper, and that the small volume of Government debt referred to above is not an important limitation on the potential available for open market operations. At any rate an examination of such evidence as appears in the Bundesbank's monthly reports suggests that in proportion to the money stock and other relevant items substantial changes in the Bank's holdings of open market paper do from time to time take place; such changes are more relevant than the total volume of Government debt. Indeed, in the light of the constraints imposed by the size of Government debt in the U.K. [44], it could be argued that the small volume of Government debt in Germany enhances the potential for open market operations by absolving the Bank from debt management considerations. This is also emphasized by the price-taking position of the Bank in the medium-term market [45]. It is a separate question, however, whether such market transactions as do take place are designed to effect monetary aggregates or interest rates.

Examining the Bank's own conception of open market policy we find the 'traditional' distinction between sales to banks and sales to the non-bank public. And until recently at any rate transactions between the Bundesbank and banks were thought of as leading 'merely . . . to a change in the composition of the banks' liquidity reserves' whereas transactions with non-banks (in short- or medium-term paper) were thought to result in changes in bank liquidity. Accordingly Bundesbank transactions with banks in short-term paper 'must be considered as relating to interest rate policy rather than to liquidity policy' and perform a function similar to discount rate changes, affecting the willingness of banks to hold different types of assets rather than their ability to hold any particular asset. The introduction of medium- and long-term paper open market transactions [46] in 1967 and increasing use of such dealings in recent years may suggest greater reliance on monetary aggregates; yet the interest policy undertones of such transactions may not be negligible, as it is possible that, though prepared to act as a price-taker in the case of such instruments (taking a direct decision on what amounts to purchase or sell, leaving it to the market to determine the price), the Bank continues to exert a strong influence on their price through appropriate manipulation of the short-term rate.

Minimum Reserve Ratios

Section 16 of the Bundesbank Act as amended in July, 1969, provides that 'in order to influence the volume of money in circulation and of credit granted, the Deutsche Bundesbank may require banks to maintain with it balances on *current account* (minimum reserves) corresponding to a certain percentage of their sight, time and savings deposit liabilities, and short- and medium-term borrowing, with the exception of liabilities to other banks also subject to the minimum reserve regulations'. The percentage fixed by the Bank must not exceed 30% for sight deposits, 20% for time deposits and 10% for savings deposits. However, for liabilities to non-residents the Bank may fix a percentage of up to 100%. Within these limits the Bank may in the light of general considerations fix different ratios, particularly for certain groups of institutions, and may exclude certain liabilities from the basis of calculation. Significantly it is also provides that 'liabilities in respect of sight deposits shall be taken to include debit balances on clearing account' (i.e., used overdrafts).

In exercising such powers the Bank grades minimum reserve ratios according to:

(a) the type and term of the liabilities (sight deposits, time deposits, etc.);

(b) the size of the institution's liabilities (institutions being divided into categories);

(c) the origin of the funds (residents or non-residents);

(d) location (depending on whether or not there is a branch establishment of the Bundesbank in that area).

In addition to such *average reserve ratios* the Bundesbank has, since 1959, from time to time imposed *marginal (incremental) reserve ratios* on particular types of liabilities, with the specific aim of discouraging certain flows, particularly increases in liabilities to foreigners [47].

As referred to earlier, the Law expressly lays down that maximum reserves are to be held exclusively in the form of balances with the Central Bank. Banks have therefore no alternative way of fulfilling their reserve requirements, such as investments in specific interest-bearing paper of the sort found in the U.K. Furthermore a general clause prohibiting the Bundesbank from paying interest on giro deposits prevents the payment of interest on reserves. This does not, however, preclude the payment of a penal rate to the Bank in the event of failure to maintain such reserves as are requested from the particular institution in question. Thus if a bank fails to maintain the full balance required under the minimum reserve regulations, interest is charged on the amount by which actual reserves of the bank fall short of the minimum reserve requirements at a penal rate of 3% above the current Bundesbank Lombard rate for periods of 30 days at a time.

As an instrument of policy, variations in reserve ratios are employed by the Bank to affect both long- and short-term developments in bank liquidity. Such changes are regarded as important in affecting the ability of the banks to increase lending and deposits as well as the structure of interest rates, in so far as they alter the costs of maintaining a certain volume of banking service. Since their introduction in mid-1948 there have been some 60 changes in minimum reserve ratios.

As investment practice varies from bank to bank and as liquidity is unevenly distributed through the banking system, banks naturally react differently to changes in ratios. In order to procure the necessary cash they will either liquidate foreign investments [48], sell domestic money market paper or borrow from the Bank. However individual banks may react, their liquidity is reduced. The decrease in buffer liquidity makes them less willing and able to grant credit; conversely, an improvement in this secondary reserve position tends to cause an increase in their credit granting [49]. In so far as banks are compelled by changes in the minimum reserve requirement to have increased recourse to Bundesbank assistance, the position of the Central Bank as 'lender of last resort' is also strengthened.

In its objectives, and in the effect which it has on 'credit', minimum reserve policy does resemble open market operations. One must, however, note that 'whereas variation in minimum reserve ratios relates to the placing of a compulsory non-interest-bearing loan with no fixed maturity period, the placing of open market paper may be regarded as a commercial mobilizable money market credit granted by the banks to the Bundesbank at market rates'. In addition, of course, variations in reserve ratios have a much more definite impact on banks' expansionary potential than open market operations in general and 'liquidity composition switching operations' in particular.

Reserve ratios on assets

In the preceding discussion our concern has been with reserve ratios relating to bank deposit liabilities. Before the advent of floating exchange rates, however, the Bundesbank showed considerable interest in examining instruments of credit policy that will enable it 'to exercise more direct influence on credit expansion' [50] than is afforded to it through control of lending via bank liquidity and through the instruments already discussed. In this context the desirability of imposing incremental reserve ratios on the increase in bank lending, as an alternative to the rigid quantitative ceilings on such lending discussed at the beginning of this section, was examined. In terms of liquidity policy, it was reasoned,

a reserve ratio on the growth of bank assets would have a similar effect to a minimum reserve on bank liabilities; any increase in the assets side of a bank's balance sheet would be subject to a certain percentage of minimum reserves. The difference as compared with the minimum reserve on liabilities (whether on the total or on the growth thereof) would be that the causal connection between credit expansion and extra minimum reserve requirements would be more apparent, for any increase in a bank's total lending would be accompanied by a rise in the minimum reserves that the institution is required to maintain, at least from the point at which an increase in lending is regarded by the Bank as unduly high and hence subjected to this special reserve burden. In the case of the minimum reserve on liabilities there is no causal relationship for the individual bank but only for the totality of banks. If credit expansion results in an increase in deposits subject to the minimum reserve, the minimum reserve requirement rises, but this need not necessarily occur at the same institution. Owing to the greater clarity of the causal connection the minimum reserve on the growth of bank assets may therefore be a more suitable instrument for influencing lending than the minimum reserve on liabilities.   [51]

Accordingly, in December, 1972, the Bundesbank proposed to the Federal Government that powers for the Bank to introduce a reserve on the increase in assets be included in the Bundesbank Act. As in the case of the alternative scheme of ceilings on lending, however, no further steps have been taken along these lines.

Controls on Capital Movements [52]

In an open economy the degree of freedom afforded to the authorities in the monetary sphere is severely limited by external factors. Accordingly, particularly under fixed exchange rates, the Bundesbank has employed various forms of regulations aiming at preventing or offsetting such destabilizing influences.

Reserve requirements on foreign liabilities

Controls under this heading operate through compulsion and inducement. As referred to above, reserve requirements to a maximum of 100% may be imposed on bank foreign-owned liabilities. Indeed, for most of the period since 1957 German banks were compelled to maintain higher average and/or marginal reserve ratios against liabilities to foreigners than against domestic liabilities [53]. In addition, however, reserve requirements are manipulated so as to induce smaller *net* inflows, by allowing banks the 'right to offset'; that is, since 1961 foreign liabilities have usually been exempt from reserve requirements to the extent that such liabilities were offset by certain types of foreign assets. Banks are thus encouraged to place funds abroad.

While such measures have also been employed in other countries, Germany has been unique in imposing reserve requirements on foreign borrowing by non-banks. Under the Bardepot Law the Government is authorized through the Bundesbank to impose minimum reserve requirements against foreign loans contracted by German companies. Thus in March, 1972, after some three years of continuous frustration of domestic policy objectives by international capital flows [54], the *cash deposit requirement* was introduced whereby a certain percentage of all borrowing abroad (other than the use of foreign trade credits with customary maturities and foreign loans tied to specified supplies of goods and services) had to be deposited in an interest-free account with the Bundesbank. The deposit requirement, fixed initially at 40%, was raised to the then statutory limit of 50% in June, 1972. An increase in the statutory ceiling to 100% was achieved in February, 1973, but the ratio itself was reduced to 20% a year later and eventually abolished in September, 1974, together with other restrictions adopted during this period [55].

Special provisions on 'last resort' lending

Effective from 1 September, 1964, the Bundesbank adopted the policy of reducing a bank's rediscount quota by the amount that gross non-resident liabilities exceeded the average of the first half of 1964. The effectiveness of this instrument was, however, rather limited in practice as banks inclined to borrow abroad tended to have the least recourse to rediscounting. Dropped in June, 1967, this regulation was revived in somewhat modified form in 1970. Under the new arrangements reductions in rediscount quotas were related to increases (relative to March, 1969) in banks' foreign sales of assets under repurchase agreements which were not subject to reserve requirements. The same penalty was imposed on banks' endorsement liabilities, arising from the rediscounting of bills of exchange abroad.

Limits on interest payment on foreign-owned liabilities
As early as mid-1960 the Bundesbank sought to discourage capital inflows by prohibiting the payment of interest on sight or time deposits of non-residents with the exception of savings deposits of individuals. At the same time banks were also forbidden to sell domestic securities subject to re-purchase agreement and money market paper to non-residents. This zero ceiling was partially revoked between May, 1962, and March, 1964, only to be resumed later in 1964 and subsequently (end-1968) to include savings deposits also. Following the 1969 revaluation and consequent massive out-flow of speculative funds, the interest ban was lifted, to be reimposed upon floating the mark in May, 1971. On the arrangements prevalent until September, 1975, all non-domestic liabilities, with the exception of savings accounts of less than DM 50,000 were subject to a zero rate of interest.

Prohibition on new foreign bank deposits
When expectations of revaluation are imminent constraints of the above character are unlikely to prevent speculative inflows. In extreme cases, therefore, such as the November, 1968, exchange crisis, German banks were forbidden to accept additional deposits from foreigners and/or to obtain new foreign loans. The prohibition ended in February, 1969, after the speculative inflow had been reversed [56].

Swaps between the Bundesbank and credit banks
Swaps of foreign for domestic currency were often employed to encourage banks to place funds abroad [57]. The Bundesbank began to offer dollar/mark swaps to the banks as early as October, 1958, charging a premium on forward marks lower than the market premium. Over the years the maturities of the swaps have ranged from two weeks to six months, the banks usually being offered a wide range. The forward mark premium offered by the Bank has of course varied in accordance with the market premium. In recent years swaps were offered during the 1967 sterling crisis, during the 1968 gold crisis

and again from August, 1968, to September, 1969, in an attempt to encourage outflows of speculative capital.

But the effect of such measures has been subject to dispute. It is claimed that during periods of heavy speculative flows (e.g. November, 1968) German banks resold on the exchange market the dollars received from swaps, and used the related forward sales of dollars to the Bundesbank as cover against forward purchases of dollars from resident customers since they could buy forward dollars in the market for less than the sale price stipulated in Bundesbank swaps. Alternatively, while placing abroad dollars acquired by swaps, banks could borrow dollars spot and repurchase them forward at a large enough discount to earn them a profit. It is perhaps significant that the Bundesbank did not offer any such swap facilities during the May to November, 1971, speculative rush.

Coupon taxes and prohibition of sale of securities to foreigners

To discourage inflows of foreign capital in the form of purchases of German bonds, a 25% *coupon tax* was introduced in 1964. This tax, deemed to have made German securities wholly unattractive up to 1969, ceased to be a prohibitive consideration in the light of inducements present in subsequent years. Accordingly, on 29 June, 1972, the Government responding to heavy speculation against sterling, decreed 'that the sale of domestic bearer bonds and bonds payable to order to non-residents be subject to *mandatory authorization*'. The measure, amounting to a ban on purchases of German bonds by foreigners, not only brought such buying to a halt but is said to have even induced sales of them by non-residents. In the period following, sales of German bonds to foreigners were only possible within the framework of 'offsetting arrangements', whereby German banks were allowed (on the basis of a general permit valid for a limited period only) to sell German bonds to foreigners to the extent that they had previously acquired *non-resident quota* by buying or redeeming foreign-owned German bonds. Furthermore, since restrictions on bond sales to non-residents tended to encourage sales of shares and investment fund units to such parties, the authorization requirement for security purchases by non-residents was, with effect from 5 February, 1973, extended to cover shares also. After some amendment in non-resident quotas in July, 1973, all mandatory authorization requirements were abolished in September, 1974 [58].

Immobilized Liquidity and Free Liquid Reserves: the Ingredients in Interpreting Present and Future

While instruments of policy have in accordance with the objectives described in the first and second section of this paper been deployed to induce required responses on the part of the banks, and, ultimately, economic units in general, the *interpretation* of policy has traditionally focused on the behaviour of two aggregates, namely

(a) Immobilized Liquidity (or 'the Central Bank Money Stock', see below), and
(b) Free Liquid Reserves

In aggregate (a) plus (b) do of course comprise *bank liquidity*. But concentration on the aggregate implies 'temporal aggregation bias' [59]. For as the Bundesbank observes,

increases in central bank money [60] and free liquid reserves are by no means equivalent; growth of central bank money indicates definitive monetary expansion whereas growth of free liquid reserves . . . points to the possibility of such expansion. [61]

For reasons that I hope will become apparent in the course of this section both of these components of bank liquidity merit consideration. But whereas now reliance is placed primarily on the former and in particular on the Central Bank Money Stock for the bulk of the period under review free liquidity loomed large in policy statements.

'Monetary policy in Germany' we were told as late as 1972, 'is guided by the basic concept of controlling the banks' supply of credit, and the resultant increase in the money stock via *bank liquidity* and, in addition, of influencing non-banks' demand for credit by changing the interest rate level. The Bundesbank has a number of instruments for varying the banks' holdings of *free liquid reserves* (i.e. such highly liquid assets as a bank can convert into central bank money at its discretion) e.g. changes in minimum reserve ratios, changes in rediscount quotas and open market policy. By raising *free liquid reserves* it can encourage banks to move out of liquid assets for the sake of obtaining a higher return, that is, to extend additional credits; up to now experience has been that the opposite reaction could be expected from a pronounced reduction in bank liquidity. As well as by quantitative measures the Bundesbank influences the holding of *free liquid reserves* by changing certain interest rates, such as when rates are raised, it becomes more attractive for the banks to hold paper representing claims on the Bundesbank, and this tends to restrict and increase the cost of bank credit to customers.' [62]

Free Liquid Reserves and the Liquidity Ratio

In formal terms free liquid reserves are described by

$$FL = BER + BDS + BFS + (\alpha RQ - DB) + (\beta RQ - A) \qquad (2.1)$$

BER = bank holdings of central bank money in excess of required reserves

BDS = domestic money market paper held by banks, i.e. all paper bought by the Bank in the open market or through rediscounting but not included in rediscount quotas

BFS = short-term external assets of banks, namely short-term claims on foreign banks (excluding any such denominated in foreign currency and payable on demand—which are regarded as working balances) plus foreign commercial and Treasury bills and discountable Treasury bonds

RQ = rediscount quotas

DB = discount borrowing

A = advances against security

α, β = utilization limits, i.e. that fraction of the rediscount quota to which banks have access in the form of discount credit and Lombard loans respectively

Within this broad definition one can trace several revisions during the period under review. Earlier definitions tended to omit or refrain from explicit reference to BER and A; between 1970 and 1972 free liquidity was defined as

$$FL = BER + BDS + BFS + (RQ - DB) + (0{\cdot}2RQ - A) \quad (2.2)$$

After the suspension of the Bundesbank's obligation to intervene against the U.S. dollar, however, banks' short-term foreign assets ceased to be thought of as a potential source of central bank money and were accordingly excluded from the definition, although presumably the holdings of such assets in currencies participating in the joint float do continue to provide a source of liquidity for the banks. In conjunction with constraints on the proportion α of rediscount quotas readily accessible to the banks for Bundesbank 'assistance', and suspension of normal Lombard credit, the relevant concept became

$$FL = BER + BDS + 0{\cdot}0BFS + (\alpha RQ - DB) + (0{\cdot}0RQ - A) \quad (2.3)$$

where α was at $0{\cdot}60$ between February and October, 1973, reduced further thereafter but raised again in November and eventually at $0{\cdot}75$ in May, 1974.

By analogy reactivation of normal Lombard credit and cancellation of limits on useable rediscount quotas (3 July, 1974) yields a liquidity concept for July, 1974, of

$$FL = BER + BDS + 0{\cdot}0BFS + (RQ - DB) + K - A \quad (2.4)$$

where K refers to bank holdings of securities eligible for advances against security but not classifying as money market paper. In so far as in all cases the primary consideration is whether any particular asset can be 'readily' employed to increase the stock of central bank money such changes in definition may be said to be 'technical' rather than 'conceptual' in character.

Comparison of (2.2) and (2.3) and (2.4), however, also reveals that an important consideration is *how readily* can a particular asset be so employed, since to the extent that *BDS* and *RQ* overlap in terms of range of securities variations in α may not imply a change in *FL* while they do imply a change in terms on which such securities are held. Implicit in (2.3), for example, seems greater willingness to accept variations in interest rates than will appear to be the case for the period to which (2.4) relates. Concentration on the aggregate does therefore imply considerable simplification; but perhaps some insight could be gained from so doing.

Ability to predictably influence the volume of credit and deposits by concentrating on bank-free liquidity depends on whether *FL* can be treated as an aggregate the supply of which is determined by the authorities and the demand for which on the part of the banks and the public respectively is stable and predictable. In so far therefore as liquidity has, certainly throughout the 1960s, served as an index of the potential available to banks for expansion, one may enquire as to whether this aggregate meets the necessary conditions.

With regard to the former, changes in reserve ratios, in rediscount quotas, in eligibility requirements for private securities included in *FL*, and transactions in open market medium-term paper do of course secure changes in volume of free liquid reserves. Indeed such inferences as can be drawn from studies which in strict monetarist tradition dismiss liquidity as an inadequate 'target' for policy and concentrate on 'proving' that the Bundesbank can and did deploy variations in reserve ratios to secure control of high powered money, do, in the light of the definition of bank liquidity as 'assets readily convertible into central-bank money', suggest that the Bank can by varying reserve ratios control free liquid reserves (offsetting changes in such components of *BL* as are not within its control).

Similarly as regards the second condition necessary to ensure Bundesbank control of intermediate variables (such as credit, deposits, and interest rates) through control of *FL*, namely that demand for free liquid reserves on the part of the banks is stable and predictable, it has been argued that:

For many years the banks reacted to fluctuations in their liquidity ratio—that is to say the proportion of their liquid assets to total deposits—by changing their lending policy . . . [63]

Indeed a definite sequence of events was posited:

The first reaction of the banks is to cut back net acquisitions of bonds, and bond holdings correlate closely with bank liquidity. This has an immediate effect on bond yields and other interest rates. The second reaction is that banks become cautious in entering into new loan commitments and this is reflected after a while on bank credit expansion.   [64]

Chart 2.3. Bank liquidity and capital market

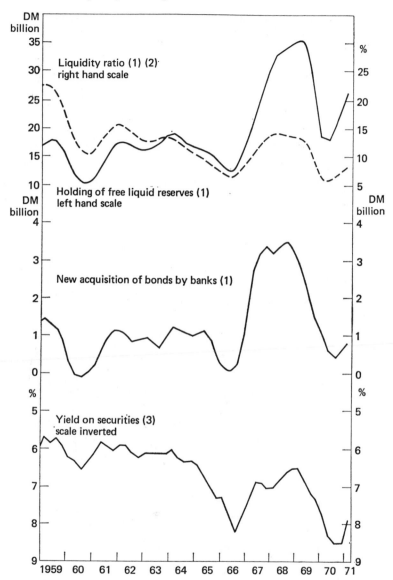

(1) Seasonally adjusted and smoothed. (2) Free liquid reserves as % of total deposits.
(3) Yield on fully-taxed bonds outstanding, quarterly averages. Partly estimated.
Source: Deutsche Bundesbank Annual Report for the year 1971.

There are, of course, lags to the process but these are determinate since

there is in general a typical time lag of about a year observed in every phase of the cycle between the change in the liquidity position of the banks and hence their credit creation potential on the one hand and the actual use of this potential on the other. [65]

Charts 2.3 and 2.4 lend some substance to such claims, though the relationship between the liquidity ratio, allowing for a one-year lag, and bank credit does not, save for the latter half of the 1960s, appear particularly stable. At any rate as the last chart suggests at the turn of the decade the relationship previously claimed will appear to have ceased to obtain.

Chart 2.4. Bank liquidity and credit expansion

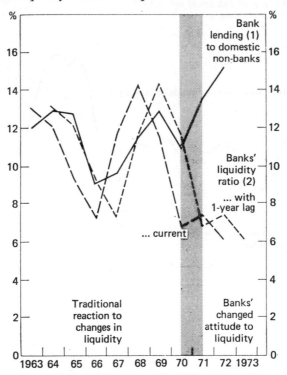

(1) Annual growth rates of bank lending, including acquisition of securities. (2) Free liquid reserves (= domestic money market paper, unused rediscount quotas, money market investments abroad, balances with the Bundesbank less minimum reserve required and less Lombard loans taken) as % of total deposits; annual averages.
Source: Deutsche Bundesbank Annual Report for the year 1972.

In the past, it was reasoned, the Bundesbank acted
on the assumption that free liquid reserves were necessary for the smooth functioning of the banking system and that it would be able to attain its monetary policy
target indirectly by influencing the amount of free liquid reserves . . . From Spring
of 1970 onwards, this basic premise of liquidity policy became increasingly question-
able . . . (since) Even when free liquid reserves had been reduced to a level which
previous experience had shown to be 'critical', credit expansion continued unabated
or even accelerated. It became evident that the basic condition for liquidity policy
in the form hitherto pursued was no longer assured. [66]

The Stock of Central Bank Money

It was in this frame that the Bundesbank move to favouring attention on the
behaviour of the Stock of Central Bank Money *CBM* occurred '. . . thus
bringing into sharper focus the question of the extent to which the central
bank makes central bank money directly available for expansion' [67].
Significantly the stock of central bank money is defined to exclude bank excess reserves and also reserves held against non-domestic liabilities and hence

$$CBM = (BIL - BFR)^{\alpha} + CC \qquad (2.5)$$

BIL = bank immobilized liquidity
BFR = bank holdings of reserves against non-domestic liabilities -
CC = currency in circulation
α = adjustment for variations (over time) in required reserve ratios (the
base year employed is January, 1974)

Thus the definition of *CBM* is such as to reflect the level as well as composition of bank-domestic liabilities, the implication being that no exclusive
attention is paid to any particular component of such liabilities such as
demand, time, or savings deposits.

In favour of the concept it may be argued that in so far as relative (base-
period) reserve ratios, applying to different types of bank deposits, can be
said to reflect an accurate evaluation of relative 'moneyness' of different types
of bank liabilities, this index of *'actual'* monetary expansion is superior
to that of other 'high-powered-money' concepts hitherto advanced. Yet if
such thinking provides the rationale for this measure certain questions must
be raised [68].

(*i*) In the first instance it must be objected that the precise definition of
Central Bank Money employed attributes an unacceptably high weight to
'currency in the hands of the public' compared with bank deposits of various
kinds. More precisely suppose that the following expression defines the
weighted money stock *WMS* considered relevant as a determinant of economic
activity

$$WMS = \sum_{j} W_j D_j + CC \qquad (2.6)$$

where D_j is a vector of quantities of the various types of bank liabilities and W_j are the 'moneyness-coefficients' corresponding to such liabilities. Then if, as seems reasonable, we accept that the coefficient on sight deposits is approximately equal to that on currency, the appropriate weighted monetary base concept is

$$CBM^\alpha = \sum_j R_j D_j + R_i CC \qquad (2.7)$$

where R_j are the reserve ratios corresponding to D_j and R_i is the reserve ratio on demand deposits. A definition of CBM such as that adopted by the Bank will then comprise an erroneous indicator unless the volume of currency in the hands of the public is a constant proportion c of the Central Bank money stock, i.e. unless

$$CC = cCBM = \frac{c}{1-c} \sum R_j D_j \qquad (2.8)$$

implying a constant currency to weighted deposits, $\sum_j W_j D_j$, ratio. As Chart 2.5 reveals [69] this was certainly not the case during the period 1961–1976. Over this period the ratio of Central Bank Money to GNP moved from 0·4027 in 1961(I) to 0·4059 in 1976(II) while the ratio of $RCBM$ to GNP rose from 0·1421 in 1961(I) to 0·1928 in 1976(II) revealing a reduction in c from 0·6470 to 0·5249.

(ii) For any particular moment in time the previous reasoning does, as stated, rest on the assumption that relative reserve ratios do reflect relative 'moneyness', i.e.

$$R_j = MW_j, \qquad (2.9)$$

where M is a scalar.

That such a hypothesis may be suspect is all too obvious to require elaboration. But a more accurate appraisal of its content cannot be secured without explicit definition of the behavioural functions of the banks and the public [70]. On the other hand it must be stressed that adjustment for over time variation in *actual* required reserve ratios does entail the additional assumption that relative 'moneyness' is temporally invariant and hence that alterations in required reserve ratios relative to those of the base period reflect non-systematic variations in demand for different bank liabilities. While for short periods of time such an assumption may be valid, over longer periods one may expect relative W_j to alter and hence a bias (additional to that identified above with respect to currency) imparted in deductions based on such a concept.

That such a change in weights can be identified empirically I have demonstrated elsewhere [71]. More significantly, however, it can easily be shown that the assumptions necessary to secure constancy of 'moneyness coefficients'

Chart 2.5. Monetary aggregates and economic activity (seasonally adjusted data)

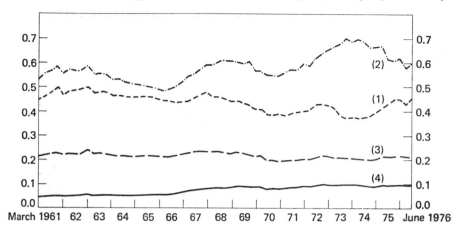

(1) $= (M_1/GNP) - 0.20$
(2) $= (M_2/GNP) - 0.40$
(3) $= (CBM/GNP) - 0.20$
(4) $= (RCBM/GNP) - 0.10$
M_1 = currency + sight deposits
M_2 = M_1 + time deposits for less than 4 years
CBM = Central Bank Money Stock
$RCBM$ = CBM − currency in circulation
GNP = GNP at current prices

	(a) Mean	(b) Stan. dev.	(b/a)
CBM/GNP	0.4089	0.0110	0.0269
M_1/GNP	0.6214	0.0335	0.0539
M_2/GNP	0.9604	0.0535	0.0557

are those that will make the construction of such a concept unnecessary since they rest on perfectly stable demand functions for the *individual components* of the weighted money stock aggregate [72].

While, however, such qualifications emphasize the need for a more accurate appraisal of the weights embodied in the construction of this aggregate [73], they do not necessarily detract from the claim that the Central Bank money stock bears a much more stable relationship to aggregate demand than is the case with *narrower* (and hence more responsive in interest induced changes) money concepts, such as M_1 and M_2. Chart 2.5 certainly supports this claim. Even more convincingly the estimates presented in Table 2.1 reveal a remarkable regularity in the behaviour of *CBM* as a function of real GNP and the price level. Consistently with Bundesbank pronouncements,

Table 2.1. *The demand for CBM and other monetary aggregates 1963(II)–1976(II)*

Functional form $\ln M_t = b_1 \ln Y_t + b_2 \ln P_t + b_3 \ln M_{t-1} + a$

(compensated for first order serial correlation)

Dependent variable	b_1	b_2	b_3	a	$1 - b_1 - b_3$	$1 - b_2 - b_3$
CBM	0·138 (2·63)	0·132 (1·90)	0·862 (14·47)	−0·104 (0·93)	0·000 (0·01)	0·006 (0·31)
M_1	0·078 (0·14)	0·318 (2·13)	0·775 (6·77)	0·592 (1·77)	0·147 (1·79)	−0·092 (1·89)
M_2	0·273 (3·14)	0·006 (0·07)¹	0·889 (12·97)	−0·735 (3·72)	−0·162 (3·83)	0·105 (2·94)

Dependent variable	ρ	Total variance	Explained variance	Residual variance	S.E. in %	$\chi^2/(d)$
CBM	0·171 (0·12)	17·76859	17·76852	0·00006	0·0019	3·320 (2)
M_1	0·200 (1·13)	21·36575	21·36552	0·00023	0·0033	9·583 (2)
M_2	0·068 (0·42)	25·77196	25·77173	0·00024	0·0030	9·244 (2)

Note: All data are in seasonally adjusted form.
Y_t = real GNP; P_t = GNP deflator
ρ = first order serial correlation coefficient
S.E. in % = standard error estimate divided by the mean of the dependent variable
$\chi^2/(d)$ = chi squared ratio of the log-likelihood values of restricted (for ρ) and unrestricted reduced forms with (d) degrees of freedom
Relationship specified $\ln M_t - \rho \ln M_{t-1} - b_1 Y_t + \rho b_1 Y_{t-1} - b_2 P_t + \rho b_2 P_{t-1} - b_3 M_{t-1} + \rho b_3 M_{t-2} - (1 - \rho) a = u_t - \rho u_{t-1}$. For each equation all parameters were estimated simultaneously by the maximum likelihood method [74].

the long run elasticities of demand for *CBM* with respect to real GNP, $b_1/(1 - b_3)$, and with respect to prices, $b_2/(1 - b_3)$, are not significantly different from unity, a feature that contrasts sharply with the estimates derived for other monetary aggregates [75].

Even so, we must observe that though focusing on the volume and growth of *CBM* appears, notwithstanding the qualifications raised above, to tell us a great deal about the degree of monetary expansion, defined to relate to the weighted money stock aggregate cited, it alas does so simultaneously and as such is endowed with no informational or predictive content over and above that gained by looking at the growth of liabilities themselves. In marked contrast the free liquid reserves relationship discussed above was interesting precisely because it was thought to provide information about the *future* course of events in the monetary sector. To put it differently, while given knowledge of the volume and composition of bank liabilities at any given moment of time there is nothing to be gained from knowledge of the Stock of Central Bank Money, save a statement of the behaviour of the public's currency ratio, free liquid reserves do (to the extent that the lagged relationship between free liquid reserves and bank credit or the money stock is stable) convey information as to how banks will behave in the future and hence of developments some time ahead.

What Happened to the Free Liquid Reserves Association?

While Chart 2.4 does suggest a very definite change to have occurred at the turn of the decade (shaded area) this change does not necessarily imply that '. . . the free liquid reserves have therefore forfeited their value as an indicator . . .' [76] of the future course of events.

Various factors may be called to explain the 1970 to 1971 change. In particular the rapid expansion of national and international money markets, encouraged no doubt by the sharp liquidity squeeze in the first half of 1970, implied the existence of new sources of 'support' when needed and accordingly a decreased need for the special support from the Central Bank by means of assets eligible there when the corresponding assurance has been given. Such developments do indeed imply a shift in the desired free liquid reserves to deposits ratio and hence an apparent lack of relationship between the free liquid reserves ratio on the one hand and bank credit or money on the other, *during the period over which the shift occurs.* Yet once the new desired free liquid reserves to deposits ratio has been reached one should expect that some relationship between FL/D and bank credit is established.

Chart 2.6 extends the period covered in 2.4 to the end of 1975. As is immediately obvious banks now operate at a much lower FL/D ratio than before. But subject to a shorter (nine months) lag a relationship between FL/D and BC is clearly identifiable. It will therefore appear that after a period of transition bank behaviour is again conditioned by a relationship between FL/D and BC no more unstable than that on which the free liquid reserves doctrine was founded.

Yet in rediscovering a relationship between free liquid reserves and bank credit we cannot but revive the question of the *exact behavioural hypothesis contained therein.*

Chart 2.6. Bank credit and free liquid reserves 1971–1975

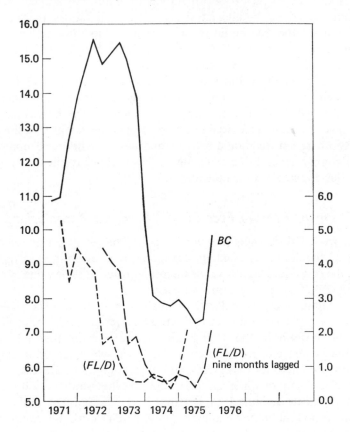

Note:

FL/D = free liquid reserves ratio, centred quarterly averages; right-hand scale
BC   = Bank credit, percentage change from corresponding previous year quarter; left-hand scale

Reflections on the Art of Central Banking

As regards the latter issue an explicit hypothesis has never to my knowledge been tendered by the Bank. Indeed

The direct connection between liquidity movements and growth of the money stock and of reserve-carrying liabilities not counting towards the money stock *was not recognisable* [77].

But until the seventies

There were two reasons for not regarding this disadvantage as ... serious ...
Firstly, it was possible to obtain information on the extent of the (actual) monetary
expansion using the various definitions of the money stock. Secondly, the trend of
free liquid reserves was interesting in terms of the effects they were expected to
produce in the future [78].

There is of course little difficulty in specifying behavioural functions that
describe bank responses *analogous* to those referred to in the previous section.
Yet to suggest that such responses conform to a *particular* time lag of whatever duration is much less palatable, since, in general, one would expect that
such lags would depend on the opportunity costs of alternative speeds of
adjustment and are therefore unlikely to be constant over time *unless* the
monetary authority's own actions are designed, consciously or unconsciously,
to secure such an outcome.

Closer inspection of the Bank's perception of free liquidity does indeed
reveal that the mechanistic relationship quoted above was not always invoked.
Thus in 1966 the Bank commented that

According to all experience there was no ground to expect that changes in the banks'
free liquidity would necessarily alter the degree of credit expansion [79].

and in 1970

The relationship between changes in bank free liquidity—the most important outcome of applying monetary policy—and the influencing of the banks' capacity to
lend (it is this after all that is ultimately intended) is far from accurately predictable
... Even when their liquidity is greatly depleted, the banks' view of the degree of
credit expansion warranted by the available liquid reserves may change; the same
liquidity ratio does not necessarily mean the same measure of willingness to step up
lending [80].

A general impression that lags invariably deviate from what was referred
to above as 'typical' is hard to avoid. But such deviations are far from
random. In the Banks' own analysis we find that lags depend on the degree
of change in policy adopted and a distinction drawn between responses to
'beginning of relaxation of financial climate' and 'intensified policy of relaxation' relating to the rate of change in free liquid reserves [81]. More
generally they depend on the relative yields and risks attaching to alternative
assets and liabilities comprised in bank portfolios. Over specific intervals of
time the combined influence of such factors may be such as to secure a
ceteris paribus association between the liquidity ratio and bank credit or bank
liabilities at some specific instant in the future. Yet any such association will
disappear when either policy or exogenous factors become too strenuous for
its *ceteris paribus* assumptions to endure.

Under this light free liquid reserves and the degree of 'actual monetary
expansion' cannot be viewed as alternatives, since (in the absence of precise

and continuous knowledge of the response functions of the banks and the public) their relative behaviour embodies information that neither of them in isolation nor any other single variable index can conceivably secure. In this respect the Bank's reliance on *both* these indices (see p. 32, above) was far from misguided; and though one may question the relative efficiency of the index of 'actual' monetary expansion chosen, *CBM*, the evidence forthcoming that free liquid reserves continue to comprise part of the information set on which policy design relies is, in my view, highly significant.

Footnotes

This paper refrains from discussion of the rule with regard to increases in the Stock of Central Bank Money, an issue I have commented upon elsewhere, Courakis (1967b).
* I am grateful to H. Bockelmann, H. J. Dudler and C. A. E. Goodhart for their comments on an earlier draft of this paper.
1. 1957 Bank Act. See Aufricht (1968) and E.C. Monetary Committee (1972). Legal competence of the Bundesbank in the monetary sphere excludes exchange rate stability for which Federal Government carries ultimate responsibility.
2. *Ibid*, article 12.
3. See, for example, Klaus & Falk (1970) particularly pp. 106–14, and also Baumgarten & Wolfgang (1971).
4. *Deutsche Bundesbank Annual Report*, 1967, p. 30.
5. *Ibid*, p. 30, emphasis added.
6. *Ibid*, pp. 29–30.
7. For discussions of central and regional government finance and expenditure policies and evaluation of the impact of such policies, see Brunner & Neumann (1971), Brunner *et al.* (1972), Biehl (1973), Gerelli (1966), Hansen (1969), Kasper (1972), Keran (1970), Kulmer (1969), Lotz (1971), Roskamp & Laumas (1967), Snyder (1970), Zeitel (1968) and Deutsche Bundesbank Monthly Reports, August, 1971; April, 1972; July, 1972; July, 1973; November, 1973.
8. *Deutsche Bundesbank Annual Report*, 1967, pp. 25–6.
9. *Deutsche Bundesbank Annual Reports*, 1970 to 1974.
10. See also Courakis (1976).
11. See also section on the art of central banking below.
12. Although 'the liquidity of the economy' remains vague endeavours to define money have, for most of the period under review, fallen short of anything wider than currency plus sight deposits. Inclusion of time deposits at less than three months' notice, it was commented in 1971, 'had to be abandoned' when it became evident that high interest elasticity of such deposits prevented this aggregate from yielding 'any reliable information concerning monetary developments'. All time deposits with less than four years' notice are, therefore, now classified as near money with the exception of savings deposits which, it is claimed, 'despite their formal short-term character are best regarded, from an economic angle, as different from time deposits'. See *Deutsche Bundesbank Monthly Report*, July, 1971, 'Longer-term Movement in the Money Stock', and also E.C. Monetary Committee (1972). Nevertheless, following the September, 1972, recommendation of the E.E.C. Commission, the Bank began to comment on the behaviour of a wider agregate M_2 that includes such near money, while as described in Section IV of this paper a yet wider aggregate is implicit in more recent policy design.
13. See also Schiller (1967).
14. See pp. 5–6 of this volume.
15. *Deutsche Bundesbank Annual Report*, 1974, p. 24.

16. With regard to this issue see, for example, *Deutsche Bundesbank Annual Report,* 1973, p. 3.

17. I am here alluding to the fact that the question of definition of 'the base' is to some extent a matter of convenience so long as the researcher remembers that alternative definitions require alternative specifications of the demand/supply relationship pertaining to the various components of the aggregate under consideration.

18. See also my 'comment' on Neumann's paper in this volume, and Richter (1974).

19. See, for example, Revell (1973) and Den Dunnen (1972).

20. Although proposals to the effect that 'credit ceiling' powers be extended to the Central Monetary Authority were made during the discussions relating to the law to promote economic stability and growth, such proposals were not acted upon.

21. *Deutsche Bundesbank Annual Report,* 1972, p. 27.

22. *Ibid.*

23. In quite exceptional circumstances the former Central Bank (Bank deutscher Länder) imposed limits on the volume of credits. Such measures were last used during the 1950–1 credit restrictions.

24. As we shall see below, the Bundesbank is statutorily obliged not to pay interest on banks' compulsory reserve holdings. Liquidity ratios such as are found, for example, in the U.K. (see Revell (1973)) and more recently in the Netherlands, do not, therefore, feature among German instruments of banking control. Yet, as is to be expected, the Bank focuses its attention on the asset holdings of banks as an index of the potential for expansion available to them.

25. See *Deutsche Bundesbank Monthly Reports,* April, 1965; July, 1970; June, 1973; and July, 1974. It should be stressed that although in official statements the term *liquidity of the banking system* has sometimes been used to describe *free liquid reserves* the former is in this paper explicitly employed to describe the sum of *free* plus *immobilized* liquidity.

26. A long-term series of 'discount' and 'Lombard' rates can be found in any issue of the Bank's *Monthly Report.* The difference between the two rates was for a long time maintained at 1% but has in recent years widened to, on occasion, 3%.

27. See also E.C. Monetary Committee (1962).

28. See *Deutsche Bundesbank Monthly Report,* October, 1971.

29. For the importance of 'announcement (type) effects' see *Deutsche Bundesbank Annual Report,* 1967, p. 4, regarding the 1966–67 monetary expansion.

30. Another form of Bundesbank intervention is the purchase of *equalization claims.* These are interest-bearing Debt-Register claims on the Länder or Federal Government. Credit institutions (and insurance companies, i.e. holders of such claims) that decide to sell equalization claims sell these to a Purchase Fund, the resources of which are derived principally from the allocation of part of the profits of the Bundesbank. In so far and so long as the resources of the Fund are not sufficient for this purpose, the Bundesbank may advance funds by purchasing equalization claims for its own account. The equalization claims temporarily acquired by the Bundesbank in this way are resold to the Fund, as soon as it again has sufficient funds at its disposal.

31. Section 20 of the Bundesbank Act imposes specific quantitative ceilings for cash advances (including Treasury bills which the Bank has bought on its own account or has promised to buy) that the Bank may provide to particular public bodies (such as the Federal Government, each of the Länder, nationalized industries, and other public corporations).

32. Suspended in May, 1973 (until further notice), they were reactivated at the end of May, 1974, when in response to extreme tightness in the money market the Bundesbank granted the banks *special* Lombard credit at a rate of 10%. Normal Lombard credit, with no limit as to the amount, was activated on 3 July, 1974, following the unrest on the credit markets resulting from the closing of the Herstatt Bank.

Initially for limited periods, this arrangement was subsequently extended until further notice.

33. In the absence of stock exchange quotation the Bank decides on the value that is to serve as a basis for lending on the collateral of the non-quoted security.

34. E.C.C. Monetary Committee 1972.

35. For definitions of liquidity see *Deutsche Bundesbank Annual Reports*.

36. Over the last few years the Bank has adopted the practice of imposing a limit on the percentage of their rediscount quotas that banks are allowed to utilize. This percentage has varied from 60% to 100% between January, 1972, and July, 1974, respectively.

37. Until 30 May, 1973, this percentage was set at 20% of rediscount quotas. Between 30 May and 3 July, 1974, the percentage was 0%, although at the end of May, 1974, *special* Lombard loans were granted at a higher rate. Normal Lombard credit was, as referred to above, resumed on 3 July, 1974, with no limit as to the amount.

38. In the revised method of calculation of quotas introduced in February, 1974, '*the individual structure* of a bank' is explicitly considered. See *Deutsche Bundesbank Monthly Report*, April, 1975, pp. 24–6.

39. See Irmler (1970) and *Deutsche Bundesbank Annual Report*, 1971, p. 17.

40. Two factors would seem to account for the relative smallness of national debt in Germany. The first is that such debt was almost completely wiped out by the two legendary inflations and the currency reforms that followed (1923 and 1948). The second is that partly as a result of very healthy economic conditions and partly owing to the independence of the monetary authority referred to above, the last two decades have not, until recently at any rate, seen substantial additions to its volume. At the end of the 1960s the aggregate public debt of the Federal Government (including special funds), the Länder governments and local authorities and including old debt dating from before the currency reform of 1948, was only about one-fifth of the GNP.

41. See also E.C. Monetary Committee (1966) and (1970).

42. E.C. Monetary Committee (1972).

43. Schloenbach (1974).

44. See, for example, Courakis (1973).

45. This should not be taken to imply that the authorities are entirely oblivious of bond price behaviour. Indeed the Bundesbank, acting on behalf of the Government, does 'in normal circumstances' offset excess demand and excess supply so as to eliminate random price fluctuations. Furthermore, 'in times of strain on the capital market, the Federal Government has temporarily extended this obligation and made more funds available to the Bundesbank, enabling it to intervene on the market for Government securities and *ensure that the market is not disturbed by sharp drops in prices*'. E.C. Monetary Committee (1970).

However, such tendencies are not allowed to impede monetary policy for, as stated elsewhere in the same source, the authorities 'considered that in the last analysis the greatest possible measure of price level stability was the most effective way of safeguarding the interests of holders of securities and, consequently, the interests of the bond market'. Thus, in general, 'fluctuations in interest' were usually accepted—indeed welcomed—except when a curb on interest rates seemed to be advisable because of the trend in economic activity.

46. *Deutsche Bundesbank Annual Report*, 1967, p. 48.

47. See also the discussion on reserve requirements on foreign liabilities below. In total the Bundesbank operates on some thirty reserve ratios at a time. See any issue of *Deutsche Bundesbank Monthly Report*.

48. Under existing arrangements regarding foreign exchange transactions such a move provides a solution to the shortage of Central Bank money facing the banking system as a whole only to the extent that such foreign investments are in currencies included in the joint float.

49. See also section on the art of central banking below.
50. For a discussion of such proposals, see Kath (1973) and Ehrlicher (1973).
51. *Deutsche Bundesbank Annual Report*, 1972, pp. 26–7.
52. See Issing (1974), E.C. Monetary Committee (1972), Mills (1968 and 1972), Porter (1972), Wadbrook (1972), Willms (1970), Whiteman (1974), Branson & Hill (1971).
53. In particular, average reserve ratios were higher for foreign-owned liabilities:

From	*To*
May, 1957	March, 1959
January, 1961	January, 1962
April, 1964	January, 1967
June, 1969	October, 1969
June, 1971	July, 1975

Marginal reserve requirements on foreign liabilities were imposed briefly in 1960, and have been applied almost continuously since December, 1968.
54. *Deutsche Bundesbank Annual Report*, 1971, pp. 35–6, and 1972, pp. 40–1.
55. *Deutsche Bundesbank Annual Report*, 1973, p. 6 and 1974, p. 20.
56. *Deutsche Bundesbank Annual Report*, 1970, pp. 16–17.
57. Similar arrangements were often effective in the Netherlands and other European countries.
58. *Deutsche Bundesbank Annual Report*, 1972, pp. 40, 55 and 73–5; 1973, pp. 6 and 26; 1974, p. 20.
59. I apologise to the reader for creating my own terminology in this case.
60. Read 'immobilized liquidity'.
61. *Deutsche Bundesbank Monthly Report*, July, 1974, p. 19.
62. *Deutsche Bundesbank Annual Report*, 1972, p. 25.
63. See Schlesinger, p. 2 above.
64. *BIS* (1972), chapter by Schlesinger & Bockelman, p. 49.
65. *Deutsche Bundesbank Annual Report*, 1966, p. 40. Also Neumann (1970).
66. *Deutsche Bundesbank Monthly Report*, July, 1974, p. 14.
67. *Ibid*, p. 15.
68. It should be stressed that similar objections can of course be raised with regard to other monetary aggregates also.
69. A more detailed discussion is provided in Courakis (1976b).
70. See Courakis (1976a).
71. Courakis (1971).
72. See Courakis (1971) and (1976b).
73. Some estimates on this issue are presented in Courakis (1976b).
74. Christ (1965), pp. 481–8 and Courakis (1976c).
75. See, however, also Courakis (1976b).
76. Schlesinger, p. 3 above.
77. *Deutsche Bundesbank Monthly Report*, July, 1974, p. 15.
78. *Ibid*.
79. *Deutsche Bundesbank Annual Report*, 1966, p. 48.
80. *Deutsche Bundesbank Annual Report*, 1970, pp. 25–6, and 1971, pp. 55–6.
81. See for example, *Deutsche Bundesbank Annual Report*, 1967, pp. 29–30.

3

Monetary Indicators in the Federal Republic of Germany*

MANFRED WILLMS

Introduction

During the last few years there has been a considerable debate among economists over the selection of an appropriate monetary indicator in Germany. In this context the questions raised have been two fold, namely:

(a) Which variable can best be used to measure the impact of monetary policy on economic activity?

(b) Does the use of more than one indicator improve information?

Variables proposed as monetary indicators are the monetary base, the money stock narrowly and broadly defined, bank credit, bank liquidity (i.e. free liquid reserves in the hands of the banks), and the calculated credit maximum (i.e. the maximum potential bank lending given the amount of reserve assets and the reserve ratio).

Bank liquidity served for a long time as the official indicator of German monetary policy. Since the early 1960s different scales of bank liquidity were used by the Deutsche Bundesbank to classify policy actions as tight or easy [1]. The German Council of Economic Advisers (Sachverständigenrat zur Begutachtung der gesamtwirtschaftlichen Entwicklung) followed the tradition of the Bundesbank and based its interpretation of monetary policy mainly on bank liquidity. In its Annual Report 1970/71 the Council stated that a reduction of bank liquidity or the liquidity ratio can be interpreted as a restrictive monetary policy because it leads to an increase of interest rates and a reduction of credit expansion. The Council also argues, however, explicitly that monetary policy cannot only be judged by the change of bank liquidity but also by the development of interest rates, and hence that these variables—liquidity and interest rates—should be used simultaneously as monetary indicators [2].

In its Annual Report 1971/72 the Council developed a new monetary indicator, the calculated credit maximum. This variable is a hypothetical magnitude of credits which can be granted when the total of liquid reserves of commercial banks equals required reserves. According to the Council the calculated credit maximum represents a reliable indicator of the impact of monetary policy [3].

It was particularly the theoretical framework and the interpretation of monetary policy advocated by the German Council of Economic Advisers which were vigorously attacked by Brunner and Neumann [4]. Brunner and Neumann demonstrated the theoretical inconsistency of the indicator candidates used by the Council and criticized heavily the simultaneous application of more than one indicator variable. The use of bank liquidity and the calculated credit maximum as monetary indicators were, on the other hand, defended mainly by economists close to the Council of Economic Advisers [5].

While economists were arguing over the selection of an adequate indicator of monetary policy, the Bundesbank made a remarkable turn in its attitude towards its traditional monetary indicator. In its Monthly Report of July, 1971, statistics of money narrowly defined were published for the first time [6]. This indicated the Bundesbank's increased attention to the indicator qualities of the quantity of money. In addition, a remarkable turn took place in its monetary policy. When in 1973 the introduction of floating exchange rates stopped the inflow of overvalued U.S. dollars, the Bundesbank used this opportunity to switch to a restrictive monetary policy in order to fight inflation. This policy was completely oriented towards the control of the monetary base. The 'Central Bank', it was commented in the 1973 Annual Report, 'now controls the creation of Central Bank money directly, whereas previously it has done so only indirectly via the free liquid reserves' [7]. Furthermore since July, 1974, the analysis of bank liquidity in the Monthly Reports has been replaced by an analysis of Central Bank money creation and free liquidity reserves [8].

The change of the intellectual climate in Germany with respect to monetary policy is also apparent in the Annual Report of the Council of Economic Advisers. While in previous years the Council analysed the calculated credit maximum as an indicator of monetary policy, the Report for 1974/75 no longer mentioned this concept.

This paper is a comprehensive theoretical analysis of indicator variables proposed to evaluate monetary policy in Germany and examines empirically various indicator candidates. In the following section a brief summary of the indicator problem is given. A simple model is constructed from which the 'ideal' indicator in the sense of Brunner/Meltzer is derived. In the third section different indicator candidates of monetary policy in Germany are examined on a theoretical basis. The fourth section presents the empirical results, while the concluding part summarizes the results and comments on their implications.

The Indicator Problem

Rational monetary policy requires information about the impact of past and current policy actions on future movements in ultimate goal variables of economic policy. Given perfect information about all structural interrelationships in the economy the exact impact of a change in any monetary policy variable on the ultimate goal variable could be expressed quantitatively. For example, let y = real income, and v_1, v_2 = instruments of monetary policy, then

$$\frac{\mathrm{d}y}{y} = \varepsilon(y, v_1)\frac{\mathrm{d}v_1}{v_1} + \varepsilon(y, v_2)\frac{\mathrm{d}v_2}{v_2} \tag{3.1}$$

would give the percentage change in y as a result of a given percentage change in v_1 and v_2.

Under perfect information (and given preferences) the monetary policy problem, or any economic policy problem, would be trivial. However, information about the structure of the economy is incomplete and does not allow for precise tracing of the effects of changes in policy variables on ultimate goal variables.

Our limited information notably does not allow for a separation of influences stemming from monetary policy actions from those of exogenous variables or other economic policy actions. In addition, varying lags in the transmission of monetary policy impulses complicate the analysis still further. In effect monetary policy actions cannot be evaluated by simply looking at the corresponding movements of the ultimate goal variable; the impact of these actions has to be judged by looking at the movement of other variables in the economic system which allow for earlier and easier measurement of the influence of policy actions.

Under incomplete information, classification of monetary policy into 'easy', 'tight' or 'neutral' can be pursued along these lines. One possibility is to use a classificatory scale. In this case, the impact of monetary policy on the economy is interpreted according to the change in the direction of a policy variable. For example, a decrease in the discount rate, the open market rate or the required reserve ratio is interpreted as an expansive monetary policy and an increase of these variables as a restrictive monetary policy. This procedure requires that only one policy variable is changed, or that the change of more than one instrument variable has an unequivocal impact on the goal variable. Besides these restrictions the information from a classificatory scale is very limited because it is not possible to derive the relative impact of different policy strategies and/or of different variables applied at a time.

A higher grade of information is provided by an ordinal scale, because it allows for a comparison of different policy strategies. Thus, an ordinal scale may be usefully applied for judging the impact of monetary policy. The problem remains then to select out of a number of candidates the optimal indicator which can be expressed in an ordinal way, and which fulfils other important requirements.

Brunner and Meltzer solve this problem by deriving a 'true' or 'ideal' indicator from a reduced system of a complete macroeconomic model [9]. Various indicator candidates are then compared with the 'true' indicator and judged according to their ranking relative to this indicator.

A similar procedure will be followed here. The condensed model of the economy consists of two markets: a goods market (3.2), and a credit market (3.3).

$$yp(y, Q) = h[m_1(i, i_f, y)B^{\text{ex}}] \tag{3.2}$$

$$m_k(i, i_f, y)B^{\text{ex}} = \lambda(i, y) \tag{3.3}$$

The left side of equation (3.2) represents the supply of goods and the right side the demand for goods. Accordingly, the left side of equation (3.3) describes the supply of (bank) credit while the right side shows the demand. The variables are: y = real income, p = price level, Q = capital stock, h = demand function for goods and services, m_1 = money multiplier, i = market interest rate, i_f = index of short-term interest rates (discount rate, Lombard rate and the rates of different types of short-term Government securities) fixed by the Bundesbank, B^{ex} = exogenous part of the monetary base, m_k = credit multiplier of the banking system, λ = demand function of the public for bank credit.

If we differentiate the above system completely with respect to the independent variables and solve it for dy/y, we get the following solution for the 'true' or 'ideal' indicator I:

$$I = \frac{dy}{y} = \varepsilon(y, B^{\text{ex}}) \left[\frac{dB^{\text{ex}}}{B^{\text{ex}}} \varepsilon(m_1, i_f) \frac{di_f}{i_f} \left(\frac{\alpha_2 \gamma_1 - \alpha_1 \gamma_2}{\alpha_2 \eta - \alpha_1} \right) \right] \tag{3.4}$$

with
$$\alpha_1 = \varepsilon(h, m_1)\, \varepsilon(m_1, i)$$
$$\alpha_2 = \varepsilon(m_k, i) - \varepsilon(\lambda, i)$$
$$\gamma_1 = \varepsilon(h, m_1)\, \varepsilon(m_1, i_f)$$
$$\gamma_2 = \varepsilon(m_k, i_f)$$
$$\eta = \varepsilon(h, B^{\text{ex}})$$

In equation (3.4) the term $\varepsilon(y, B^{\text{ex}})$ is the elasticity of real income with respect to the exogenous monetary base. $\varepsilon(m_1, i_f)$ is the elasticity of the money multiplier with respect to the index of interest rates which are fixed by the Bundesbank. dB^{ex}/B^{ex} and di_f/i_f are the rates of change of the exogenous monetary base and of the index of policy determined interest rates, respectively. The terms in the parentheses are other elasticities related to the goods and credit markets of the model.

A Theoretical Comparison of Alternative Indicator Candidates

The true indicator (i.e. the change in the ultimate goal variable) requires information which is not available for decision makers in monetary policy. The question is to what extent do different indicators which are used for judging monetary policy actions deliver reliable information in the sense that they consistently provide information about the direction, or better, about the magnitude of the future change in the true indicator. In the following analysis different indicator candidates of German economic authorities are examined with respect to their coincidence with the true indicator.

Monetary Base

The exogenous part of the monetary base B^{ex} is the amount of high-powered money in the economy adjusted for legal reserves and borrowings of commercial banks through the discount window. It is calculated by adjusting the monetary base for the impact of changes of legal reserve requirements and the quantitative effect of changes in the discount rate.

From the sources side the total amount of base money B is defined as

$$B = IR + RF + GC - ND + O \qquad (3.5)$$

where IR denotes net international reserves, RF the refinancing of commercial banks through discounts and advances, GC the stock of Government securities including the net amount of mobilization papers in the hands of the Central Bank, ND the net deposits of governments at the Central Bank and O other assets net of other liabilities plus coins in circulation.

From the uses side the monetary base is defined as follows

$$B = C + R \qquad (3.6)$$

where C stands for currency in the hands of the public and R for reserves at commercial banks, i.e. the sum of required R^r and excess reserves R^e.

The monetary base B differs in two respects from B^{ex} used in equations (3.2) to (3.4). First B^{ex} includes the impact of the required reserve policy on the total amount of base money. This effect is measured by calculating the reserves which are liberated or impounded by changes in the required reserve ratios [10]. Secondly, B^{ex} is adjusted for source components which are not directly controlled by the monetary authorities and thus must be explained by behavioural relationships. In the German monetary system the endogenous components of the monetary base are RF and large parts of GC. These components are endogenous because the Bundesbank determines the discount rate, the Lombard rate and the rate of mobilization and liquidity papers, while the banks decide which volume of base money they want to borrow at the Bundesbank under given conditions [11].

If the above adjustments are taken into account the exogenous part of the monetary base is

$$B^{\mathrm{ex}} = B - B^{\mathrm{r}} - RF + GB \qquad (3.7)$$

where B^{r} represents the required reserve adjustment component and GB the stock of mobilization and liquidity papers in the hands of commercial banks. Equation (3.7) shows that money market transactions between commercial banks and the Central Bank do not influence B^{ex}.

It must be asked now whether the rate of change of B^{ex} provides reliable information about the impact of monetary policy under the above hypothesis of the structure of the economy.

It is obvious from equation (3.4) that $\mathrm{d}B^{\mathrm{ex}}/B^{\mathrm{ex}}$ plays an important role in the 'true' indicator. However, this equation contains in addition a term which reflects the impact of changes of policy determined interest rates on the money multiplier and the subsequent feedback effects. The additional term in the brackets reduces somewhat the capacity of the exogenous monetary base as an indicator. Without that term which reflects monetary policy actions influencing i_f, the rate of change in B^{ex} would be very close to the movement of the ideal indicator. The importance of the term disappears if monetary policy were to be altered towards an exclusive use of instruments which control directly the quantity of high-powered money or if the impact of changes in the policy determined interest rates on the money multiplier could be correctly predicted and thus their influence be separated from other influences.

Money

The two types of money are examined:

$$M_1 = C + D \qquad (3.8)$$
$$M_2 = C + D + T \qquad (3.9)$$

where

$C =$ currency in the hands of the public
$D =$ demand deposits and
$T =$ time deposits

Both types of money are related to the exogenous monetary base by the corresponding multipliers. The multipliers are expressions of different 'wealth' coefficients which reflect the behaviour of the banking system and the general public. The balance sheet of the banking system plays an important role in the determination of the multipliers. The subsequent analysis uses the following simplified balance sheet:

$$R^r + R^e + GB + K = D + T + RF \tag{3.10}$$

where R^r is the total amount of required reserves, R^e are excess reserves and K are bank credits. Dividing both sides of (3.10) by $D + T$ turns the balance sheet equation into a constraint for the relationship of bank behaviour coefficients.

$$r^r + r^e + g + k = 1 + f \tag{3.11}$$

Introducing coefficients for the currency ratio c ($c = C/D$), the time/deposit ratio t ($t = T/D$) and a ratio for the required reserves adjustment component r ($r = R/(D + T)$) and rearranging equations (3.6), (3.7), (3.8), (3.10), and (3.11) leads to the following relationships:

$$M_1 = \frac{1 + c}{(1 - k - r)(1 + t) + c} B^{ex} \tag{3.12}$$

$$M_2 = \frac{1 + c + t}{(1 - k - r)(1 + t) + c} B^{ex} \tag{3.13}$$

The quotients in front of B^{ex} are the money multipliers m_1 (equation (3.12)) and m_2 (equation (3.13)).

For the 'wealth' coefficients in the above money multipliers the following behavioural and functional dependencies are postulated:

$$c = c(i, y) \qquad \frac{\partial c}{\partial i} < 0, \frac{\partial c}{\partial y} > 0 \tag{3.14}$$

$$t = t(i, y) \qquad \frac{\partial t}{\partial i} < 0, \frac{\partial t}{\partial y} > 0 \tag{3.15}$$

$$k = k(i, i_f, r^r) \qquad \frac{\partial k}{\partial i} > 0, \frac{\partial k}{\partial i_f} < 0, \frac{\partial k}{\partial r^r} = -1 \tag{3.16}$$

$$r = r(r^r) \qquad \frac{dr}{dr^r} = 1 \tag{3.17}$$

Under these assumptions equations (3.12) and (3.13) may be written in a condensed form as:

$$M_1 = m_1(i_f, r^r, i, y) B^{ex} \tag{3.12a}$$

$$M_2 = m_2(i_f, r^r, i, y) B^{ex} \tag{3.13a}$$

Differentiation of (3.12a) and (3.13a) yields:

$$\frac{dM_1}{M_1} = \frac{dB^{ex}}{B^{ex}} + \varepsilon(m_1, i_f)\frac{di_f}{i_f} + \varepsilon(m_1, i)\frac{di}{i} + \varepsilon(m_1, y)\frac{dy}{y} \tag{3.18a}$$

and:

$$\frac{\mathrm{d}M_2}{M_2} = \frac{\mathrm{d}B^{\mathrm{ex}}}{B^{\mathrm{ex}}} + \varepsilon(m_2, i_f)\frac{\mathrm{d}i_f}{i_f} + \varepsilon(m_2, i)\frac{\mathrm{d}i}{i} + \varepsilon(m_2, y)\frac{\mathrm{d}y}{y} \qquad (3.18\mathrm{b})$$

The terms

$$\varepsilon(m_1, r^{\mathrm{r}})\frac{\mathrm{d}r^{\mathrm{r}}}{r^{\mathrm{r}}} \quad \text{and} \quad \varepsilon(m_2, r^{\mathrm{r}})\frac{\mathrm{d}r^{\mathrm{r}}}{r^{\mathrm{r}}}$$

have been omitted since the respective elasticities are zero (see Appendix C, 5) [12].

A comparison of (3.18a) and (3.18b) with (3.4) shows that if the money stock, narrowly or broadly defined, is taken as an indicator of the impact of monetary policy, its properties are not the same as those of the 'true' indicator. First of all, equations (3.18a) and (3.18b) do not include the ratio of elasticities related to $\mathrm{d}i_f/i_f$ which is found in the true indicator. Since this ratio will normally be smaller than unity, the two money supply indicators will tend to overestimate the impact of policy measures which affect i_f.

Secondly, the equations for the rates of change of the money stock deviate from the 'true' indicator by the expressions

$$\varepsilon(m_i, i)\frac{\mathrm{d}i}{i} \quad \text{and} \quad \varepsilon(m_i, y)\frac{\mathrm{d}y}{y}$$

These expressions reflect the feedback effects of monetary policy via the interest rate and output.

The elasticities of the money multipliers with respect to the interest rate and real income are weighted sums of more detailed elasticities (see Appendix C). They differ for m_1 and m_2. This is due to the fact that $\varepsilon(m_1, t) < 0$ under reasonable assumptions and $\varepsilon(m_2, t) > 0$. For example, $\varepsilon(m_1, i)$ is definitely positive for m_1. For m_2, however, the interest rate elasticity could become negative. The impact of a change in the t-ratio on the two money multipliers also affects $\varepsilon(m, y)$ in a different way. While $\varepsilon(m_1, y)$ is negative, $\varepsilon(m_2, y)$ may be positive.

Using the so derived properties of the multipliers for judging the rate of change of the two types of money as indicators leads to the following results. For M_1 the impact of the market interest rate on the multiplier underestimates the effect of an expansionary monetary policy. This is the case because the decline of the market interest rate as a result of such a policy will reduce the multiplier. The course of monetary policy will in a similar way be underestimated with respect to the feedback effect of y. The increase in y due to an expansive monetary policy will reduce the multiplier for m_1. Thus, there is a tendency to underestimate the impact of an expansive monetary policy (to overestimate a restrictive policy) when relying on M_1 as an indicator. However, $\varepsilon(m_1, i)$ is certainly rather small. Therefore, the influence of an induced change in i on the degree of deviation of dM_1/M_1 from the 'true' indicator may be assumed to be very small also. Little is known, on the other hand, about the magnitude of a change in y due to an expansive monetary policy and/or to exogenous influences.

For M_2 the elasticity $\varepsilon(m_2, i)$ may be negative and $\varepsilon(m_2, y)$ positive, depending on the size of $\varepsilon(m_2, t)$ and $\varepsilon(t, i)$ and $\varepsilon(t, y)$, respectively. If these assumptions about the elasticities hold, then dM_2/M_2 would tend to overestimate the impact of an expansive monetary policy. This overestimation would probably be rather strong at the end of boom periods. In this phase of the business cycle t tends to increase substantially because economic units augment their time deposits due to a lack of investment opportunities in real capital. At the same time, the growth rate of real income is declining. Both effects lead to a substantial increase in $\varepsilon(t, y)$ and thus in $\varepsilon(m_2, y)$. These implications make M_2 a less reliable indicator of monetary policy than the money stock narrowly defined.

Bank Credit

In order to examine the quality of commercial bank credit as a monetary indicator, we relate the credit supply equation of the banking system to the exogenous part of the monetary base:

$$K = \frac{k(1 + t)}{(1 - k - r)(1 + t) + c} B^{\text{ex}} \tag{3.19}$$

Substituting this equation into the basic model and solving for the rate of change of bank credit as a monetary indicator leads to

$$\frac{dK}{K} = \frac{dB^{\text{ex}}}{B^{\text{ex}}} + \varepsilon(m_k, r^r)\frac{dr^r}{r^r} + \varepsilon(m_k, i_f)\frac{di_f}{i_f} + \varepsilon(m_k, i)\frac{di}{i} + \varepsilon(m_k, y)\frac{dy}{y} \tag{3.20}$$

Equation (3.20) differs from the equations for the two forms of the money supply by the existence of $\varepsilon(m_k, r^r)$ which equals -1. $\varepsilon(m_1, r^r)$ and $\varepsilon(m_2, r^r)$, on the other hand, are zero and have therefore been omitted in equations (3.18a) and (3.18b) as well as in the equation for the true indicator (3.4). An expansionary required reserves policy will as a result lead to an overestimation of the course of monetary policy if the rate of change of bank credit is used as a monetary indicator. In addition, the same objections which were expressed when evaluating the money stock(s) as indicator(s) hold in principle for bank credit, as may be seen from the following discussion.

Analysing in detail the elasticities of the credit multiplier with respect to the interest rate and real income shows that the indicator properties of bank credit are rather similar to the indicator properties of M_2. The fact that

$\varepsilon(m_k, t)$ is positive makes the sign of $\varepsilon(m_k, i)$ and $\varepsilon(m_k, y)$ ambiguous. If $\varepsilon(m_k, t)$ is relatively large the interest rate and real income elasticity of the credit multiplier can become negative. In this case the rate of change of bank credit overestimates the influence of an expansionary monetary policy. As $\varepsilon(m_k, t)$ varies substantially over the business cycle, dK/K may sometimes overestimate and sometimes underestimate the impact of monetary policy. Therefore, bank credit will not yield consistent information and, hence, is not as good a monetary indicator as money.

Free Liquid Reserves

The definition, and hence the composition, of free liquid reserves has been changed quite often by the Bundesbank. In the subsequent analysis free liquid reserves L are defined as

$$L = R^e + GB + \overline{RF} - RF \tag{3.21}$$

where $\overline{RF}$ stands for the rediscount quota fixed by the Bundesbank. $\overline{RF} - RF$ then gives the amount by which the banking system can still refinance itself in order to expand its total volume of assets.

Rearranging equation (3.21) and relating it to the exogenous part of the monetary base by the multiplier m_l for free liquid reserves leads to the following relationship between L and B^{ex}:

$$L = \frac{(1 - k - r^r + \bar{f})(1 + t)}{(1 - k - r)(1 + t) + c} B^{ex} \tag{3.22a}$$

where $\bar{f}$ equals the ratio of the rediscount quota RF to $D + T$ and the other coefficients are defined as above. Equation (3.22) may be written as:

$$L = m_l(r^r, i_f, i, y) B^{ex} \tag{3.22b}$$

From (3.22b) follows:

$$\frac{dL}{L} = \frac{dB^{ex}}{B^{ex}} + \varepsilon(m_l, r^r)\frac{dr^r}{r^r} + \varepsilon(m_l, i_f)\frac{di_f}{i_f} + \varepsilon(m_l, i)\frac{di}{i} + \varepsilon(m_l, y)\frac{dy}{y} \tag{3.23}$$

Equation (3.23) shows that free liquid reserves like bank credit overestimate the impact of a required reserve policy in comparison with the 'true' indicator since $\varepsilon(m_l, r^r)$ is smaller than zero while in the true indicator it equals zero. In the case of a discount rate policy the effect on free liquid reserves differs from those on other indicators. While the elasticities of the money and the credit multiplier with respect to the discount rate are negative, $\varepsilon(m_l, i_f)$ is positive. Thus, while money and bank credit overestimate the effect of the discount rate policy in relation to the 'true' indicator, it is underestimated in the case of free liquid reserves.

A further deviation from the results obtained for the other monetary indicators occurs if the impact of the market interest rate is considered. Contrary to the other indicator candidates the elasticity of the free liquid reserve multiplier with respect to this interest rate is negative. This is due to the fact that $\varepsilon(m_l, k)$, the elasticity of the free liquid reserves multiplier with respect to the bank credit ratio, is negative and relatively large in size and k is positively related to i. The corresponding elasticity $\varepsilon(k, i)$ is hence of great importance for the determination of the indicator quality of dL/L. If i declines due to an expansionary monetary policy the liquid reserves multiplier increases and thus the rate of change of free liquid reserves. In this case dL/L indicates at first correctly the course of monetary policy. The increase of the interest rate at a later stage of an expansive monetary policy phase will, however, let the impact of this policy appear smaller than it really is.

It should be remembered that, here as well as in the case of M_1, M_2 and K, an exogenous change in credit demand altering i and going along with monetary policy measures will lead to a misjudgement of the impact, or even the direction, of these measures. (Likewise will an exogenous change in y.)

Since $\varepsilon(m_l, i)$ is greater than $\varepsilon(m_1, i)$ and $\varepsilon(m_2, i)$ and probably greater than $\varepsilon(m_k, i)$, the exogenous and feedback effects on i will lead to a deviation of the percentage change in L from the change in the true indicator which is larger than in the case of M_1, M_2 and K. Since $\varepsilon(m_l, i)$ is negative and $\varepsilon(m_l, y)$ positive, the use of L as an indicator will tend to overestimate the thrust of an expansive monetary policy.

Calculated Credit Maximum

The calculated credit maximum is derived from the following simplified balance sheet of the commercial banking sector:

$$K + LS = D + T + \overline{RF} \tag{3.24}$$

where K stands for credit, LS for liquidity balance, D for demand deposits, T for time deposits and $\overline{RF}$ for the rediscount quota.

$$LS = R^r + R^e + GB + \overline{RF} - RF \tag{3.25}$$

LS differs from free liquid reserves by the inclusion of the total amount of required reserves R^r.

The amount of credit which can be offered by the banking system as a whole reaches a maximum when banks hold no excess reserves and no mobilization and liquidity papers, and when they take full advantage of the rediscount quota, i.e. when $\overline{RF} - RF = 0$.

Equation (3.25) can then be re-written as

$$LS = R^r \tag{3.25a}$$

Defining

$$R^r = r^r(D + T) \tag{3.26a}$$

and

$$\overline{RF} = \tilde{f}(D + T) \tag{3.26b}$$

substituting these expressions into (3.24) and rearranging them yields

$$K^x = \frac{1 - r^r + \tilde{f}}{r^r} LS \tag{3.27}$$

where K^x is the calculated credit maximum. Considering that from a comparison between (3.21) and (3.25) it follows that $LS = L + R^r$ for the regular case (i.e. banks do not give credits up to the maximum amount), the calculated credit maximum can be related to B^{ex} in a similar way as free liquid reserves (compare equation (3.22)):

$$K^x = \frac{(1 - r^r + \tilde{f})(1 - k + \tilde{f})(1 + t)}{r^r[(1 - k - r)(1 + t) + c]} B^{ex} \tag{3.28}$$

Differentiation of the condensed version of (3.28)

$$K^x = m_x(r^r, i_f, i, y) B^{ex} \tag{3.28a}$$

yields:

$$\frac{dK^x}{K^x} = \frac{dB^{ex}}{B^{ex}} + \varepsilon(m_x, r^r)\frac{dr^r}{r^r} + \varepsilon(m_x, i_f)\frac{di_f}{i_f} + \varepsilon(m_x, i)\frac{di}{i} + \varepsilon(m_x, y)\frac{dy}{y} \tag{3.29}$$

Comparing this indicator with the 'true' indicator leads to results very similar to those obtained for free liquid reserves. The calculated credit maximum overestimates the impact of the required reserves policy and underestimates the effect of the discount rate policy, provided the assumptions of the previous section hold. Since $\varepsilon(m_x, k)$ is negative and $k = k(i)$ with $\partial k/\partial i > 0$ the elasticity of the multiplier for the calculated credit maximum with respect to the market interest rate is also negative. A negative interest elasticity and a positive income elasticity of the multiplier imply an overestimation of the impact of an expansionary monetary policy if K^x is used as an indicator. Hence, the same objections which have been raised against the use of free liquid reserves as an indicator may be brought up against the use of the calculated credit maximum.

Summarizing the propositions of the theoretical analysis renders the following results. Under the given hypothesis of the structure of the economy and the assumption of a single policy goal (here growth of real income), money narrowly defined is the best monetary indicator. The exogenous monetary base (B^{ex}) is also a good indicator but it neither catches up the effects of a change in the required reserves policy nor in the rediscount policy. It can therefore not be employed as an indicator. Less reliable information is given if money broadly defined and bank credit are used as monetary indicators. The most unreliable and inconsistent information of the impact of monetary policy is obtained from free liquid reserves and the calculated credit maximum.

An Empirical Evaluation of Alternative Monetary Indicators

An appropriate testing of the quality of alternative monetary indicators in the context of the above model would require the following procedure. First, calculate the dependence of the ultimate goal variable (here y) on a change in a monetary policy variable PV, e.g. calculate the regression coefficients for equation:

(a) $$Y = a + bPV + e$$

or

(b) $$Y_t = a + b_1 PV_t + b_2 PV_{t-1} + \ldots + b_n PV_{t-n+1} + e_t$$

or any other form (e.g., logarithmic, first differences, growth rates). Second, follow the same procedure for the alternative monetary indicators MI as dependent variables, e.g.

(c) $$MI_i = a_i + b_i PV.$$

Third, compare the coefficient(s) of the equations for the monetary indicators with those of the equation for the goal variable; the indicator candidate which regularly and consistently produces coefficients which are closest to those of the goal variable is to be chosen as the best approximation of the true indicator. Unfortunately this procedure cannot be followed in this section. Data on monetary policy measures are often not available and, in some cases, cannot be expressed in quantitative terms. Hence, the first part of the way a change in monetary policy takes to the ultimate goal variable, namely the way to a change in the indicator, has been omitted in our empirical testing. The subsequent analysis concentrates on the relation between the indicator candidates and the goal variable. This approach implicitly restricts itself to testing the criterion of *stability* and *consistency* of the ratio between the coefficients of indicators and those of the goal variable. The additional information about the relative *size* of the coefficients which a comparison of (a) and (c) would yield cannot be obtained by this procedure.

Two approaches have been employed side by side to test the alternative indicator candidates against the criterion of stability and consistency in their relation to the goal variable. First, the Almon-lag technique [13], second, the Koyck-lag approach [14]. Both assumed that a dependent variable Y (here nominal GNP) is determined by the weighted sum of past values of an independent variable, X (here the monetary indicators). While the Koyck approach assumes a geometric lag distribution, the Almon approach simply assumes that the successive weights lie on a polynomial of n-th degree, the degree of the polynomial can be chosen freely in accordance with various hypotheses.

In the empirical testing the many possibilities of the Almon technique have been used. Polynomials of second and third degree have been tested, alternative assumptions about the length of the lag period have been made, original data as well as first differences and growth rates were applied. Table 3.1 summarizes the results of the regression which yielded the best

Table 3.1. *Regression estimates of changes in nominal GNP on changes in alternative monetary indicators*
(Almon Lag, Polynomial of Second Degree, 1959(I)–1973(IV))[a],[b]

First Differences	M_1	B	M_2	LS	K^x	K	L
t	0·347 (0·411)	2·620 (1·757)	2·580 (3·682)	−0·044 (−0·927)	−0·045 (−3·003)	0·040 (0·399)	−1·120 (−2·062)
$t - 1$	0·651 (2·211)	1·743 (3·112)	1·023 (4·895)	−0·260 (−1·100)	−0·022 (−4·768)	0·123 (3·717)	−0·699 (−3·180)
$t - 2$	0·933 (1·703)	1·244 (1·455)	−0·011 (−0·028)	−0·081 (−0·360)	−0·006 (−0·899)	0·160 (2·627)	−0·383 (−1·709)
$t - 3$	1·195 (1·897)	1·124 (1·114)	−0·521 (−1·051)	0·095 (0·375)	0·004 (0·414)	0·148 (1·995)	−0·166 (−0·601)
$t - 4$	1·437 (3·504)	1·382 (1·827)	−0·508 (−1·320)	0·267 (1·208)	0·006 (0·961)	0·090 (1·592)	−0·046 (−0·203)
$t - 5$	1·657 (4·227)	2·019 (2·506)	0·029 (0·126)	0·436 (1·814)	0·002 (0·432)	−0·016 (−0·372)	−0·023 (−0·109)
$t - 6$	1·857 (1·448)	3·035 (1·454)	1·089 (1·481)	0·601 (1·222)	−0·009 (−0·554)	−0·170 (−1·347)	−0·098 (−0·187)
Sum	8·078 (7·136)	13·167 (6·511)	3·683 (9·499)	0·616 (0·475)	−0·070 (−3·021)	0·375 (6·723)	−2·527 (−2·288)
Constant	0·109 (0·061)	−1·050 (−0·506)	3·234 (3·022)	11·985 (8·726)	13·135 (13·576)	0·482 (0·344)	12·874 (12·471)
R^2	0·602	0·528	0·687	0·052	0·288	0·734	0·131
Durbin–Watson	0·638	0·486	0·726	0·255	0·415	0·857	0·280

(a) 1959(I)–1972(IV) for free liquid reserves (L). Since the Bundesbank changed the coverage of L (exclusion of short-term foreign assets of domestic banks, because of the floating exchange rates) consistent data are available only until 1972(IV).
(b) Figures in parenthesis are the t-values; critical value = 1·68. R^2 is the degree of explanation of the dependent variable, adjusted for degrees of freedom.

results among the various equations tested. First differences of quarterly data on an annual basis (i.e. $Q_{i,t} - Q_{i,t-1}$) were applied. The length of the distributed lag is seven quarters, i.e. effects up to one-and-a-half years after the period of a change in an indicator variable are included in the estimation. The polynomial is of second degree. The degree of explanation of the variance in ΔY [15] is on the whole unsatisfactory. Only the R^2-values of the credit volume and M_2 lie substantially above 0·6, while the values for LS and L seem to cast doubt on the proposition that there exists a relation between these two magnitudes and GNP at all. The coefficients of multiple determination are, however, only one criterion to be used in judging the quality of the regression, the 't'-values of each individual coefficient are the other. With 46 degrees of freedom the critical value for a 5% confidence interval is given with approximately 1·68.

For the sums of the coefficients, i.e., for the long-term effects, all indicator variables, except LS, produce t-statistics above the critical value (Table 3.2). Two of the t-values are, however, related to coefficients with an unexpected sign (K^x, L). For the individual periods the picture is quite different. Only a minority of the total number of coefficients is statistically significant. Judging from the number of significant coefficients per indicator, M_1 fares best with five out of seven. All coefficients also have the right sign.

Table 3.2. *Values of t-statistics of alternative monetary indicators*

Period	M_1	B	M_2	LS	K^x	K	L
t	0·41	1·76x	3·68x	−0·93	−3·00x	0·40	−2·06x
$t - 1$	2·21x	3·11x	4·89x	−1·10	−4·77x	3·72x	−3·18x
$t - 2$	1·70x	1·45	−0·03	−0·36	−0·90	2·63x	−1·71x
$t - 3$	1·90x	1·11	−1·05	0·37	0·41	1·99x	−0·60
$t - 4$	3·50x	1·83x	−1·32	1·21	0·96	1·59	−0·20
$t - 5$	4·23x	2·51x	0·13	1·81x	0·43	−0·37	−0·11
$t - 6$	1·45	1·45	1·48	1·22	−0·55	−1·35	−0·19
Sum	7·14x	6·51x	9·50x	0·47	−3·02	6·72x	−2·29x

x = significant

The same is true for B which ranks second with four significant coefficients. Next follow K and L with three each. L, however, displays for all coefficients (including the significant ones) the wrong sign, while for K the significant coefficients have the expected sign and negative values appear only at the end of the lag period. The somewhat odd phenomenon of three negative coefficients in the middle of the lag period surprises when evaluating M_2. These negative coefficients are preceded by highly significant coefficients at the beginning of the period. K^x shows two statistically significant coefficients, both have, however, the wrong sign, as have two other coefficients which are not significant. The most disappointing result is produced by *LS* which offers only one significant coefficient.

Finally, it should be noted, that the Durbin–Watson statistic points to a rather high degree of autocorrelation in the residuals. In the Almon procedure, however, this does not mean that the estimates are biased; it only indicates that the standard errors of the regression coefficients (and indirectly of the distributed lag weights) are understated [16] or, in other words, that the *t*-statistics are overstated.

A summary of the results from the Almon technique would lead to the, admittedly, rather tentative conclusion that M_1 and *B* must be considered the most reliable indicators among our selection. *K* and M_2 seem to be quite reliable for long-run observations; however, they are not consistent over the short- and medium-run. The remaining indicator candidates do not seem to be acceptable since they either displayed the wrong sign or showed a low degree of reliability over the period covered by the regressions.

The results of testing the Koyck distribution are summarized in Table 3.3. Again first differences have been taken in order to ensure comparability with the Almon results. The degree of explanation of the dependent variable (ΔY) is on the whole again disappointing. Regressions on original data produced generally much better R^2-values (between 0·990 and 0·995), as would be expected.

Table 3.3. *Regression estimates of changes in nominal GNP on changes in alternative monetary indicators*
(Koyck lag, 1959(I)–1973(IV))[a],[b]

First Differences	M_1	B	M_2	LS	K^x	K	L
Constant	1·882	0·650	3·647	3·310	4·957	0·739	5·742
	(1·112)	(0·407)	(2·903)	(2·119)	(2·796)	(0·587)	(4·368)
Δ monetary indicator	1·005	4·124	2·897	−0·877	−0·031	0·276	2·119
	(1·141)	(3·037)	(5·717)	(−2·008)	(−2·457)	(6·023)	(4·562)
Δ GNP$_{t-1}$	0·823	0·669	0·149	0·878	0·699	0·290	−0·321
	(5·692)	(4·706)	(0·892)	(6·921)	(4·720)	(2·031)	(−3·465)
R^2	0·460	0·529	0·658	0·486	0·504	0·672	0·462
Durbin–Watson	0·459	0·577	0·648	0·499	0·503	0·713	0·507
Average lag[c]	4·6	2·0	0·2	7·2	2·3	0·4	—[d]

[a] 1959(I)–1972(IV) for free liquid reserves *L*. Compare footnote (*a*) Table 3.1.
[b] Figures in parenthesis are the *t*-values, critical value = 1·68. R^2 is the degree of explanation of the dependent variable, adjusted for the degrees of freedom.
[c] Rounded; for the calculation see footnote [17].
[d] Result would be negative.

The Durbin–Watson statistics are very low for all regressions, they all point to strong positive autocorrelation. The reason may be that even the first differences reflect the prevalence of trends and cycles which were particularly strongly felt in regressions on the original data. The interpretation of the coefficients must therefore be handled with due care.

Looking at the coefficients for the alternative indicator candidates it is noted that they do not have the expected sign in the case of LS (liquidity balance) and K^x (calculated credit maximum); both are, however, statistically significant at the 5% level. The coefficient of M_1 is the only one in our choice which is not significant; a result which contrasts sharply with that obtained under the Almon technique.

Comparing the size of the coefficient for M_1 with the coefficients for B and M_2 as well as with the Almon results for M_1 it must be assumed that the coefficient is largely understated here; one would expect it to be in the neighbourhood of 3.5. Similarly, the size of the coefficient for K relative to those of B and M_2 appears to be surprisingly small when held against economic reasoning. It is, however, highly significant and it was small in the Almon testing procedure as well.

The coefficients for ΔY_{t-1} determine the average lag [17], which is frequently calculated in connection with the Koyck technique. It furnishes information similar to the calculation of the whole lag distribution. With the exception of M_2 and L these coefficients lead to average lags of reasonable size. The explanation for the impossibly short lag in the case of M_2 may be seen in the fact that the coefficient is statistically not significant. For L the coefficient would lead to a negative average lag; no explanation could be found for this result.

Looking at the relative size of the average lags it is surprising that the value for B is smaller than the value for M_1. Economic reasoning would suggest rather the opposite since, surely, the 'way' from a change in B to a change in Y is supposed to be longer than the 'way' from M_1 to Y.

A summary of the results from the Koyck procedure leads again to rather tentative conclusions. K and M_2 appear to be the most reliable monetary indicators. This may be concluded from looking at the degree of explanation of the dependent variable as well as at the size of the t-statistics. M_1 fares rather poorly in this testing technique. The result was somewhat better for M_1 in the case of original data rather than first differences. L obtains much better results here than in the Almon tests; the negative coefficient for ΔY_{t-1}, however, casts some doubt on the reliability of the other coefficients. LS and K^x can hardly be recommended as indicators because of their wrong sign.

On the whole the econometric testing led to results which are less conclusive than the theoretical reasoning. It may be argued that the turmoil in the money and credit markets at the end of the testing period (1969–73) which affected Germany more than most other countries has perturbed not only the participants in these markets but also the data setting. But, of course, a good indicator should be capable of giving consistent and reliable information even in these situations.

Appendix A

List of Symbols

B = monetary base

B^{ex} = exogenous part of the monetary base

B^r = required reserves adjustment component

C = currency in circulation

c = C/D

D = demand deposits

f = $RF/(D + T)$

$\tilde{f}$ = $\overline{RF}/(D + T)$

GB = stock of mobilization and liquidity papers in the hands of commercial banks

GC = stock of Government securities in the hands of the Central Bank

g = $GB/(D + T)$

h = coefficient of demand function for goods and services

I = the 'true' indicator

IR = net international reserves

i = market interest rate

i_f = index of short-term interest rates fixed by the Bundesbank, e.g. discount rate, Lombard rate, rates of Government securities

K = bank credits

K^x = calculated credit maximum

k = $K/(D + T)$

L = free liquid reserves

LS = liquidity balance

M_1 = money supply narrowly defined, e.g. currency plus demand deposits

M_2 = M_1 plus time deposits

m_1 = money multiplier for M_1

m_2 = money multiplier for M_2

m_k = multiplier for bank credits

m_l = multiplier for free liquid reserves

m_x = multiplier for the calculated credit maximum

O = other assets of commercial banks net of liabilities

p = price level

Q = capital stock

R^e = excess reserves
R^r = required reserves
RF = refinancing of commercial banks through discounts and advances
$\overline{RF}$ = rediscount quota
r^e = $R^e/(D + T)$
r^r = $R^r/(D + T)$
T = time deposits
t = T/D
V_1, V_2 = instruments of monetary policy
y = real income
λ = coefficient of demand for bank credit

Appendix B

Derivation of Multipliers

1. *The money multiplier* (M_1)
    (1) $M = C + D$
    (2) $c = C/D$ currency ratio
    (1a) $M = (1 + c)D$
    (3) $t = T/D$ time/deposit ratio
    (4) $R^r + R^e + GB + K = D + T + RF$ consolidated balance of commercial banking system

   (4a) $r^r + r^e + g + k = 1 + f$
   (5) $B^{ex} = B - B^r - RF + GB$
   (6) $B = C + R^r + R^e$
   From (2)–(6) follows:
   (7) $D = \dfrac{1}{(1 - k - r)(1 + t) + c} B^{ex}$

   hence

   (1b) $M = \dfrac{1 + c}{(1 - k - r)(1 + t) + c} B^{ex}$

2. *The money multiplier* (M_2)
    (1) $M_2 = C + D + T$
    (1a) $M_2 = (1 + c + t)D$

   hence:

   (1b) $M_2 = \dfrac{1 + c + t}{(1 - k - r)(1 + t) + c} B^{ex}$

3. *The credit multiplier*

   (1) $K = D + T + RF - R^r - R^e - GB$

   (1a) $K = (1 + f - r^r - r^e - g)(D + T)$

   (1b) $K = \dfrac{k(1 + t)}{(1 - k - r)(1 + t) + c} B^{ex}$

4. *The multiplier for free liquid reserves*

   (1) $L = R^e + GB + RF - RF$

   (1a) $L = (r^e + g + \tilde{f} - f)(D + T)$

   (1b) $L = \dfrac{(1 - k - r^r + \tilde{f})(1 + t)}{(1 - k - r)(1 + t) + c} B^{ex}$

5. *The multiplier for the calculated credit maximum*

   (1) $K^x = \dfrac{1 - r^r + \tilde{f}}{r^r} LS$

   (2) $LS = R^r + R^e + GB + \overline{RF} - RF$

   (2a) $LS = (r^r + r^e + g + \tilde{f} - f)(D + T)$

   (1a) $K^x = \dfrac{(1 - r^r + \tilde{f})(1 - k + \tilde{f})(1 + t)}{r^r[(1 - k - r)(1 + t) + c]} B^{ex}$

Appendix C

Elasticities of the multipliers with respect to different variables.
(* = results obtained by making realistic assumptions with respect to the size of the coefficients)

1. *Elasticities with respect to c*
   $\varepsilon(m_1, c) < 0^*$, $\varepsilon(m_2, c) < 0^*$, $\varepsilon(m_k, c) < 0$, $\varepsilon(m_l, c) < 0$, $\varepsilon(m_x, c) < 0$

2. *Elasticities with respect to t*
   $\varepsilon(m_1, t) < 0$, $\varepsilon(m_2, t) > 0$, $\varepsilon(m_k, t) > 0$, $\varepsilon(m_l, t) > 0$, $\varepsilon(m_x, t) > 0$

3. *Elasticities with respect to k*
   $\varepsilon(m_1, k) > 0$, $\varepsilon(m_2, k) > 0$, $\varepsilon(m_k, k) > 0$, $\varepsilon(m_l, k) < 0^*$, $\varepsilon(m_x, k) < 0^*$

4. *Elasticities with respect to i_f*
   $\varepsilon(m_1, i_f) < 0$, $\varepsilon(m_2, i_f) < 0$, $\varepsilon(m_k, i_f) < 0$, $\varepsilon(m_l, i_f) > 0^*$, $\varepsilon(m_x, i_f) > 0^*$

5. *Elasticities with respect to r^r*
   $\varepsilon(m_1, r^r) = 0$, $\varepsilon(m_2, r^r) = 0$, $\varepsilon(m_k, r^r) = \varepsilon(k, r^r) = -1$, $\varepsilon(m_l, r^r) < 0$, $\varepsilon(m_x, r^r) < 0$

6. *Elasticities with respect to i*

   $\varepsilon(m_1, i) > 0$, $\varepsilon(m_2, i) > 0^*$, $\varepsilon(m_k, i) > 0^*$, $\varepsilon(m_l, i) < 0^*$, $\varepsilon(m_x, i) < 0^*$

7. *Elasticities with respect to y*

   $\varepsilon(m_1, y) < 0$, $\varepsilon(m_2, y) > 0^*$, $\varepsilon(m_k, y) > 0^*$, $\varepsilon(m_l, y) > 0^*$, $\varepsilon(m_x, y) > 0^*$

Footnotes

* For research assistance and valuable comments on an earlier draft of this paper the author is very much indebted to Diplom-Volkswirt Klaus-Walter Riechel, Member of the Institute of Economic Policy at the University of Kiel.

1. For an analysis and application of bank liquidity as a monetary indicator in Germany see *Deutsche Bundesbank Monthly Report*, April, 1965, pp. 29–37, and Neumann, (1972), and Courakis, pp. 31–7 above.

2. Sachverständigenrat zur Begutachtung der gesamtwirtschaftlichen Entwicklung, *Jahresgutachten 1970/71*, Stuttgart, Mainz 1970, pp. 40–6 and pp. 100–102.

3. Sachverständigenrat zur Begutachtung der gesamtwirtschaftlichen Entwicklung, *Jahresgutachten 1971/72*, Stuttgart, Mainz 1971, pp. 55–60 and pp. 168–9.

4. See Brunner, & Neumann, (1972a), (1972b) and (1972c).

5. Ketterer, (1971), & Pohl, (1972).

6. *Deutsche Bundesbank Monthly Report*, July, 1971.

7. *Deutsche Bundesbank Annual Report*, 1973, p. 3.

8. *Deutsche Bundesbank Monthly Report*, July, 1974, pp. 14–23.

9. See Brunner, & Meltzer, (1976).

10. For the calculation procedure see Andersen, & Jordan, (1968).

11. For a detailed analysis of the institutional setting of the money supply process in Germany, see Siebke, & Willms, (1974).

12. It should be noted that throughout the paper it is assumed that neither a required reserves policy nor a shift in the composition between D and T leads to a change in the average required reserves ratio, in which case B^{ex} would also change.

13. See Almon, (1965).

14. See Koyck, (1954).

15. Adjusted for the degrees of freedom.

16. Almon, (1965) p. 187.

17. Let z = coefficient for the lagged dependent variable (here ΔY_{t-1}), then the average lag is determined by:

$$a = \frac{z}{1 - z}$$

Monetary Indicators in the Federal Republic of Germany— a Comment

PETER A. BULL

Following Brunner and Meltzer, Professor Willms attempts to 'grade' various monetary indicators in Germany by their ability to track money GNP. The monetary indicators he examines are: the monetary base; a narrow and a broad definition of money stock; bank credit; free liquid reserves in the hands of the banks; and the 'calculated credit maximum'— the largest amount that bank lending could be, given the amount of reserve assets and the reserve ratio.

The empirical section of his paper shows mixed results. When he uses Almon lags, the money stock on the narrow definition and the monetary base appear to be the best indicators; with Koyck lags, the money stock on the broad definition and bank lending seem best.

However, there are a number of points of definition and analysis that may surprise the reader. Some of them are detailed below.

(a) In equation (3.3), why is the supply of bank credit a function of real income?

(b) In equation (3.7), the 'exogenous' monetary base includes the whole stock of Government securities held by the banks less Government securities which they have lodged as collateral with the Bundesbank, which means (as Professor Willms points out) that rediscounting has no effect on the exogenous monetary base. But the Bundesbank presumably chooses its discount and Lombard rates and the rates at which it deals in Government paper so as to influence the amount of base money which the banks want to borrow.

(c) In equations (3.8)–(3.10) it is perhaps slightly puzzling that C and T represent the ratios of cash holdings and time deposits to sight deposits only (and not to all deposits). More puzzling are some of the partial derivatives in the block of equations (3.14)–(3.17) which form a set of assumptions. Why, for example, is the proportion of time deposits lower, the higher are interest rates other than those fixed by the Bundesbank? Why, in equation (3.16), is a change in the reserve requirement matched wholly in bank lending? Why not partly in excess reserves? Similarly, in equation (3.17), why are reserves held by the banks dependent on the reserve requirement only, and not for instance on interest rates? In equation (3.3) they appear to be a function of interest rates, and also in equations (3.12a) and (3.13a), where the 'multiplier' relating the exogenous monetary base to the money stock depends on the reserve requirement.

(d) It is not clear why a decline in market interest rates, following an easing of monetary policy will make the money stock understate the effect of an expansionary policy. Some of Professor Willms' equations suggest that it will have no effect on the money stock (see above); on page 56, he expects that it would reduce it, presumably because there would be less opportunity cost to holding spare reserve assets (and with market interest rates lower, the public would hold a larger proportion of their bank deposits at sight which in Germany requires more reserves to be held). But it does not follow from this that the change in the money stock on the narrow definition *understates* the expansionary effect of policy. If the effect of policy is to make the banks want to hold more reserve assets, through its effect on interest rates, policy is that much less expansionary. To follow on with the argument on page 56, it seems odd to suggest that the change in the money stock understates the expansionary effect of policy because a higher real income makes people want to hold more money balances (as I think Professor Willms is suggesting). Later on p. 57, and accepting Professor Willms' argument for money on the narrow definition, I do not see why looking at the proportionate change in the money stock on the wide definition should *overstate* the expansionary effect of policy, since he rather suggests that the relevant elasticities have the same sign as for narrowly defined money. But, of course, he may be correct that the velocity of circulation, particularly of broadly defined money, falls at the end of a boom.

(e) Professor Willms' definition of 'bank credit' (page 57) is not clear—from the balance sheet identity (equation (3.10)) it appears to be all lending by the banks to (or purchase of any sort of claim on) the domestic private and overseas sectors and the public sector other than debt which can be lodged with the Bundesbank.

(f) Not surprisingly, free liquid reserves of the banks are dependent on interest rates generally and those fixed by the Bundesbank, in equation (3.22a). But apparently they were not regarded as so dependent in equation (3.17). And why should the 'multiplier' attached to free liquid reserves decrease when the reserve requirement rises, as the text on p. 58 suggests? Why should it increase the Bundesbank's rediscount rate?

(g) In equation (3.28a), I am not clear why the 'calculated credit maximum' should be a function of interest rates and real income, given the exogenous monetary base: as I understand, it is calculated in an entirely mechanical way from the monetary base and required reserves. (Of course, this does not imply that actual lending is determined mechanically by these things.)

4

A Theoretical and Empirical Analysis
of the German Money Supply Process*

MANFRED J. M. NEUMANN

Introduction

The purpose of the paper is to investigate in detail the main forces which
shaped the money supply processes in the Federal Republic of Germany
during the period 1958 to 1972. A credit market hypothesis of the money
supply process will be developed taking into account the specific institutional
pattern of the German monetary system. This frame will then be used as the
basis for the empirical investigation. We will decompose the growth of the
money supply into the contribution of proximate determinants and compare
the behaviour of these determinants over various subperiods of special
interest. Finally, we will estimate a reduced-form money supply equation
resulting from our hypothesis in order to gain information on the responses
of monetary growth to changes in ultimate determinants.

A Credit Market Hypothesis of the German Money Supply Process

Outline of the General Structure

The money supply hypothesis formulated in this paper belongs to the family
of hypotheses built on the foundations provided by the Brunner–Meltzer non-
linear money supply hypothesis [1]. Originally, the Brunner–Meltzer framework was designed to explain the monetary processes of economies like the
U.S. which by European standards is relatively little affected by balance of
payments flows. Later on Brunner extended the framework so that the major
aspects and properties of open economies are incorporated [2]. Other economists, in applying the general Brunner–Meltzer frame to specific countries,

have worked along the same lines [3], and their work has influenced in one way or another the present paper.

The characteristic peculiarity of a credit market hypothesis of the money supply is to be seen in the concentration of the proximate interest rate determination in a credit market instead of the Keynesian money market. The money supply process and thus the development of the money stock, bank credit and interest rates are explained simultaneously by the interaction of commercial banks and the public on the credit market, subject to constraints imposed on them by the monetary authorities and by institutional regulations set by the Government.

We define as a first approximation the credit market as a market where the public's stock supply of domestic earning assets meets the stock demand of banks for those assets. The public's stock supply of domestic earning assets σ consists mainly of its desired bank loan position and, in addition, of its implicit stock supply of domestic securities to banks. Without presenting a complete specification in this section we describe the public's asset supply by the following function:

$$\sigma = \sigma(i, S, \ldots), \qquad \sigma_1 < 0 < \sigma_2$$

where i is an index of domestic credit market rates, S is the outstanding stock of domestic securities and the dots indicate that arguments are still missing. The partial derivates σ_1 and σ_2 indicate that the public's asset supply in our hypothesis responds negatively to changes of the credit market rate and positively to changes of the outstanding stock of securities.

The bank's demand for domestic earning assets DEA may be described by the product of the monetary base B and an earning asset multiplier a.

$$DEA = aB$$

Quite generally we define the monetary base as monetary liabilities of the monetary authorities to banks and the domestic public, i.e. as the sum of bank reserves and currency. The asset multiplier will be defined later as a rational function of various allocation parameters supposed to characterize important aspects of the portfolio behaviour of banks and the public. Thus the asset multiplier depends besides other arguments on interest rates and reserve requirement ratios r,

$$a = a(i, r, \ldots), \qquad a_1 > 0 > a_2$$

Equating the asset supply function to the asset demand function gives the credit market equilibrium and permits the derivation of an equilibrium solution for the index of credit market rates

$$i = i(S, r, \ldots), \qquad i_{1,2} > 0$$

This solution will be used to obtain a solution for the money supply. Like the banks' asset demand the money supply will be described by the product of the monetary base and a multiplier m, the money multiplier. This multiplier again summarizes the portfolio decisions of banks and the public. Thus we may write:

$$m = m(i, r, \ldots), \qquad m_1 > 0 > m_2$$

and consequently the money supply function

$$M = m(i, r, \ldots)B$$

where M denotes the money stock. Replacing, finally, the credit market rate by the solution obtained from the credit market equation gives a solution for the money supply in terms of policy parameters and other variables which can be viewed to be exogenous to the current monetary processes.

Money Stock and Monetary Base

The property distinguishing money from other assets is its dominating use as a medium of exchange which can be explained by the relatively low information and transaction costs associated with the use of those assets [4]. In general, one cannot infer from the medium of exchange property that the sum of assets exhibiting that property gives the most appropriate approximation of the money stock. In the German case, however, it can be demonstrated that it is this collection of assets which explains best the movement of the general price level and of economic activity.

Thus we define the money stock narrowly as the sum of currency C held by the domestic public and its demand deposits D with commercial banks

$$M = C + D \tag{4.1}$$

The domestic public includes private households and enterprises as well as local communities but excludes the Federal Government and the eleven state governments which legally are forced to hold their demand deposits with the Deutsche Bundesbank, i.e. the German Central Bank. The inclusion of local communities into the domestic public seems to be justified as these agents in general do not behave differently from private households or enterprises with regard to the management of expenditure and cash holdings.

The monetary base we have already defined quite generally as monetary liabilities of the monetary authorities to banks and the domestic public. In the Federal Republic the Deutsche Bundesbank is the only monetary authority. Independent of instructions from the Federal Government the Bank has to 'safeguard the currency' and to regulate the expansion of money and credit accordingly [5]. The monetary liabilities of the Bank to commercial banks and the domestic public consist of the bank notes in circulation and deposit liabilities but exclude the coins in circulation. The right of coinage still belongs to the Government. The Bundesbank, however, has a say in the respective decisions of the Government and, as a matter of fact, has always kept the issuance of coins under close control. To take account of the coins in circulation we extend our definition of the monetary base by including in addition assets which are treated by the monetary authority as perfect substitutes to its monetary liabilities.

Thus we define the monetary base B from the uses-side as

$$B = R + C \qquad (4.2)$$

where R denotes the base money reserves of commercial banks and C the currency held by the public. Note that C does not include the Bundesbank's deposit liabilities to private households and enterprises which have always been of negligible amount [6].

To derive the sources side of the monetary base we add to both sides of the Bundesbank's balance sheet the amount of coins in circulation, rearrange the various items in a convenient manner and solve the identity for the sum of the uses of the base. This gives:

$$B = IR + RF + MOBC - NPD - SCD - SWAP + OAN \quad (4.3)$$

where IR denotes net international reserves adjusted for swap arrangements with commercial banks, RF the borrowing to banks through discounts and advances, $MOBC$ the Central Bank's portfolio of mobilization and liquidity paper, NPD public deposits net of book credits and treasury bill holdings, SCD special cash deposits of enterprises for borrowing abroad, $SWAP$ the volume of swap contracts and OAN other assets net of other liabilities.

The monetary base defined describes the supply of base money by the Bundesbank, but from this it does not follow that it provides the most adequate foundation for an informative money supply hypothesis. There are two problems.

(a) The definition does not take account of the Bundesbank's required reserves policy and therefore does not reflect the actual impulse behaviour of the Bank.

(b) There are source components included which are influenced by current monetary processes and thus make it advisable to exclude them from the base and to explain them by behaviour functions.

The first problem can easily be taken care of by introducing the well-known concept of liberated reserves. The reserves liberated or impounded by a reduction of required reserve ratios or an increase, respectively, are given by

$$\Delta L_t = \sum_{j=1}^{n} (r_{t-1}^j - r_t^j) D_{t-1}^j, \quad \text{with } j = 1, \ldots, n \qquad (4.4)$$

The index j indicates that the reserve ratios are differentiated for various types of non-bank liabilities. Cumulating over time gives a stock variable L

$$L_t = \sum_{t=0}^{t} \Delta L_t \tag{4.5}$$

which, when added to both sides of the monetary base, leads to the extended monetary base, B^e.

$$B^e = R + C + L \tag{4.6}$$

$$B^e = IR + RF + MOBC - NPD - SCD - SWAP + OAN + L \tag{4.7}$$

Equation (4.6) describes the uses side and equation (4.7) the sources side.

Let us now take up the endogeneity–exogeneity issue and first single out those source components which can clearly be viewed as exogenous or predetermined relative to current monetary processes. These are the components NPD, SCD, $SWAP$, OAN, and L. Net public deposits, NPD, are defined as gross deposits of public authorities and agencies minus book credits and Treasury bill holdings. NPD is under the joint control of the Government and the Bundesbank and, by the way, has never become negative, thus reflecting the favourable state that budget deficits are not financed by base money creation but by selling debt to commercial banks and the public. The imposition of special cash deposits, SDC, is a new policy instrument. L reflects the required reserves policy. Swap operations $SWAP$ with commercial banks have been used as an instrument for the shorter-run management of international reserves until the Bundesbank in 1969 found this to be a defective device when banks became used to immediately reimporting funds they were supposed to export under the swap arrangement. Finally the item OAN, other assets net of other liabilities, may also be treated as exogenous, as it consists in the main of securities purchased, coins in circulation, land and buildings of the Bank, capital and reserves among other items.

This leaves us with the source components IR, RF and $MOBC$. Of these three RF and $MOBC$ are clearly influenced by the current monetary process and therefore endogenous. As regards the banks' refinancing RF through discounts and advances the Bundesbank sets the discount and the Lombard rate and it is up to the banks to decide in assessment of the whole situation, especially in assessment of the prices of competing liabilities and of financial assets, which volume of borrowing from the Central Bank they want to carry. However, it has to be considered that the banks' borrowing decisions are subject to a quantity constraint as the Bundesbank determines the upper limit by setting rediscount quotas which are varied quite heavily from time to time. While during the 1960s this constraint was of no real importance, as banks always used to have relatively high unused quotas at their disposal, even during periods of monetary restraint, it has become more and more biting in the 1970s, when the Bundesbank gradually cut back gross rediscount quotas by one half between 1970 and 1973. Since autumn 1972 unused quotas have been practically exhausted. Nevertheless it seems to be justified to treat

RF as an endogenous source component for the period under consideration in this study.

The Bundesbank's open market portfolio of mobilization and liquidity paper *MOBC* is also influenced by the current monetary process. The Bundesbank fixes rates at which it is willing to buy or sell any amount of specified open market paper the economic agents may offer or demand; moreover, open market operations are concentrated in the money market. The bulk of operations is carried out with mobilization and liquidity paper. Mobilization paper consists of Treasury bills and non-interest bearing Treasury bonds which the Treasury has to hand over to the Bundesbank upon request up to the nominal amount of the Bank's equalization claim against the Federal Government (DM 8·1 billion). This claim originates from the Monetary Reform provisions of 1948. In addition, the Government has to hand over to the Bank another DM 8 billion of Treasury bills if necessary; this paper is called liquidity paper.

, Although the buying and selling rates fixed for open market paper are not identical to the discount or the Lombard rate of the Bank, they have always been kept in an almost fixed relation to these rates thus inducing banks to keep their borrowing through the discount window in line with their portfolio of open market paper. For the purpose of our hypothesis it is advisable to split the Bundesbank's portfolio *MOBC* into an endogenous and an exogenous component as follows:

$$MOBC = MOBT - MOBP - MOB \qquad (4.8)$$

where *MOBT* denotes the fixed total volume of open market paper, *MOBP* the holdings of the domestic public and of foreigners and *MOB* the holdings of banks. *MOBT* is exogenous, *MOB* is endogenous, and *MOBP* can also be treated as being exogenous for two reasons. First, the Bundesbank started offering open market paper to the domestic public only in 1971, and the amounts purchased since then are still very limited. Secondly, since about 1969 foreign monetary authorities acquired mobilization paper from the Bundesbank in exchange for their currency, these amounts are controlled, of course, by the Bank and these operations do not change the German monetary base.

Before turning to the source component international reserves, let us condense those domestic source components which shall be treated as being exogenous to the current domestic monetary process.

$$NDC = MOBT - MOBP - NPD - SCD - SWAP + L + OAN \qquad (4.9)$$

This condensed source component will be called net domestic component. Equation (4.9) allows simplification of the sources statement of the extended monetary base to:

$$B^e = IR + RF - MOB + NDC \qquad (4.10)$$

The last source component to be discussed, IR, net international reserves adjusted for the volume of swap arrangements with commercial banks, can be analysed with the aid of the balance of payments constraint.

$$\Delta IR = CAB - GDNI + \Delta(FL - FA)^{P} + \Delta(FL - FAS - FAL)^{B} \qquad (4.11)$$

where CAB denotes the current account balance, $GDNI$ the Government's direct net transactions with foreign countries, FL foreign liabilities, FA foreign assets, split into short-term and long-term assets (S or L), and the indices P and B indicate the ownership of the domestic public and of banks, respectively. Of these balance of payments items only CAB and $GDNI$ can safely be assumed to be exogenous relative to the current monetary process. Nevertheless, in this study we shall also treat the domestic public's foreign position as if it were exogenous. The reason is that we lack reliable stock data of the public's foreign assets and foreign liabilities. I hope that this unsatisfactory treatment can be eliminated in the future by introducing an estimated time-series based on some auxiliary hypotheses.

The banks' portfolio of foreign assets is split into a portfolio of short-term foreign assets, adjusted for the volume of swap operations FAS and into a portfolio of long-term foreign assets FAL; the dividing line is a maturity of six months. FAS is clearly endogenous and the same may be true of FAL, if one is concerned with its longer-run behaviour. For a short-run analysis, however, it seems to be advisable to treat FAL as a relatively exogenous item. One reason for this is given by the fact that long-term foreign asset portfolios of German banks almost exclusively consist of loan assets. The costs of information and adjustment are in general much higher in the foreign loan business than in the foreign securities business, thus there might be a significant threshold of reaction delaying the adjustment. More importantly, commercial banks started the long-term business with foreigners on a significant scale only in 1968–69. For all the years before, the portfolio FAL, statistically observed for the total commercial banking system, belonged almost entirely to one state-owned bank, namely the Kreditanstalt für Wiederaufbau (Reconstruction Loan Corporation) and was due to politically determined development aid programmes. Even nowadays approximately 50% of the total items are due to development aid. Finally, we will treat commercial banks' foreign liabilities FL as endogenous.

By suitably summing over time we obtain from equation (4.11)

$$IR = \int CAB \, dt - \int GDNI \, dt + (FL - FA)^{P} - FAL^{B} + (FL - FAS)^{B} \quad (4.12)$$

Lumping together the exogenous components into an expression NIR

$$NIR = \int CAB \, dt - \int GDNI \, dt + (FL - FA)^{P} - FAL^{B} \qquad (4.13)$$

which may be called adjusted international reserves gives

$$IR = NIR + (FL - FAS)^{B} \qquad (4.12a)$$

D

Using equation (4.12a) we can rewrite equation (4.10), i.e. the source equation of the extended base, as follows:

$$B^e = NIR + NDC + (FL - FAS)^B + RF - MOB \qquad (4.14)$$

Summarizing our analysis so far of the various sources of the extended monetary base we may conclude that there are two major source components which have to be considered as being endogenous, namely the borrowing of commercial banks from the Bundesbank, as reflected by changes of RF and MOB, and the banks business relations with foreigners, as reflected by changes of FL^B and FAS^B.

The question then is what consequences have to be drawn from this for the construction of our money supply hypothesis. Do we have, as is commonly done in the literature, to adjust the base in such a way that we end up with a truly exogenous base, or could we equally well build a money supply hypothesis on the extended monetary base as it stands?

It seems to me that the construction of a money supply hypothesis centred on the extended base could well be justified on theoretical grounds:

(a) From the fact that the extended base contains endogenous as well as exogenous source components it cannot be inferred that the base itself is endogenous, for the simple reason that it may actually be a policy-controlled aggregate. This would clearly be the case, if the authorities were able to compensate for any undesired change of endogenous source components.

(b) Even if the extended base were completely endogenous, it would not follow from this that a money supply hypothesis built on it must lead to statements or predictions about the behaviour of the money stock differing from those derivable from a similarly constructed hypothesis centred on an exogenous base [7]. The reason is that the latter hypothesis would simply be an enlargement of the former.

In spite of that we will proceed to construct an hypothesis using an adjusted monetary base because such an enlarged hypothesis provides additional information by explaining two important sources of base money supply. However, within the general frame we will also make use of the extended monetary base and the associated extended-multiplier approach for the explanation of observed money supply movements in terms of its proximate determinants. This will be very useful because it will give us some insight into the relative merits of alternative multiplier approaches in serving as schemes for the regular short-term observation of money supply movements and their proximate determinants.

We adjust the extended monetary base by subtracting RF and FL^B and by adding MOB and FAS^B. Thus the adjusted monetary base is given by

$$B^a = R + C + L - RF + MOB - (FL - FAS)^B \qquad (4.15)$$

$$B^a = NIR + NDC \qquad (4.16)$$

where (4.15) defines the uses side and (4.16) the sources side.

Supply and Demand of Earning Assets (the Credit Market)

The credit market is the outcome of an aggregation over three markets; the loan market, the market of Government securities and the market of privately issued securities (industrial bonds). Thus it may be defined as the market where the domestic public supplies DM-denominated earning assets to domestic banks and foreigners. Accordingly, the credit market rate i to be proximately determined by the credit market equation is an appropriately weighted index of credit market rates.

The net stock supply of earning assets σ by the domestic public is given by

$$\sigma = L^P + GS + PS - S^P - S^F \qquad (4.17)$$

where L^P denotes the public's desired loan liability position, S^P the public's stock demand for domestic securities, S^F the respective stock demanded by foreigners, GS the outstanding stock of Government securities, and PS the outstanding stock of privately issued securities. The sum of the terms GS, PS, S^P, and S^F describes the stock of domestic securities not absorbed by the domestic public and by foreigners, thus forming an implicit stock supply of earning assets to banks [8]. Note that GS is exogenous; the same applies, as a preliminary treatment, to S^F.

The public's supply behaviour may be approximated by

$$\sigma = \sigma(i - \pi, i_f, c, p, P, GS, W) \qquad \sigma_{2,3,4,6,7} > 0 > \sigma_{1,5} \qquad (4.18)$$

where π is the anticipated rate of inflation, i_f an index of foreign interest rates on comparable earning assets, c special cash deposits ratio on private borrowing abroad, p the output price level, P the market value of a unit of real capital, and W total real wealth.

Thus it is stated that the domestic stock supply of earning assets will decrease, if the real rate of interest increases and/or the competing rate for borrowing abroad decreases, as long as the respective rate differential is not eliminated by a compensating management of the special cash deposits ratio. An increase p of output prices or of the Government's stock supply of bonds GS will increase the domestic earning asset supply, while an increase in the value of real capital P will lead to a decrease of σ, because an increasing P means that financing via the issuance of equity becomes cheaper, on the one hand, and that the implicit stock supply of securities is reduced, on the other, owing to increased substitution of real capital by financial assets. Finally, there is the wealth effect, consisting of two adverse effects: a positive direct effect of increasing wealth and a weaker negative effect via the induced increased demand for Government securities (see equation (4.17)).

The stock demand for domestic earning assets DEA by commercial banks can be described by the product of the adjusted monetary base and an earning asset multiplier a^a,

$$DEA = a^a B^a \qquad (4.19)$$

The structure of the earning asset multiplier is determined by the structure of the consolidated balance sheet of the commercial banking system. This is given by

$$RR + ER + MOB + FAS + FAL + DEA$$
$$= D + T + BS + FL + RF \qquad (4.20)$$

where RR denotes required reserves, ER excess reserves including banks' vault cash holdings, T time and savings deposits of the domestic public, subject to reserve requirements, and BS the outstanding stock of bank securities.

Solving equation (4.20) for DEA and making use of the multiplier definition

$$a^a = DEA/B^a \qquad (4.21)$$

we derive with the aid of equation (4.15)

$$a^a = \frac{D + T + BS + FL + RF - MOB - FAS - FAL - RR - ER}{RR + ER + C + L - RF + MOB - FL + FAS} \qquad (4.22)$$

The movement of the various components of the numerator and of the denominator, and therefore the movement of the asset multiplier, depends on relevant portfolio behaviour of banks and the public. In the next two sections we will describe that behaviour by appropriately defined allocation ratios which are supposed to respond to specified stimuli.

Commercial Banks' Behaviour

The banks' demand for base money holdings may be split into a demand for required reserves and a demand for excess reserves. German banks are required to hold interest-free deposits on Bundesbank accounts against total liabilities, maturing within less than four years, *vis-à-vis* domestic and foreign nonbanks as well as foreign banks. We describe the demand for required reserves by

$$RR = r(D + T + FD) \qquad (4.23)$$

where r is the average required reserve ratio and FD denotes foreign deposits subject to reserve requirement. Note that FD describes only a fraction of total foreign liabilities FL of banks. The main reason for this is that foreign liabilities resulting from interest arbitrage deals are exempted from the reserve requirement.

The Bundesbank differentiates the liabilities subject to reserve requirement by various criteria, the rationality of which may be questioned, and thus manages to operate with more than 30 different reserve ratios. We will not introduce all these very nice complications but restrict ourselves to three summary required reserve ratios, one for domestic demand deposits r^d, one for domestic time and saving deposits r^t, and one for foreign deposits r^f.

$$r = r^d \frac{D}{D+T+FD} + r^t \frac{T}{D+T+FD} + r^f \frac{FD}{D+T+FD} \qquad (4.24)$$

These three reserve ratios will be treated as policy parameters.

The concept of liberated reserves has already been introduced as a means of transferring the short-run effects of changes in minimum reserve policy from the money multiplier into the monetary base. Accordingly we define a parameter l

$$l = \frac{L}{D+T+FD} \qquad (4.25)$$

which can also be split into three parameters l^d, l^t, and l^f:

$$l = l^d \frac{D}{D+T+FD} + l^t \frac{T}{D+T+FD} + l^f \frac{FD}{D+T+FD} \qquad (4.26)$$

In the short run, any change of the reserve ratios r^d, r^t, and r^f is approximately matched by an opposite change in l^d, l^t, and l^f.

It is productive for banks to hold excess reserves although this productivity has always been relatively low for German banks because they have in general been able to raise sufficient funds when needed by selling paper through the discount window or in the open market. Defining the excess reserve ratio as

$$e = ER/(D+T+FD) \qquad (4.27)$$

we state the desired excess reserve ratio to be determined by

$$e = e(i,d) \qquad e_1 < 0 < e_2 \qquad (4.28)$$

d denotes an index of the costs of borrowing from the Bundesbank via rediscounting or selling open market paper. If the costs of borrowing from the Bundesbank are increasing, banks will increase their relative demand for excess reserves.

The borrowing from the Bundesbank in our hypothesis takes place through rediscounting, Lombarding and selling open market paper and could therefore be described by one condensed allocation ratio. However, this would preclude us from empirical testing. Therefore we define two separate ratios:

$$b = RF/(D+T+FD) \qquad (4.29)$$

$$mob = MOB/(D+T+FD) \qquad (4.30)$$

and approximate the desired behaviour of these ratios by

$$b = b(i, i_e, sw, d, Q) \qquad b_{1,2,3} > 0 > b_4 \text{ subject to } Q \qquad (4.31)$$

$$mob = mob(i, i_e, sw, d) \qquad mob_{1,2,3} < 0 < mob_4 \qquad (4.32)$$

where i_e denotes the Eurodollar market rate and sw the swap rate in the open market, giving the premium or discount on forward exchange.

Q is the policy constraint on rediscounting and Lombarding as given by the rediscount quotas. A reduction of the credit market rate and of the Eurodollar market rate reduces, according to our hypothesis, the relative demand of banks for borrowing from the Bundesbank.

The demand of banks for foreign assets may be described by the ratios

$$fal = FAL/FL \qquad (4.33)$$

$$fas = FAS/FL \qquad (4.34)$$

connecting the portfolios of foreign assets with foreign liabilities. We treat the ratio fal as given in the short run [10]. The desired short-term foreign assets ratio depends in addition to the stimuli already introduced on ex, the anticipated change of the exchange rate, expressed in DM per unit of foreign currency.

$$fas = fas(i, i_e, sw, d, ex) \qquad fas_{2,3,5} > 0 > fas_{1,4} \qquad (4.35)$$

An increasing expectation of a revaluation of the DM reduces the relative demand for short-term foreign assets.

The supply behaviour of banks as regards their liabilities can be described by price setting functions explaining the adjustment of the yields offered to the public. We introduce three functions

$$i_t = i_t(i, i_e, sw) \qquad i_{t1,2,3} > 0 \qquad (4.36)$$

$$i_b = i_b(i) \qquad i_{b1} > 0 \qquad (4.37)$$

$$i_a = i_a(i, i_e, sw, ex) \qquad i_{a1,2,3,4} > 0 \qquad (4.38)$$

where i_t denotes an index of interest rates offered on domestic time and savings deposits, i_b an index of interest rates offered on bank bonds, and i_a an index of interest rates offered on foreign deposits. We assume that i_b does not depend on the external rate because the bulk of bank securities is issued by mortgage banks which do not engage in foreign operations. Note that the yield offered on foreign deposits depends positively on the anticipated change of exchange rates, reflecting the reduction of this yield during periods of heavy speculation on a revaluation of the DM, if the Bundesbank does not intervene by prohibiting any interest payment on such deposits.

The price setting functions imply that the banks are free in setting interest rates which has not always been the case. Under the Interest Rates Order of the Federal Banking Supervisory Office ceilings on these rates had to be observed until 1966–7. The ceilings were not fixed but moved in a somewhat delayed way with the discount rate.

Behaviour of the Domestic Public and of Foreigners

The relative demand for base money by the domestic public is described by the currency ratio k

$$k = C/D \qquad (4.39)$$

which is determined in the long run by institutional developments like the propagated substitution of cash payment by cheque payment. In the short run the desired currency ratio depends on the yields offered on competing financial assets and on wealth

$$k = k(i_t, i_b, W) \qquad k_{1,2} > 0 > k_3 \qquad (4.40)$$

The postulated positive response of the currency ratio to changes in interest rates may be somewhat surprising [11] but reflects our hypothesis that the interest elasticity of the demand for demand deposits is numerically larger than the interest elasticity of the demand for currency.

The domestic public's relative demand for time deposits and for savings deposits is lumped together in the time/deposit ratio

$$t = T/D \qquad (4.41)$$

The short-term movement of this ratio can be expected to be dominated by the very sensitive demand for time deposits by enterprises. Thus we write

$$t = t(i_t, i_b, i, i_e, sw, P, ex, W) \qquad t_{1,6,8} > 0 > t_{2,3,4,5,7} \qquad (4.42)$$

If the yield on competing domestic and foreign financial assets as well as on real capital increases, time deposits will be substituted by such assets. Also the anticipated change of exchange rates plays a role in these portfolio decisions.

The relative demand for bank securities [12] as described by the bank securities ratio bs

$$bs = BS/D \qquad (4.43)$$

is approximated by a function similar to (4.42).

$$bs = bs(i_t, i_b, i, i_e, sw, P, ex, W) \qquad bs_{2,6,8} > 0 > bs_{1,3,4,5,7} \qquad (4.44)$$

Finally, there is the demand of foreign banks and public for deposit liabilities of German banks. We define a foreign liabilities ratio fd

$$fd = FL/D \qquad (4.45)$$

The desired foreign liabilities ratio depends on German and foreign interest rates

$$fd = fd(i_a, i, i_e, sw, ex) \qquad fd_1 > 0 > fd_{2,3,4,5} \qquad (4.46)$$

This behaviour function applies accordingly to the ratios fd^1 and fd^2,

$$fd^1 = FD/D \qquad (4.47)$$

$$fd^2 = (FL - FD)/D \qquad (4.48)$$

where FD describes foreign liabilities subject to reserve requirement.

Note that in our hypothesis the foreign liabilities ratio represents the demand of foreigners for German deposit liabilities where the corresponding supply behaviour of German banks is given by the price setting function (4.38). This treatment of fd differs from the treatment Siebke and Willms have given to this ratio, interpreting it as describing demand of German banks for foreign liabilities. It seems to me that in doing this we would run into difficulties in explaining the heavy speculative inflow of foreign funds to German banks which carried a 100% reserve requirement and as such were of little use to the banks.

Money Multipliers, Asset Multipliers and Proximate Determinants of the Money Supply

Having defined allocation ratios we can specify the asset and money multipliers. As we wish to make use of an extended multiplier approach as well as of an adjusted multiplier approach for the explanation of observed money supply movements in terms of proximate determinants, we define two alternative money multipliers

$$m^e = M/B^e \tag{4.49a}$$

$$m^a = M/B^a \tag{4.49b}$$

where m^e is the extended money multiplier and m^a the adjusted money multiplier. Appropriate substitution of M, B^e and B^a by expressions containing allocation ratios gives

$$m^e = \frac{1+k}{\Delta^e} \tag{4.50a}$$

$$m^a = \frac{1+k}{\Delta^a} \tag{4.50b}$$

where

$$\Delta^e = k + (r^d + l^d) + t(r^t + l^t) + fd^1(r^f + l^f) + e(1 + t + fd^1)$$

and

$$\Delta^a = \Delta^e - (b - mob)(1 + t + fd^1) - fd(1 - fas)$$

Accordingly, the adjusted asset multiplier, as given by equation (4.22), can be specified

$$a^a = \frac{(1+b-mob-e)(1+t+fd^1)+fd^2+bs-r^d-tr^t-fd^1r^f-fd(fas+fal)}{\Delta^a}$$

$$\tag{4.51}$$

The money and asset multipliers can be transformed into multiplier functions by making use of suitable equilibrium conditions, equating actual with desired allocation ratios

$$m^e = m^e(i, i_a, i_b, i_e, sw, ex, P, W, d, r^d, r^t, r^f, l^d, l^t, l^f) \qquad (4.52a)$$

$$m^a = m^a(i, \ldots, l^f) \qquad (4.52b)$$

$$a^a = a^a(i, \ldots, l^f) \qquad (4.53)$$

The multiplier functions contain the same argument although with different weights. In the next two sections we will use these functions in solving for the credit market rate and the money supply.

The decomposition of the money supply into proximate determinants which will serve as a useful means to the empirical description of the money supply process remains to be explained. Based on the extended or the adjusted multiplier approach the money supply can be expressed as the product of a multiplier and the respective base

$$M = m^e B^e \qquad (4.54a)$$

$$M = m^a B^a \qquad (4.54b)$$

As we are interested in relative changes of the money supply and its proximate determinants, we rewrite both equations in logarithmic form and differentiate for time z. This gives

$$\frac{d \ln M}{dz} = \frac{d \ln m^e}{dz} + \frac{d \ln B^e}{dz} \qquad (4.55a)$$

$$\frac{d \ln M}{dz} = \frac{d \ln m^a}{dz} + \frac{d \ln B^a}{dz} \qquad (4.55b)$$

Making use of the multiplier definitions (4.50a and b) and of the base definitions from the sources side (4.14) and (4.16) we can decompose the relative changes of the multipliers and of the bases as follows

$$d \ln m^e = \varepsilon(m^e, k) d \ln k \text{ plus similar terms for } t, fd^1, fd^2, r^d,$$

$$r^t, r^f, l^d, l^t, l^f, \text{ and } e \qquad (4.56a)$$

$$d \ln m^a = \varepsilon(m^a, k) d \ln k \text{ plus similar terms for } t, fd^1, fd^2, r^d,$$

$$r^t, r^f, l^d, l^t, l^f, e, b, mob, \text{ and } fas \qquad (4.56b)$$

$$d \ln B^e = \varepsilon(B^e, NIR) d \ln AIR \text{ plus similar terms for } NDC, RF,$$

$$MOB, FL, \text{ and } FAS \qquad (4.57a)$$

$$d \ln B^a = \varepsilon(B^a, NIR) d \ln AIR + \varepsilon(B^a, NDC) d \ln NDC \qquad (4.57b)$$

The base elasticities are equal to the quotients of the source components in question and the respective base aggregate. The signs of the multiplier elasticities are exhibited in Tables II and III of Appendix A, while their precise values, as indeed those pertaining to other such tables, can be obtained from the author on request.

Comparing the elasticities of the alternative money multipliers we find that the respective elasticities exhibit algebraically a very similar structure and carry with one exception the same sign. Both multipliers respond negatively to changes of k, t, r^d, r^t, r^f, l^d, l^t, l^f, and e. The adjusted money multiplier reacts in addition positively on changes of b and fd^2 and negatively on changes of *mob* and *fas*. With respect to changes of fd^1 the multipliers react differently, $\varepsilon(m^a, fd^1)$ is positive while $\varepsilon(m^e, fd^1)$ is negative. This difference in reaction is due to the explicit exclusion of FD as a source component from B^a resulting in a partial positive reaction of m^a on changes of fd^1 which dominates the total reaction of m^a.

Finally note that the asset multiplier elasticities in general are numerically larger than the corresponding money multiplier elasticities.*

Solution for the Credit Market Rate

Equating the supply function and the demand function for domestic earning assets gives the credit market equation which can be solved for the equilibrium credit market rate.

$$\ln \sigma = \varepsilon(s, i - \pi) j \ln i + \varepsilon(s, i - \pi)(1 - j) \ln \pi$$
$$+ \varepsilon(s, i_f) \ln i_f + \varepsilon(s, c) \ln c + \varepsilon(s, p) \ln p$$
$$+ \varepsilon(s, P) \ln P + \varepsilon(s, W) \ln W + \ln GS \qquad (4.58)$$

where $j = i/(i - \pi) > 1$. The signs of the elasticities are identical to the signs of the derivatives already stated.

The demand function is derived by substituting function (4.53) for a^a in equation (4.19). In logarithmic form we have

$$\ln DEA = \ln B^a + \varepsilon(a^a, i) \ln i + \varepsilon(a^a, i_e) \ln i_e$$
$$+ \varepsilon(a^a, sw) \ln sw + \varepsilon(a^a, ex) \ln ex + \varepsilon(a^a, P) \ln P$$
$$+ \varepsilon(a^a, W) \ln W + \varepsilon(a^a, d) \ln d + \varepsilon(a^a, r^d) \ln r^d$$
$$\text{plus similar terms for } r^t, r^f, l^d, l^t, \text{ and } l^f \qquad (4.59)$$

The total elasticities of the demand function depend on the asset multiplier elasticities with respect to the allocation ratios, and the elasticities of the desired allocation ratios with respect to interest rates and other determinants. The signs of the total elasticities are exhibited in Table IV of Appendix A. Note that several order constraints are introduced in order to derive unequivocal responses.

According to our hypothesis the demand for domestic earning assets responds positively to changes of the credit market rate, the base, wealth and the market value of real capital (per unit). It responds negatively to changes of the Eurodollar rate, required reserve ratios and the discount rate.

From equating (4.58) and (4.59) the following solution for the credit market rate is obtained

---

* The precise values of these elasticities can be obtained from the author on request. [Ed.]

$$\ln i = \varepsilon(i, B^a) \ln B^a + \varepsilon(i, i_e) \ln i_e + \varepsilon(i, sw) \ln sw$$
$$+ \varepsilon(i, i_f) \ln i_f + \varepsilon(i, d) \ln d + \varepsilon(i, \pi) \ln \pi$$
$$+ \varepsilon(i, p) \ln p + \varepsilon(i, P) \ln P + \varepsilon(i, W) \ln W$$
$$+ \varepsilon(i, GS) \ln GS + \varepsilon(i, c) \ln c + \varepsilon(i, ex) \ln ex$$
$$+ \varepsilon(i, r^d) \ln r^d \text{ plus similar terms for } r^t, r^f, l^d, l^t, \text{ and } l^f \quad (4.60)$$

The signs of the responses of the credit market rate to changes in its determinants are exhibited in Table V of Appendix A.

The credit market rate responds negatively to changes in the exogenous base and positively to changes in the discount rate and in reserve requirement rates thus assuring efficiency to monetary policy. Increases in the anticipated rate of inflation and of the output price level contribute to a rising credit market rate. The same can be said about the influence of foreign interest rates and of the anticipation of changes of the exchange rate. Thus increasing anticipation of a revaluation of the DM induces bank and nonbank behaviour which leads to downward pressure on the credit market rate.

Solution for the Money Supply

In logarithmic form the money supply function following from (4.54b) and (4.52b) is

$$\ln M = \ln B^a + \varepsilon(m^a, i) \ln i + \varepsilon(m^a, i_e) \ln i_e + \varepsilon(m^a, sw) \ln sw$$
$$+ \varepsilon(m^a, ex) \ln ex + \varepsilon(m^a, P) \ln P + \varepsilon(m^a, W) \ln W$$
$$+ \varepsilon(m^a, d) \ln d + \varepsilon(m^a, r^d) \ln r^d \text{ plus similar terms for}$$
$$r^t, r^f, l^d, l^t, \text{ and } l^f \quad (4.61)$$

This equation corresponds to the earning asset demand equation (4.59); again the elasticities summarize the responses of the money multiplier to changes in the allocation ratios and the responses of these ratios to changes in its determinants. The structure and the signs of the total responses are given in Table VI of Appendix A.

The final step to be done is the substitution of the solution for the credit market rate into equation (4.61).

$$\ln M = \varepsilon(M, B^a) \ln B^a + \varepsilon(M, i_e) \ln i_e + \varepsilon(M, sw) \ln sw$$
$$+ \varepsilon(M, ex) \ln ex + \varepsilon(M, P) \ln P + \varepsilon(M, W) \ln W$$
$$+ \varepsilon(M, p) \ln p + \varepsilon(M, \pi) \ln \pi + \varepsilon(M, i_f) \ln i_f$$
$$+ \varepsilon(M, GS) \ln GS + \varepsilon(M, d) \ln d + \varepsilon(M, c) \ln c$$
$$+ \varepsilon(M, r^d) \ln r^d \text{ plus similar terms for}$$
$$r^t, r^f, l^d, l^t, \text{ and } l^f \quad (4.62)$$

As a result we obtain an equilibrium solution for the money supply reflecting the interaction of the money supply, domestic earning assets and the interest rate on the credit market. Once again signs of the elasticities are presented in Table VII of Appendix A, while precise expressions relating to them can be obtained from the author on request. Preliminary regression estimates of simplified versions of this equation are given on p. 104.

Empirical Analysis

We start the empirical analysis by breaking down monetary growth into the contributions of its proximate determinants. We consider the total period as well as selected sub-periods. The selection of sub-periods is not led by an interest into specific historical situations but by theoretical considerations. If it is true that monetary processes are of a systematic rather than of a chance nature, as it is contended by monetary theory, then we should be able to observe a systematic variation in the contribution of important proximate determinants when sub-periods are discriminated by relevant criteria. Therefore we differentiate between periods of high or accelerating monetary growth and periods of low or decelerating monetary growth, between periods of rising and of declining domestic interest rates and between periods of rising and declining international reserve flows.

Movement of the Money Stock and of Other Monetary Variables Over the Period 1958–72

During the period under consideration the money stock grew from DM 35 billion in early 1958 to DM 134 billion by the end of 1972. The average annual rate of growth was 8·6%, moving between 1·6% at minimum and 14·5% at maximum [13].

There were four decelerations of monetary growth and four accelerations. The movement of the money stock has always been in a very close association

Table 4.1 *Annual Rates of Change in M, B^b, and B^a*

	Money stock	Extended base	Adjusted base
Average	8·63	8·39	3·43
Maximum	14·51	15·50	35·78
Minimum	1·55	2·30	−37·14
Standard deviation	3·05	2·47	13·23

with the movement of the extended monetary base in the Federal Republic. The extended base grew from 1958 to 1972 by almost the same annual rate as the money stock, reaching a level of DM 81 billion by the end of 1972 compared to DM 22 billion in early 1958.

In contrast to the money stock and the extended base the adjusted monetary base moved wildly. Its coefficient of variation was 3·85 and thus more than ten times the respective coefficients of variation of the money stock (0·30) and of the extended base (0·35).

The marked difference in the movement of B^e and B^a is necessarily reflected in the movements of the corresponding money multipliers m^e and m^a. The extended multiplier is numerically very stable [14] as can be seen from Tables I and II of Appendix B where information on the values, rates of change and variation of the money multipliers and their components is supplied. Both multipliers rose over the total period; however, the average rise of m^e was negligible (0·2%) compared to the average rise of m^a (5·2%).

The currency ratio k declined over the whole period almost continuously, from 0·78 to 0·47. This downward trend had been suspended in 1961 for several quarters when the banks introduced the five-day week, thus forcing the public to increase its average currency holdings. The time/deposit ratio has increased over the whole period exhibiting a wider range of variation than the currency ratio. Note that for statistical reasons we have lumped together the time/deposit ratio with part of the foreign deposit ratio [15].

The average required reserve ratio r varied between 0·05 and 0·13, reflecting the heavy use the Bundesbank made of this instrument [16]. The sum of the ratios r and l is relatively stable although still varying, mainly for two reasons:

(a) There are interdeposit flows which show up when the respective individual required reserve ratios are different.

(b) The direct base money impact of changes in reserve requirements is approximately eliminated by the ratio l but not completely.

The excess reserve ratio e decreased slightly over the whole period, but is really negligibly small. The main variation observed is due to short periods of heavy speculative capital inflows from abroad.

The borrowing ratios b and mob varied considerably around trends. The ratio b moved upward from 0·01 to 0·07 while the ratio mob moved downward from 0·09 to 0·01. As we will see in detail in a later section, borrowing from the Bundesbank played an important role in dampening monetary fluctuations.

The foreign deposit ratio fd was very stable at a level of 0·17 from 1958 to 1967 with the exception of a short speculative period in 1960–61. Since mid-1968 foreigners became used to speculating on repeated revaluation of the DM and thus fd jumped within two years to a new level of 0·40 fluctuating narrowly around this level since mid-1970. The ratio of short-term foreign assets of banks fas exhibits considerable fluctuation. Between 1958 and 1967 it increased from 0·5 to 1·0; thereafter it started declining reaching the original level of 0·5 by the end of 1972.

Two Alternative Approaches to Proximate Determination of the Money Stock

Within the general framework of our money supply hypothesis we have formulated two alternative multiplier approaches for the analysis of monetary growth in terms of proximate determinants. Both approaches are similarly structured; the main difference is that in the adjusted multiplier approach the commercial banks' borrowing from the Bundesbank, their acquisition of short-term foreign assets and the demand of foreigners for German deposit liabilities appear in ratio form in the multiplier, while they appear as base source components in the case of the extended multiplier approach.

Although the broad informational content as regards proximate determination of the money stock and its change can be expected to coincide, the observed contribution of single determinants can be very different in absolute value from one approach to the other. This leads us to question which of the two schemes is the more reliable for the organization of empirical observations. The answer to this question is important, not only on academic grounds but also on the grounds that such a scheme may usefully serve as an analytical means for monetary policy management.

The only criterion I can see for deciding this issue is the relative degree of stability or regularity in the empirical relations stated by the competing

Table 4.2. *Coefficients of variation of the respective multiplier or base elasticities and contributions to monetary growth*

Proximate determinant	Multiplier or base elasticities		Contributions to monetary growth	
	Approach		Approach	
	m^e	m^a	m^e	m^a
k	−0·08	−0·48	1·04	1·04
$t + fd^1$	−0·16	−0·16	−1·82	−1·84
$r + l$	−0·12	−0·39	5·47	13·36
e	−0·15	−0·38	9·71	7·83
RF	0·73		2·31	
b		1·02		6·02
MOB	−0·83		4·19	
mob		−0·68		4·05
FL	0·48		1·04	
fd		0·96		2·39
FAS	−0·44		−1·75	
fas		−0·73		11·00
NIR	0·20	0·19	2·87	3·34
NDC	1·18	1·64	−6·36	−4·55

* The coefficient of variation is defined as the quotient of the standard deviation and the arithmetic mean.

approaches. The reason for this is that our construction of a money supply hypothesis is based on the contention that monetary processes are systematic processes implying stable patterns of regularities for the proximate determinants of the money supply.

Tables III and IV of Appendix B give information on the means and standard deviations of the multiplier and base elasticities for both approaches. It turns out that the elasticities relevant within the extended multiplier approach in most cases exhibit a much smaller range of variation than the corresponding elasticities of the adjusted multiplier approach. This result is not very surprising, because we already know that m^e and B^e show a more stable behaviour than m^a and B^a. For instance, the coefficient of variation in the case of m^e was 0·02 compared with 0·28 for m^a.

To facilitate comparison coefficients of variation for the total period are presented in Table 4.2. The first two columns give the coefficients of the multiplier and base responses to changes in their components. In the cases of six of the ten proximate determinants the coefficient of variation of the response is numerically much smaller for the m^e-approach than for the m^a-approach; in three cases it is about the same and in only one case is it markedly larger. This establishes that within the frame of an extended multiplier approach in general more stable and thus more predictable responses of the money supply to changes in proximate determinants are derived than within the frame of the adjusted multiplier approach. This is also reflected by the last two columns of Table 4.2 which give the coefficients of variation observed for the contributions of the determinants to monetary growth.

Finally, we summed the variances of the average contributions of the determinants over the period 1959 to 1972, separately for both approaches, and computed the sum of covariances. This led to Σ Cov. $= -965$ for the m^a-approach, and to Σ Cov. $= -398$ for the m^e-approach, indicating a much higher negative covariation of the determinants' contributions within the m^a-approach than within the m^e-approach.

Summarizing the evidence presented it seems safe to conclude that the extended multiplier approach is a more reliable device for the empirical analysis of money supply growth in terms of proximate determinants than the adjusted multiplier approach. The Deutsche Bundesbank and the German Council of Economic Experts would therefore be well advised to consider adopting the extended multiplier approach as an instrument for the current diagnosis of monetary events.

In the following sections we will nevertheless make use of both approaches in order to give the reader more information on their relative performance. It will become apparent that in general it does not make a big difference which approach is used as long as one is not concerned with the absolute values of the determinants' contributions but with their relative order of magnitude.

Determinants of the German Money Supply in the Long Run

The last column of Table V in Appendix B gives information on the long-run contributions of the proximate determinants of the money supply. It appears that over the period 1959 to 1972 the monetary growth (8·6% p.a.) was completely dominated by the growth of the extended monetary base (8·4% p.a.) which reflects the monetary impulse emitted by the Bundesbank. Thus the behaviour of banks and of the public, as summarized by the extended money multiplier, was of no relevance for the long-run expansion of the money supply, although it must be recognized that banks in addition influence the money supply via their borrowing from the Central Bank and via operations in foreign assets.

In order to gain a better insight into the main determinants we have reorganized in Table 4.3 the various proximate determinants by exhibiting suitable combinations. The contribution of the domestic public combines the behaviour of the currency and the time/deposit ratio; the contribution of the domestic operations of banks combines their reserve and borrowing behaviour; the contribution of international reserve flows combines the behaviour of foreigners as regards German deposit liabilities; the behaviour of German banks as regards short-term foreign assets and the behaviour

Table 4.3.

	m^e-approach	m^a-approach
$\hat{M}$	8·63	
Contribution of:		
Domestic public	−0·01	0·38
Domestic operations of banks	3·53	3·14
Exogenous domestic source component	−1·77	−3·53
International reserve flows	6·89	8·66

of the exogenous part of the source component net international reserves. Finally, there is the contribution of the exogenous domestic source component of the base. According to the m^e- as well as the m^a-approach, the contribution of the domestic public to the long-run growth of the money supply was negligible. In fact, the contributions of the currency ratio and of the time/deposit ratio tend to offset each other in the long run.

The most important long-run determinants were clearly the international reserve flows, supplemented by the banks' borrowing from the Bundesbank. Taken together these two determinants accounted for an average growth of the money supply of more than 10% p.a. However, they were partly neutralized by a respective negative contribution of the exogenous domestic source component. Note that more than two-thirds of the contribution of international reserve flows resulted from current account surpluses.

Thus we may conclude that the long-run growth of the German money supply in the past was predominantly guaranteed by the adherence of the German authorities to an undervalued currency and to the granting of an automatic recourse to the Central Bank within the limits of relatively large rediscount quotas.

Periods of Monetary Acceleration versus Periods of Monetary Deceleration

The basic information is supplied by Table V of Appendix B. As usual we note again that the extended monetary base, reflecting the total impulse emitted by the Bundesbank, dominated the growth of the money supply during accelerations as well as during decelerations. The extended money multiplier contributed very little but moved procyclically. This is mainly due to the procyclical behaviour of the domestic public via the currency ratio and the time/deposit ratio.

Table 4.4. *Periods of monetary acceleration and deceleration*

	Acceleration (1)	Deceleration (2)	Difference (1) − (2)
	m^e-approach		
$\hat{M}$	9·55	7·10	2·45
Contribution of:			
Domestic public	0·59	−1·01	1·60
Domestic operations of banks	0·64	8·36	−7·72
Exogenous domestic source component	−3·98	1·91	−5·89
International reserve flows	12·32	−2·15	14·47
	m^a-approach		
Domestic public	1·13	−0·88	2·01
Domestic operations of banks	−1·42	10·72	−12·14
Exogenous domestic source component	−7·51	3·10	−10·61
International reserve flows	17·22	−5·61	11·61
Approx. error	0·20	−0·36	

Our prevailing observation that the international reserve flows constitute the most important determinant of monetary growth is again confirmed. Moreover, it is this determinant which was almost exclusively responsible for the occurrence of monetary accelerations and decelerations in the past, as can be judged from the last column of Table 4.4. The difference between its average contributions during periods of monetary acceleration and deceleration is positive and nine times the difference between the corresponding contributions of the domestic public, in the case of the m^e-approach, and more than five times in the case of the m^a-approach. We also note that the exogenous part and the endogenous part of the international reserve flows behaved equally in this respect.

The procyclical influence of international reserve flows and of the domestic public on the growth of the money supply was partly offset—contrary to what commonly is believed—by an anticyclical behaviour of the banking system and by the exogenous domestic source component. The average contribution of the banks' domestic operations was practically zero during periods of acceleration but more than plus 8% during periods of deceleration, when the banks economized on their holdings of excess reserves and borrowed heavily from the Bundesbank by selling bills and open market paper. The

Table 4.5. *Contributions of alternative source components during different phases of monetary policy*

	Terminating deceleration	Opening Terminating Phases of Monetary acceleration		Opening deceleration
		m^e-approach		
$\hat{M}$	5·24	7·52	10·69	8·93
Contribution of:				
Domestic public	−2·41	−0·96	1·60	0·17
Domestic operations of banks	9·07	−4·79	4·72	10·73
Exogenous domestic source component	−2·31	−8·21	1·10	5·31
International reserve flows	0·89	20·96	3·28	−7·30
		m^a-approach		
Domestic public	−2·16	0·46	1·63	0·20
Domestic operations of banks	13·34	−9·68	5·94	13·75
Exogenous domestic source component	0·15	−13·76	0·14	6·76
International reserve flows	−5·04	30·13	3·19	−12·04
Approx. Error	−1·05	0·59	−0·03	0·25

exogenous domestic source component contributed negatively to monetary growth during periods of acceleration and positively, although on a moderate scale, during periods of deceleration.

To push our empirical investigation into the behaviour of proximate determinants during periods of monetary acceleration and deceleration a step further we have selected sub-periods, namely, what we call opening and terminating phases of acceleration or deceleration. Opening phases are defined as being the first three-quarters of an acceleration or deceleration, and terminating phases the respective last three-quarters [17]. The information gained by this procedure is summarized in Table 4.5; for more details see Tables VI and VII of Appendix B.

We have already noted a procyclical behaviour of the domestic public and find now that this occurs predominantly during the terminating phases of a deceleration or acceleration. According to the m^e-approach the average contribution of the public during terminating phases of deceleration was -2.4 but 1.6 during terminating phases of acceleration. Moreover, although on a very moderate scale, the domestic public seems to contribute positively to monetary growth during opening phases of deceleration and negatively during opening phases of acceleration.

The dampening behaviour of commercial banks via their domestic operations, on the other hand, took place primarily during the opening phases of monetary acceleration or deceleration. During terminating phases of acceleration the banks even behaved procyclically, contributing on the average almost 5% to the growth rate of the money supply. Also the exogenous domestic source component contributed predominantly during opening phases of acceleration or deceleration to a dampening of the variation in monetary growth, but moved procyclically during the respective terminating phases.

Finally, there are the international reserve flows which constituted the crucial determinant responsible for the opening of periods of accelerating or decelerating monetary growth. As can be judged from Table 4.6, there is no other proximate determinant displaying similarly high differences in its average contributions to monetary growth between the sub-periods considered.

Periods of Rising Interest Rates versus Periods of Decreasing Interest Rates

Periods of rising domestic interest rates were to a large extent periods of decelerating monetary growth while periods of decreasing interest rates were mainly periods of accelerating monetary growth. Thus the information gained by differentiating sub-periods following the criterion of changes in domestic interest rates is roughly the same as in the previous section, as can be seen from comparing Table 4.6 with Table 4.4.

We do not repeat the general observations but concentrate on two special observations, namely (a) the contribution of the currency ratio, and (b) the contribution of the banks' borrowing from the Bundesbank.

Table VIII of Appendix B shows that the average contribution of the currency ratio to the growth of the money supply was positive during periods of decreasing interest rates and doubled its contribution during periods of rising interest rates. As the elasticity of the money multiplier with respect to the currency ratio is negative, our observation indicates that the average decrease of the currency ratio was much smaller during periods of rising

Table 4.6. *Periods of decreasing and rising interest rates*

	Decreasing (1)	Rising (2)	Difference (1) − (2)
		m^e-approach	
$\hat{M}$	9·13	8·20	0·93
Contribution of:			
Domestic public	0·29	−0·28	0·57
Domestic operations of banks	−1·57	7·95	−9·52
Exogenous domestic source component	−3·97	0·14	−3·11
International reserve flows	14·39	0·38	14·01
		m^a-approach	
Domestic public	0·97	−0·13	1·10
Domestic operations of banks	−4·87	10·08	−14·95
Exogenous domestic source component	−7·86	0·22	−8·08
International reserve flows	20·22	−1·34	21·56
Approx. error	0·71	−0·63	

interest rates than during periods of decreasing interest rates. This confirms, although not conclusively, our hypothesis of a positive interest elasticity of the currency ratio.

The apparently high positive interest rate responsiveness of commercial banks' borrowing from the Bundesbank should also be noticed. As can be derived from Table VIII of Appendix B the average contribution to monetary growth through selling of bills and mobilization paper was during periods of rising interest rates more than double the long-run contribution (7·8% as compared to 3·3%, m^e-approach); during periods of decreasing interest rates banks reduced their borrowing drastically, thus contributing negatively to monetary growth (−2·0%). In general both sources of borrowing behaved similarly.

Periods of Rising International Reserves versus Periods of Decreasing International Reserves

It is very well established by monetary theory that given a system of fixed exchange rates no single country can escape from the international path of inflation in the long run because the balance of payments constraint enforces an automatic adjustment of domestic monetary growth. It has also been repeatedly asserted by Government officials as well as by academic economists that this is true even in the shorter run due to 'offsetting capital flows'. However, the notion of offsetting capital flows is not very well founded; Brunner has demonstrated this thesis to be an essentially impressionistic idea without analytic support and has presented evidence refuting the theory from Italian and German experience [18].

Clearly, the denial of the thesis that under fixed exchange rates monetary policy loses any effectiveness even in the shorter run does not mean to deny that the pressure for domestic adjustment may become overwhelming when the discrepancy between the international and the domestic rate of inflation becomes large enough to raise a widespread speculation on a correction of the official exchange rates. The recent German experience offers indeed dramatic evidence on this. But it has also to be noted that before these developments occurred there was always a considerable margin for an autonomous shorter-run monetary policy.

Table 4.7. *Periods of rising and decreasing international reserves*

	Rising	Decreasing	Heavily* Rising	Heavily* Decreasing
	m^e-approach			
$\hat{M}$	8·34	9·15	9·59	6·51
Contribution of:				
Domestic public	−0·22	0·33	0·31	−0·49
Domestic operations of banks	0·58	8·82	−1·48	20·03
Exogenous domestic source component	−7·00	7·66	−15·81	7·79
International reserve flows	14·98	−7·67	26·59	−20·88
	m^a-approach			
Domestic public	0·35	0·43	1·26	0·01
Domestic operations of banks	−1·62	11·69	−7·08	31·18
Exogenous domestic source component	−10·29	8·63	−23·11	12·79
International reserve flows	19·95	−11·65	37·83	−36·27
Approx. error	0·01	−0·06	0·70	−1·21

* Periods exhibiting rates of change of more than DM 5 billion for corresponding quarters.

During the 1960s the German authorities effectively managed to lag behind the international development of inflation and thus to maintain an undervalued currency. It is most noteworthy that the average growth rate of the German money supply was below its long-run value during periods of rising international reserves (8·3%) to be compared with 8·6%) and above it during periods of decreasing international reserves (9·2%); see Table IX of Appendix B. Thus total domestic forces operating on the money supply overcompensated the foreign forces in the shorter run. The first two columns of Table 4.7 show that the exogenous domestic source component and the domestic operations of banks were the most important compensating sources. Clearly, if we concentrate on shorter sub-periods of very large capital inflows or outflows [19], as presented by the last two columns of Table 4.7, we observe a partial compensation only.

Further information on the major compensating sources is supplied by Tables 4.8 and 4.9. Table 4.8 shows the covariances between the international reserve flows and changes in the exogenous domestic source component NDC as well as changes in the total domestic component DC of the extended base. All covariances are negative, but it should be

Table 4.8. *Covariances* between international reserve flows and $\Delta\,NDC$ and $\Delta\,DC$ for periods of rising and decreasing international reserves*

	1959–72	Rising	Decreasing
ΔNDC	−208	−236	− 37
ΔDC	−977	−975	−4003

* Measured in percent of the variance of the sum of the covariating components.

noted that the covariances between ΔIR and ΔDC are numerically much larger than the corresponding covariances between ΔIR and ΔNDC. This reflects the important compensating role played by the borrowing behaviour of banks.

To differentiate more sharply between the exogenous domestic source component on the one hand and commercial banks' borrowing on the other as regards their importance in compensation for the impact of international reserve flows, we have regressed separately changes of these sources on changes of international reserves. The resulting regression coefficients or, as we call them, coefficients of compensation are presented in Table 4.9.

First we note that the coefficient of compensation ΔDC with respect to changes in the total domestic component estimated for the total period is exactly the same as the one which has been estimated for a somewhat different

Table 4.9. *Coefficients of compensation with respect to international reserve flows*

Compensation by	Coefficient of compensation	t-value	R^2
	Period: 1959–1972		
ΔNDC	−0·557	−15·346	0·808
$\Delta RF - \Delta MOB$	−0·303	−7·295	0·486
ΔDC	−0·859	−36·488	0·959
	Periods of rising international reserves		
ΔNDC	−0·597	−11·517	0·789
$\Delta RF - \Delta MOB$	−0·205	−3·866	0·284
ΔDC	−0·798	−22·922	0·936
	Periods of decreasing international reserves		
ΔNDC	−0·249	−4·107	0·312
$\Delta RF - \Delta MOB$	−0·769	−8·801	0·799
ΔDC	−1·018	−27·354	0·975

period by Manfred Willms, namely −0·86 [20]. The coefficient indicates that on the average DM 86 out of each DM 100 change in international reserves were compensated by opposite changes in the total domestic component. On the interpretation of Willms this reflects the compensating behaviour of the monetary authorities. I find it difficult, however, to follow that interpretation, if one argues—as we do—within a framework which treats the Central Bank borrowing of commercial banks as only indirectly controlled [21]. It was for this reason that I have split ΔDC into ΔNDC and $\Delta(RF - MOB)$. From this split we obtain the result that during the period 1959–72 about two-thirds of the average compensation were carried out by the exogenous domestic source component but one-third by the banks' borrowing behaviour.

Considering sub-periods we find that during periods of rising international reserves 80% of these increases were compensated by opposite movement of the total domestic component and as much as three-quarters of the compensation was due to the behaviour of the exogenous domestic source component. However, the picture was radically different during periods of decreasing international reserves. First of all, we observe that during those periods the movement of international reserve flows was fully compensated by the total domestic component of the extended monetary base; the estimated coefficient of compensation is −1·02. Secondly, we find that in comparison to other periods the exogenous domestic component and the borrowing component swapped their parts. The borrowing component then overtook three-quarters of the total compensation.

The Controllability of the Monetary Base

The issue of the controllability of the German money supply growth in the shorter run, where the shorter run is measured in quarters rather than in months or weeks, can be usefully reduced to an issue of the controllability of the extended monetary base because the extended money multiplier has always remained numerically very stable and thus predictable within a narrow margin.

Our empirical observations on the German money supply process can be exploited to reach a tentative conclusion on the controllability issue, but it should be noted that we have to differentiate control from controllability. We are not in a position to answer the question whether the Bundesbank actually controlled the money supply or the monetary base in the past. Our knowledge of the actual impulse behaviour of the Bundesbank, reflected by the movement of the extended monetary base, is not sufficient information; in addition we would have to know precisely what the intended behaviour of the Bank was.

Table 4.10. *Coefficients of compensation of* $\Delta(B^e - NDC)$ *by* ΔNDC

	Coefficient of compensation	t-value	R^2
Period 1959–72	−0·773	−23·371	0·906
Periods of rising international reserves	−0·724	−15·893	0·875
Periods of decreasing international reserves	−0·900	−10·913	0·861
Periods of monetary acceleration	−0·749	−24.129	0·893
Periods of monetary deceleration	−0·987	−22·431	0·941

However, the controllability question, namely, whether or at least to what degree the extended monetary base was controllable in the past, can be tentatively answered. For instance, if we were to observe that the Bundesbank, by suitably changing the exogenous domestic source component NDC, compensated fully or even overcompensated any change in the sum of the remaining exogenous or endogenous source components of the extended base, then we could conclude without doubt that the Bank had full control over base money creation and thus over the money supply [22]. On the other hand, if we were to observe a coefficient of compensation of −0·8 or of −0·1, in these cases we could only conclude that the Bank was able to compensate on the average for 80% or 10% of the total change in the remaining sources of base money creation. But we should note that such observations do not rule out the possibility that the Bank had the power to fully compensate for undesired changes in the remaining source components.

For the empirical investigation into the controllability issue we have to separate the source components directly controlled by the Bundesbank from all other source components. For the reader's convenience the source equation of the extended monetary base is repeated:

$$B^e = NIR + (FL - FAS)^B + RF - MOB + NDC \qquad (4.14)$$

The only source component directly controlled by the Bank is NDC, the exogenous domestic source component; all other sources are either endogenous and thus only indirectly influenced by the Bank or exogenous to the Bank. We emphasize that the exogenous part of international reserves is not under the direct control of the Bank as long as fixed exchange rates are maintained; this has been overlooked by Willms in his investigation of the controllability issue [23]. Regressing ΔNDC on $\Delta(B^e - NDC)$, or equivalently, on $\Delta[NIR + (FL - FAS)^B + RF - MOB]$ led to the coefficients of compensation presented in Table 4.10.

The results may be summarized as follows:

(a) Measured over the total period 1959–72 the Bundesbank has been able to compensate on average for 77% of the summed changes in source components of the base not under its direct quantity control. This points to a relative high degree of controllability [24].

(b) The estimated coefficients of compensation are lower for periods of rising international reserves or of accelerating monetary growth than for periods of decreasing international reserves or decelerating monetary growth.

This asymmetry in the coefficients can be interpreted very differently. On one interpretation it can be regarded as confirming evidence for the contention that in open economies the monetary authorities are better equipped to fight deflation rather than inflation. On an alternative interpretation—based on the *a priori* assumption that the authorities can always fully neutralize undesired monetary developments—one reaches the conclusion that the observed asymmetry simply reflects the deliberate cyclical behaviour of the authorities who apparently believe a continuous alternation of monetary acceleration and deceleration to be preferable to a more steady growth of the money supply.

Estimates of Money Supply and Interest Rate Functions

Preliminary estimates of somewhat simplified money supply and interest rate functions are reported in Tables 4.11 and 4.12. Again both approaches have been used, the adjusted as well as the extended multiplier approach. Before commenting on the results, let us very briefly describe the data.

All the estimates are based on seasonally non-adjusted quarterly data, making use of seasonal dummies which are not reported. The monetary base and the money stock data are either daily or weekly averages. While the discount rate is measured daily, the credit market rate and the Eurodollar rate are measured weekly. The credit market rate is approximated by the effective yield on outstanding Government bonds, the Eurodollar rate used is the interest rate on three months Eurodollar deposits in London. Finally, there is gross national income Y; the data are those estimated by the Deutsches Institut für Wirtschaftsforschung (Berlin).

The money supply functions estimated are either based on the extended base or the adjusted base. In the variable K_2 the adjusted base—after having been purged from liberated reserves—is combined with the direct influence of required reserve rates on the money multiplier. Comparing the first three

Table 4.11. *Money supply functions*, period 1960–72*

No.	1	2	3	4	5	6
K_2	0·412*	0·299*	0·179*			
$\ln B^e$				1·000*	1·019*	0·988*
$\ln d$		−0·145	−0·690*		−0·003	−0·042*
$\ln i_e$		−0·509*	0·532*		−0·020	
$\ln i$			1·748*			0·105*
Const.	7·027*	7·823*	6·714*	0·476*	0·292*	0·466*
$\bar{R}^2$	0·59	0·75	0·88	1·00	1·00	1·00
Standard error	0·185	0·146	0·101	0·014	0·013	0·013
DW	0·72	0·77	1·09	1·02	1·28	1·26

* Asterisks indicate significance on the 5% error level.
$$K_2 = \ln B^a + \varepsilon(m^a, r)\ln r$$

functions we find that the inclusion of the discount rate, the Eurodollar rate and the credit market rate improves the estimated relationship, with co-efficients being significantly different from zero on the 5% level and displaying the hypothesized signs.

But clearly the first three money supply functions cannot compete with the last three. Substituting B^e for K_2 leads to better estimates. The elasticity of the money stock with respect to the extended base appears to be unity (function 4) and adding the discount rate as well as the Eurodollar rate does not make a big difference. This was to be expected as the influence of the Eurodollar and the discount rate should be much higher in the case of the adjusted money multiplier than in the case of the extended money multiplier. Leaving the reduced form by including the credit market rate (function 6) gives a positive interest elasticity of about 0·1 for the extended money multiplier, while the corresponding interest elasticity of the adjusted money multiplier appears to be more than fifteen times the former elasticity. Finally it may be noted that the overall quality of the money supply functions 4 to 6 again points to the conclusion that the extended money multiplier approach is superior to any other analytic approach in serving as a foundation and device for money supply management. This can be said although the estimates still contain serial correlation [25].

The estimated interest rate functions do look very bad [26]. Using the adjusted multiplier approach (see functions 1 to 4 in Table 4.12) one does not find the

Table 4.12. Interest rate functions*, period 1960–72

No.	1	2	3	4	5	6
K_4	0·011	0·000				
$\ln B^a$			−0·010	0·006		
$\varepsilon(a^a, r)\ln r$			0·152*	−0·045		
$\ln B^c$					−0·751*	−0·124
$\ln Y_{-1}$	0·302*	0·177*	0·132	0·217*	1·015*	0·294
$\ln d$		0·257*		0·284*		0·252*
Const.	−1·754*	−0·497*	0·315	−1·018	−1·010	−0·392
$\bar{R}^2$	0·57	0·84	0·64	0·84	0·61	0·84
Standard error	0·083	0·050	0·076	0·050	0·079	0·050
DW	0·23	0·34	0·26	0·37	0·34	0·35

* Asterisks indicate significance on the 5% error level.
$$K_4 = \ln B^a + \varepsilon(a^a, r)\ln r$$

hypothesized negative elasticity of the credit market rate with respect to the base; instead, the influence of the adjusted base appears to be practically equal to zero. This, it seems to me, is a result difficult to understand for every student of economics. I have been more puzzled, because in 1971 Manfred Willms published an interest rate function, similar to function 1, which gave the expected negative elasticity [27].

Willms had:

$$\ln i = -0.219 - 0.427^* \ln B^n + 0.603^* \ln Y$$
$$\bar{R}^2 = 0.61, \text{ Standard error} = 0.07, DW = 0.32$$

Willms' period of observation was 1960,1 to 1970,2. Thus I re-estimated function 1 for the same period and obtained

$$\ln i = -1.860 + 0.10[\ln B^a + \varepsilon(a^a, r)\ln r] + 0.313^* \ln Y_{-1}$$
$$\bar{R}^2 = 0.40, \text{ Standard error} = 0.09, DW = 0.20,$$

again a positive elasticity of the credit market rate with respect to the adjusted base. Clearly, the discrepancies in the estimates must be due to the still differing definitions of the base. There are two differences between both definitions:

(*a*) Willms subtracted from the sources base not only the net short-term foreign liabilities of banks but in addition those of nonbanks.

(*b*) Willms specified incorrectly the influence of the required reserve policy on the credit rate by including liberated reserves in his net monetary base.

While such a procedure is appropriate in the case of the estimation of money supply functions, it becomes incorrect when applied to the estimation of interest rate or earning asset demand functions. It was for this reason that we first purged B^a from liberated reserves and then combined it with the expression $\varepsilon(a^a, r) \ln r$.

For the very reason just discussed it would also be inappropriate to use for the explanation of the credit market rate the extended base, even within the frame of the extended multiplier approach. Nevertheless, one is able to obtain better-looking results if one is prepared to accept the extended base (see especially function 5 in Table 4.12). Clearly, the interest rate functions presented are unsatisfactory and raise questions about earlier empirical results from the German study. More detailed empirical as well as analytical investigation into the interest rate determination will be necessary and it can only be hoped that competing research on this problem for other European countries will serve as a fruitful encouragement.

Appendix A

Table I. List of symbols

B = monetary base
B^a = adjusted monetary base
B^e = extended monetary base
BS = bank securities in circulation
C = currency holdings of the public
CAB = current account balance
D = demand deposits of the domestic public
DEA = domestic earning assets held by banks
ER = excess reserves including vault cash
FA = foreign assets
FAL = long-term foreign assets
FAS = short-term foreign assets
FD = foreign deposits subject to reserve requirement
FL = foreign liabilites
$GDNI$ = Government's direct net transactions with foreign countries
GS = outstanding stock of Government securities
IR = net international reserves
L = liberated reserves
L^p = public's desired loan liability position
M = money stock
MOB = banks' holdings of open market paper
$MOBC$ = Bundesbank's holdings of open market paper
$MOBP$ = public's holdings of open market paper

$MOBT$ = total stock holdings of open market paper
NDC = net domestic component of B^a
NIR = adjusted international reserves
NPD = net public deposits
OAN = other assets net
P = per unit market value of real capital
PS = outstanding stock of privately issued securities
R = base money holdings of banks
RR = required reserves
RF = borrowings through rediscounting and Lombarding
SF = domestic securities held by foreigners
SP = domestic securities held by domestic public
SCD = special cash deposits
$SWAP$ = swap contracts
T = time deposits of the domestic public
W = wealth
a^a = adjusted asset multiplier
b = borrowing ratio
bs = bank securities ratio
c = special cash deposits ratio
d = discount rate
e = excess reserve ratio
ex = anticpated change of exchange rate
fal = ratio of long-term foreign assets
fas = ratio of short-term foreign assets
fd = foreign deposits ratio
i = credit market rate
i_a = interest rate on foreign deposits
i_b = interest rate on bank securities
i_e = Eurodollar rate
i_f = interest rate on long-term foreign assets
i_t = interest rate on domestic time deposits
j = $i/(i - \pi)$
k = currency ratio
l = liberated reserves ratio
m^a = adjusted money multiplier
m^e = extended money multiplier
p = output price level
r = required reserve ratio
t = time/deposit ratio
sw = swap rate in the open market
σ = public's supply of domestic earning assets
π = anticipated rate of inflation
α = $(a^a + 1)/a^a$

Table II. Extended multiplier approach: multiplier elasticities with respect to proximate determinants

$\varepsilon(m^e, k) < 0; m^e > 1$ $\varepsilon(m^e, r^t) < 0$
$\varepsilon(m^e, t) < 0$ $\varepsilon(m^e, l^t) < 0$
$\varepsilon(m^e, fd^1) < 0$ $\varepsilon(m^e, r^f) < 0$
$\varepsilon(m^e, r^d) < 0$ $\varepsilon(m^e, l^f) < 0$
$\varepsilon(m^e, l^d) < 0$ $\varepsilon(m^e, e) < 0$

The elasticities are obtained by differentiating the multiplier for the component in question and multiplying the result by the quotient of the component and the multiplier.

Table III. Adjusted multiplier approach: multiplier elasticities with respect to proximate determinants

1. Money Multiplier Elasticities

$\varepsilon(m^a, k) < 0; \ m^a > 1$ $\varepsilon(m^a, r^t) < 0$

$\varepsilon(m^a, t) < 0;$ $\varepsilon(m^a, l^t) < 0$

$\quad r^t + l^t + e + mob > b$ $\varepsilon(m^a, r^f) < 0$

$\varepsilon(m^a, fd^1) > 0;$ $\varepsilon(m^a, l^f) < 0$

$\quad 1 + b > r^t + l^t + e + mob + fas$ $\varepsilon(m^a, e) < 0$

$\varepsilon(m^a, fd^2) > 0; \ 1 > fas$ $\varepsilon(m^a, b) > 0$

$\varepsilon(m^a, r^d) < 0$ $\varepsilon(m^a, mob) < 0$

$\varepsilon(m^a, l^d) < 0$ $\varepsilon(m^a, fas) < 0$

2. Asset Multiplier Elasticities

Some of the following elasticities are multiples of the respective money multiplier elasticities; the multiplying factor is $\alpha = (a^a + 1)/a^a$.

$\varepsilon(a^a, k) < 0, \ m^a > 1$ $\varepsilon(a^a, l^d) < 0$

$\varepsilon(a^a, t) > 0, \ 1 + l^t + b(a^a + 1)$ $\varepsilon(a^a, r^t) < 0$

$\quad > (r^t + l^t + e + mob)$ $\varepsilon(a^a, l^t) < 0$

$\quad (a^a + 1)$ $\varepsilon(a^a, r^f) < 0$

$\varepsilon(a^a, fd^1) > 0, \ (a^a + 1)(1 + b)$ $\varepsilon(a^a, l^f) < 0$

$\quad > (a + 1)(r^t + l^t + e + mob + fas)$ $\varepsilon(a^a, e) < 0$

$\quad + l^t + fal$ $\varepsilon(a^a, b) > 0$

$\varepsilon(a^a, fd^2) > 0, \ (a + 1)(1 - fas) > fal$ $\varepsilon(a^a, mob) < 0$

$\varepsilon(a^a, bs) > 0$ $\varepsilon(a^a, fas) < 0$

$\varepsilon(a^a, r^d) < 0$ $\varepsilon(a^a, fal) < 0$

Table IV. Responses of the adjusted asset multiplier to changes in interest rates and other determinants

$\varepsilon(a^a, i) \ > 0$

provided $\varepsilon(t, i_t) \, \varepsilon(i_t, i) > |\, \varepsilon(t, i_b) \, \varepsilon(i_b, i) + \varepsilon(t, i)\,|$

$\quad \varepsilon(bs, i_b) \, \varepsilon(i_b, i) > |\, \varepsilon(bs, i_t) \, \varepsilon(i_t, i) + \varepsilon(bs, i)\,|$

$\quad \varepsilon(fd, i_a) \, \varepsilon(i_a, i) > |\, \varepsilon(fd, i)\,|$

$\quad \bar{\varepsilon}(a^a, i) - \varepsilon(a^a, k) \, \bar{\varepsilon}(k, i) > |\, \varepsilon(a^a, k) \, \bar{\varepsilon}(k, i)\,|$

$\varepsilon(a^a, i_e) \ < 0$

provided $\varepsilon(t, i_t) \, \varepsilon(i_t, i_e) < |\, (t, i_e)\,|$

$\quad \varepsilon(fd, i_a) \, \varepsilon(i_a, i_e) < |\, (fd, i_e)\,|$

$\quad |\, \bar{\varepsilon}(a^a, i_e) - \varepsilon(a^a, b) \, \varepsilon(b, i_e) - \varepsilon(a^a, mob) \, \varepsilon(mob, i_e)\,|$

$\quad\quad > \varepsilon(a^a, b) \, \varepsilon(b, i_e) + \varepsilon(a^a, mob) \, \varepsilon(mob, i_e)$

$\varepsilon(a^a, \ sw) < 0$

Structure and order constraints are similar to those given for $\varepsilon(a^a, i_e)$.

$\varepsilon(a^a, \ ex) < 0$

provided $|\, \varepsilon(fd, ex)\,| > \varepsilon(fd, i_a) \, \varepsilon(i_a, ex)$

$\varepsilon(a^a, P) > 0$

$\varepsilon(a^a, w) > 0$

provided $\varepsilon(a^a, t) \, \varepsilon(t, W) + \varepsilon(a^a, bs) \, \varepsilon(bw, W) > |\, \varepsilon(a^a, k) \, \varepsilon(k, W)\,|$

$\varepsilon(a^a, d) < 0$

provided $|\, \varepsilon(a^a, e) \, \varepsilon(e, d) + \varepsilon(a^a, b) \, \varepsilon(b, d) + \varepsilon(a^a, mob) \, \varepsilon(mob, d)\,|$

$\quad\quad > \varepsilon(a^a, fas) \, \varepsilon(fas, d)$

$\varepsilon(a^a, r^d) < 0$

Similar solutions for r^t, r^f, l^d, l^t and l^f.

Table V. Responses of the credit market rate to changes in determinants

$\varepsilon(i, B^a) < 0$

$\varepsilon(i, i_e) > 0$

$\varepsilon(i, sw) > 0$

$\varepsilon(i, ex) > 0$

$\varepsilon(i, i_f) > 0$

$\varepsilon(i, d) > 0$

$\varepsilon(i, \pi) > 0$

$\varepsilon(i, p) > 0$

$\varepsilon(i, P) < 0$

$\varepsilon(i, W) > 0$

provided ε (s,W) $> \varepsilon(a^a, W)$

$\varepsilon(i, GS) > 0$

$\varepsilon(i, c) > 0$

$\varepsilon(i, r^d) > 0$

Similar solutions for r^t, r^f, l^d, l^t, and l^f.

Table VI. Responses of the adjusted money multiplier to changes in interest rates and other determinants

Total elasticities are indicated by carrying a bar where necessary.

$\varepsilon(m^a, i) > 0$

provided $\bar{\varepsilon}(m^a, i) - \varepsilon(m^a, k) \bar{\varepsilon}(k, i) - \varepsilon(m^a, t) \bar{\varepsilon}(t, i)$
$> | \varepsilon(m^a, k) \bar{\varepsilon}(k, i) + \varepsilon(m^a, t) \bar{\varepsilon}(t, i) |$

$\varepsilon(m^a, i_e) > 0$

provided $\varepsilon(m^a, t) \bar{\varepsilon}(t, i_e) + \varepsilon(m^a, b) \varepsilon(b, i_e) + \varepsilon(m^a, mob) \varepsilon(mob, i_e)$
$> | \varepsilon(m^a, fd^1) \varepsilon(fd^1, i_e) + \varepsilon(m^a, fd^2) \varepsilon(fd^2, i_e) + \varepsilon(m^a, fas) \varepsilon(fas, i_e) |$

$\varepsilon(m^a, sw) > 0$

Structure and order constraint are similar to those given for $\varepsilon(m^a, i_e)$.

$\varepsilon(m^a, ex) < 0$

provided $| \bar{\varepsilon}(m^a, ex) - \varepsilon(m^a, t) \varepsilon(t, ex) | > \varepsilon(m^a, t) \varepsilon(t, ex)$

$\varepsilon(m^a, P) < 0$

$\varepsilon(m^a, W) < 0$

provided $| \varepsilon(m^a, t) \varepsilon(t, W) | > \varepsilon(m^a, k) \varepsilon(k, W)$

$\varepsilon(m^a, d) < 0$

$\varepsilon(m^a, r^d) < 0$

Similar solutions for r^t, r^f, l^d, l^t, and l^f.

Table VII. Responses of the money stock to changes in ultimate determinants

Each of the following elasticities contains a factor q:

$$q = \frac{\varepsilon(m^a, i)}{\varepsilon(a^a, i) - \varepsilon(s, i - \pi)j}, \qquad l > q > 0$$
as $\varepsilon(a^a, i) > \varepsilon(m^a, i)$

$\varepsilon(M, B^a) > 0$

$\varepsilon(M, i_e) > 0$

$\varepsilon(M, sw) > 0$

$\varepsilon(M, ex) > 0$

$\varepsilon(M, i_f) > 0$

$\varepsilon(M, P) < 0$

$\varepsilon(M, W) > 0$

$\varepsilon(M, p) > 0$

$\varepsilon(M, \pi) > 0$

$\varepsilon(M, GS) > 0$

$\varepsilon(M, c) > 0$

$\varepsilon(M, d) < 0$

$\varepsilon(M, r^d) < 0$

Similar solutions for r^t, r^f, l^d, l^t, and l^f.

Note that the negative signs of the last two elasticities implies a $q < 0.88$ as the average value of α is 1.14.

Appendix B

Table I. Money multipliers and their components

Quarterly data

		Period		
		1959–65	1966–72	1958–72
m^e	average	1·63	1·61	1·62
	st. dev.	0·02	0·02	0·03
k	average	0·64	0·53	0·60
	st. dev	0·03	0·04	0·08
$t + fd^1$	average	2·73	3·63	3·13
	st. dev.	0·17	0·21	0·50
r	average	0·09	0·07	0·08
	st. dev.	0·02	0·02	0·02
$r + l$	average	0·09	0·08	0·08
	st. dev.	0·00	0·00	0·00
e	average	0·01	0·01	0·01
	st. dev.	0·00	0·00	0·00
m^a	average	1·66	2·42	2·00
	st. dev.	0·13	0·55	0·55
b	average	0·02	0·04	0·03
	st. dev.	0·01	0·02	0·02
mob	average	0·03	0·01	0·02
	st. dev.	0·01	0·00	0·02
fd	average	0·17	0·30	0·23
	st. dev.	0·02	0·11	0·01
fas	average	0·60	0·66	0·63
	st. dev.	0·16	0·17	0·16

*Table II. Annual rates of change of the money multipliers and their components**

Quarterly data   percent p.a.

		Period		
		1959–65	1966–72	1959–72
$\hat{m}^e$	average	0·56	−0·07	0·24
	st. dev.	1·96	2·12	2·03
$\hat{k}$	average	−3·29	−3·35	−3·32
	st. dev.	3·74	2·94	3·30
$\widehat{t + fd^1}$	average	2·45	3·03	2·74
	st. dev.	3·72	5·51	4·62

		Period 1959–65	1966–72	1959–72
$\hat{r}$	average	−1·00	1·88	0·44
	st. dev.	19·80	20·70	19·94
$\widehat{r+l}$	average	−1·19	−0·12	−0·66
	st. dev.	1·79	3·46	2·76
$\hat{e}$	average	−0·23	−2·56	−1·39
	st. dev.	7·01	15·59	11·93
m^a	average	4·75	5·55	5·15
	st. dev.	5·80	17·12	12·86
$\hat{b}$	average	10·06	6·97	8·52
	st. dev.	43·40	41·12	41·54
$\widehat{mob}$	average	−30·82	0·32	−15·25
	st. dev.	32·09	117·14	85·76
$\widehat{fd}$	average	1·38	12·68	6·94
	st. dev.	13·07	16·03	15·47
$\widehat{fas}$	average	1·38	−3·33	−0·97
	st. dev.	47·89	31·86	40·01

* For corresponding quarters, assuming continuous growth as described by an exponential function.

Table III. Money multiplier elasticities with respect to proximate determinants
Quarterly data

		Period 1959–65	1966–72	1958–72
$\varepsilon(m^e, k)$	average	−0·2451	−0·2125	−0·2302
	st. dev.	0·0070	0·0112	0·0187
$\varepsilon(m^e, t + fd^1)$	average	−0·2660	−0·3452	−0·3004
	st. dev.	0·0149	0·0241	0·0469
$\varepsilon(m^e, r + l)$	average	−0·3185	−0·3869	−0·3479
	st. dev.	0·0122	0·0250	0·0419
$\varepsilon(m^e, e)$	average	−0·0449	−0·0535	−0·0485
	st. dev.	0·0035	0·0071	0·0073
$\varepsilon(m^a, k)$	average	−0·2588	−0·4864	−0·3585
	st. dev.	0·0460	0·1721	0·1708
$\varepsilon(m^a, t + fd^1)$	average	−0·3069	−0·2935	−0·3020
	st. dev.	0·0258	0·0640	0·0472
$\varepsilon(m^a, r + l)$	average	−0·3265	−0·5860	−0·4422
	st. dev.	0·0355	0·1575	0·1738
$\varepsilon(m^a, e)$	average	−0·0461	−0·0804	−0·0613
	st. dev.	0·0064	0·0203	0·0231

E

			Period	
		1959–65	1966–72	1958–72
$\varepsilon(m^a, b)$	average	0·0682	0·3355	0·1911
	st. dev.	0·0374	0·2064	0·1952
$\varepsilon(m^a, mob)$	average	−0·1154	−0·0436	−0·0889
	st. dev.	0·0383	0·0352	0·0606
$\varepsilon(m^a, fd)$	average	0·0701	0·2079	0·1331
	st. dev.	0·0305	0·1566	0·1280
$\varepsilon(m^a, fas)$	average	−0·1048	−0·3082	−0·1976
	st. dev.	0·0285	0·1449	0·1435

Table IV. Base elasticities

Quarterly data

			Period	
		1959–65	1966–72	1958–72
$\varepsilon(B^e, RF)$	average	0·0647	0·2059	0·1294
	st. dev.	0·0295	0·0864	0·0943
$\varepsilon(B^e, MOB)$	average	−0·1157	0·0281	−0·0840
	st. dev.	0·0433	0·0191	0·0698
$\varepsilon(B^e, FL)$	average	0·1704	0·3198	0·2382
	st. dev.	0·0182	0·1257	0·1146
$\varepsilon(B^e, FAS)$	average	−0·1024	−0·1963	−0·1449
	st. dev.	0·0263	0·0565	0·0639
$\varepsilon(B^e, NIR)$	average	0·8415	0·6389	0·7546
	st. dev.	0·0980	0·1171	0·1516
$\varepsilon(B^e, NDC)$	average	0·1408	0·0598	0·1064
	st. dev.	0·0812	0·1546	0·1256
$\varepsilon(B^a, NIR)$	average	0·8561	0·9401	0·8938
	st. dev.	0·0817	0·2346	0·1723
$\varepsilon(B^a, NDC)$	average	0·1431	0·0575	0·1047
	st. dev.	0·0816	0·2326	0·1713

Table V. Money supply and proximate determinants—periods of monetary acceleration versus periods of monetary deceleration

A. *Extended-multiplier approach*

Average annual percentage rates of change*

	Periods of		
	Acceleration[1] 35 quarters	Deceleration[2] 21 quarters	Total period 56 quarters
M	9·55 (2·78)	7·10 (2·99)	8·63 (3·05)
Contribution of			
m^e	0·61 (1·98)	−0·37 (2·05)	0·24 (2·03)
B^e	8·94 (2·43)	7·47 (2·31)	8·39 (2·47)
k	0·93 (0·80)	0·50 (0·75)	0·77 (0·80)
$t + fd^1$	−0·34 (1·29)	−1·51 (1·34)	−0·78 (1·42)
$r + l$	0·11 (1·21)	0·32 (0·66)	0·19 (1·04)
e	−0·08 (0·64)	0·31 (0·67)	0·07 (0·68)
ε	−0·01 (0·07)	0·01 (0·08)	−0·00 (0·07)
RF	0·61 (4·12)	5·76 (6·94)	2·54 (5·86)
MOB	−0·00 (3·31)	1·97 (2·15)	0·73 (3·06)
FLB	4·64 (4·17)	3·77 (5·05)	4·32 (4·49)
$FASB$	−1·76 (3·05)	−3·24 (5·31)	−2·32 (4·06)
NIR	9·44 (12·67)	−2·68 (13·04)	4·89 (14·01)
NDC	−3·98 (11·59)	1·91 (9·86)	−1·77 (11·25)

B. Adjusted-multiplier approach

Average annual percentage rates of change*

	Periods of Acceleration[1] 35 quarters	Deceleration[2] 21 quarters	Total period 56 quarters
M	9·55	7·10	8·63
	(2·78)	(2·99)	(3·05)
Contribution of			
m^a	2·59	9·41	5·20
	(11·23)	(14·04)	(12·86)
B^a	6·95	−2·31	3·43
	(11·86)	(13·68)	(13·23)
k	1·46	0·53	1·11
	(1·23)	(0·70)	(1·15)
$t + fd^1$	−0·33	−1·41	−0·73
	(1·28)	(1·18)	(1·34)
$r +$	−0·07	0·40	0·11
	(1·72)	(0·86)	(1·47)
e	−0·07	0·43	0·12
	(0·84)	(1·03)	(0·94)
b	−1·43	6·77	1·65
	(7·57)	(11·42)	(9·94)
mob	0·15	3·12	1·26
	(5·85)	(2·75)	(5·10)
fd	1·05	1·41	1·20
	(2·75)	(3·16)	(2·87)
fas	1·70	−1·50	0·50
	(5·30)	(5·30)	(5·50)
ε	0·20	−0·36	−0·00
	(2·53)	(2·57)	(2·53)
NIR	14·47	−5·52	6·96
	(22·48)	(10·07)	(23·24)
NDC	−7·51	3·10	−3·53
	(17·46)	(10·81)	(16·06)

* Computed from weighted annual percentage rates of change for corresponding quarters, assuming a continuous growth as described by an exponential function. Standard deviations in parentheses.

(1) 1959/1–1959/3   (2) 1959/4–1960/4
    1961/1–1962/2   1962/3–1963/2
    1963/3–1965/2   1965/3–1967/2
    1967/3–1969/3   1969/4–1970/3
    1970/4–1972/4

Table VI. Money supply and proximate determinants—terminating phases of monetary acceleration versus opening phases of monetary deceleration

A. *Extended-multiplier approach*

Average annual percentage rates of change*

	Terminating[1] Phases of Acceleration 12 quarters	Opening[2] Deceleration 12 quarters	1959–72 56 quarters
M	10·69	8·93	8·63
	(2·51)	(1·92)	(3·05)
Contribution of			
m^e	1·25	0·94	0·24
	(2·32)	(1·55)	(2·03)
B^e	9·44	8·00	8·39
	(1·27)	(2·33)	(2·47)
k	1·15	0·90	0·77
	(1·01)	(0·69)	(0·80)
$t + fd^1$	0·45	−0·73	−0·78
	(0·82)	(0·95)	(1·42)
$r + l$	0·03	0·33	0·19
	(1·22)	(0·62)	(1·04)
e	−0·38	0·41	0·07
	(0·86)	(0·88)	(0·68)
ε	0·01	0·03	−0·00
	(0·08)	(0·09)	(0·07)
RF	2·44	7·05	2·54
	(4·04)	(7·16)	(5·86)
MOB	2·63	2·94	0·73
	(3·15)	(2·15)	(3·06)
FLB	3·63	4·37	4·32
	(3·99)	(5·57)	(4·49)
$FASB$	−1·21	−4·77	−2·32
	(2·73)	(5·07)	(4·06)
NIR	0·86	−6·90	4·89
	(5·85)	(11·63)	(14·01)
NDC	1·10	5·31	−1·77
	(11·46)	(6·78)	(11·25)

B. *Adjusted-multiplier Approach*

Average annual percentage rates of change*

	Terminating[1] Phases of Acceleration 12 quarters	Opening[2] of Deceleration 12 quarters	1959–72 56 quarters
M	10·69 (2·51)	8·93 (1·92)	8·63 (3·05)
Contribution of			
m^a	9·50 (7·86)	12·80 (12·52)	5·20 (12·86)
B^a	1·19 (9·74)	−3·87 (13·79)	3·43 (13·23)
k	1·08 (0·68)	0·95 (0·44)	1·11 (1·15)
$t + fd^1$	0·55 (0·89)	−0·75 (0·99)	−0·73 (1·34)
$r + l$	−0·12 (1·48)	0·39 (0·93)	0·11 (1·47)
e	−0·47 (1·08)	0·60 (1·36)	0·12 (0·94)
b	2·39 (4·48)	8·32 (11·05)	1·65 (9·94)
mob	4·14 (3·69)	4·46 (2·68)	1·26 (5·10)
fd	0·92 (2·18)	1·57 (3·44)	1·20 (2·87)
fas	1·21 (5·25)	−2·98 (4·30)	0·50 (5·50)
ε	−0·03 (1·01)	0·25 (2·34)	−0·00 (2·53)
NIR	1·06 (6·11)	−10·63 (18·86)	6·96 (23·24)
DNC	6·76 (8·39)	6·76 (8·39)	−3·53 (16·06)

* See corresponding footnote of Table V(A)
(1) i.e. last three quarters.   (2) i.e. first three quarters.
   1959/1–1959/3   1959/4–1960/2
   1961/4–1962/2   1962/3–1963/1
   1964/4–1965/2   1965/3–1966/1
   1969/1–1969/3   1969/4–1970/2

Table VII. Money supply and proximate determinants—terminating phases of monetary deceleration versus opening phases of monetary acceleration

A. *Extended-multiplier approach*

Average annual percentage rates of change*

	Terminating[1] Phases of Deceleration 9 quarters	Opening[2] Acceleration 9 quarters	1959–72 56 quarters
M	5·24	7·52	8·63
	(2·83)	(2·45)	(3·05)
Contribution of			
m^e	−1·67	−0·23	0·24
	(2·06)	(1·60)	(2·03)
B^e	6·91	7·75	8·39
	(3·07)	(2·75)	(2·47)
k	−0·00	0·76	0·77
	(0·40)	(0·94)	(0·80)
$t + fd^1$	−2·41	−1·20	−0·78
	(1·14)	(1·08)	(1·42)
$r + l$	0·37	0·07	0·19
	(0·83)	(1·15)	(1·04)
e	0·36	0·14	0·07
	(0·82)	(0·39)	(0·68)
ε	0·02	−0·00	−0·00
	(0·12)	(0·04)	(0·07)
RF	7·37	−1·68	2·54
	(10·00)	(5·16)	(5·86)
MOB	0·97	−3·32	0·73
	(2·09)	(2·42)	(3·06)
FLB	6·28	6·87	4·32
	(6·52)	(5·51)	(4·49)
$FASB$	−3·16	−3·94	−2·32
	(7·38)	(2·60)	(4·06)
NIR	−2·23	18·03	4·89
	(20·36)	(16·28)	(14·01)
NDC	−2·31	−8·21	−1·77
	(13·71)	(13·77)	(11·25)

B. *Adjusted-multiplier approach*

Average annual percentage rates of change*

	Terminating[1] Phases of Deceleration 9 quarters	Opening[2] Acceleration 9 quarters	1959–72 56 quarters
M	5·24	7·52	8·63
	(2·83)	(2·45)	(3·05)
Contribution of			
m^a	13·24	−4·63	5·20
	(20·77)	(14·12)	(12·86)
B^a	−7·99	12·15	3·43
	(19·22)	(14·79)	(13·23)
k	0·01	1·61	1·11
	(0·54)	(1·75)	(1·15)
$t + fd^1$	−2·17	−1·15	−0·73
	(0·96)	(1·02)	(1·34)
$r + l$	0·59	−0·12	0·11
	(1·07)	(1·65)	(1·47)
e	0·53	0·16	0·12
	(1·34)	(0·53)	(0·94)
b	10·23	−4·61	1·65
	(16·56)	(11·47)	(9·94)
mob	1·99	−5·11	1·26
	(2·58)	(6·86)	(5·10)
fd	3·17	3·29	1·20
	(3·94)	(3·64)	(2·87)
fas	−0·07	0·93	0·50
	(7·10)	(5·12)	(5·50)
ε	−1·05	0·59	−0·00
	(3·88)	(4·64)	(2·53)
NIR	−8·14	25·91	6·96
	(29·67)	(30·34)	(23·24)
NDC	0·15	−13·76	−3·53
	(16·02)	(22·99)	(16·06)

* See corresponding footnote of Table VA.
(1) i.e. last three quarters.   (2) i.e. first three quarters.
    1960/2–1960/4   1961/1–1961/3
    1966/4–1967/2   1967/3–1968/1
    1970/1–1970/3   1970/4–1971/2

Table VIII. Money supply and proximate determinants—periods of rising interest rates versus periods of decreasing interest rates

A. Extended-multiplier approach

Average annual percentage rates of change*

	Periods of		Total period
	Rising[2]	Decreasing[3]	
	Interest rates[1]		
	30 quarters	26 quarters	56 quarters
M	8·20	9·13	8·63
	(2·44)	(3·67)	(3·05)
Contribution of			
m^e	−0·11	0·65	0·24
	(1·80)	(2·26)	(2·03)
B^e	8·31	8·48	8·39
	(2·30)	(2·70)	(2·47)
k	0·55	1·02	0·77
	(0·64)	(0·90)	(0·80)
$t + fd^1$	−0·83	−0·73	−0·78
	(1·20)	(1·66)	(1·42)
$r +$	0·09	0·31	0·19
	(0·93)	(1·15)	(1·04)
e	0·07	0·07	0·07
	(0·82)	(0·47)	(0·68)
ε	0·01	−0·02	−0·00
	(0·08)	(0·06)	(0·07)
RF	5·75)	−1·17	2·54
	(5·73)	(3·27)	(5·86)
MOB	2·04	−0·78	0·73
	(2·25)	(3·22)	(3·06)
FLB	4·29	4·34	4·32
	(5·16)	(3·67)	(4·49)
$FASB$	−2·42	−2·20	−2·32
	(4·74)	(3·21)	(4·06)
NIR	−1·49	12·25	4·89
	(11·45)	(13·22)	(14·01)
NDC	0·14	−3·97	−1·77
	(9·85)	(12·51)	(11·25)

B. *Adjusted-multiplier approach*

Average annual percentage rates of change*

	Periods of		Total period
	Rising[2]	Decreasing[3]	
	Interest rates[1]		
	30 quarters	26 quarters	56 quarters
M	8·20	9·13	8·63
	(2·44)	(3·67)	(3·05)
Contribution of			
m^a	11·10	−1·61	5·20
	(11·09)	(10·96)	(12·86)
B^a	−2·90	10·74	3·43
	(11·98)	(10·73)	(13·23)
k	0·68	1·61	1·11
	(0·70)	(1·37)	(1·15)
$t + fd^1$	−0·81	−0·64	−0·73
	(1·17)	(1·53)	(1·34)
$r + l$	0·04	0·18	0·11
	(1·28)	(1·69)	(1·47)
e	0·10	0·14	0·12
	(1·17)	(0·60)	(0·94)
b	6·69	−4·17	1·65
	(9·86)	(6·24)	(9·94)
mob	3·25	−1·02	1·26
	(2·74)	(6·20)	(5·10)
fd	1·60	0·74	1·20
	(3·37)	(2·13)	(2·87)
fas	0·18	0·86	0·50
	(5·21)	(5·89)	(5·50)
ε	−0·63	0·71	−0·00
	(2·68)	(2·19)	(2·53)
NIR	−3·12	18·62	6·96
	(17·18)	(24·13)	(23·24)
NDC	0·22	−7·86	−3·53
	(11·44)	(19·47)	(16·06)

* See corresponding footnote of Table V(A).
(1) As measured by annual rates of change for corresponding quarters.

(2) 1959/4–1960/4	(3) 1959/1–1959/3
1962/2–1963/3	1961/1–1962/1
1964/2–1966/4	1963/4–1964/1
1969/2–1970/4	1967/1–1969/1
1972/4	1971/1–1972/3

Table IX. Money supply and proximate determinants—periods of rising international reserves versus periods of decreasing international reserves

A. *Extended-multiplier approach*

Average annual percentage rates of change*

	Periods of		Total period
	Rising[1]	Decreasing[2]	
	International reserves		
	36 quarters	20 quarters	56 quarters
M	8·34	9·15	8·63
	(3·32)	(2·57)	(3·05)
Contribution of			
m^e	−0·20	1·03	0·24
	(2·14)	(1·63)	(2·03)
B^e	8·54	8·12	8·39
	(2·72)	(1·99)	(2·47)
k	0·72	0·84	0·77
	(0·83)	(0·76)	(0·80)
$t + fd^1$	−0·94	−0·51	−0·78
	(1·59)	(1·02)	(1·42)
$r + l$	0·02	0·49	0·19
	(1·20)	(0·55)	(1·04)
e	0·00	0·19	0·07
	(0·63)	(0·76)	(0·68)
ε	−0·00	−0·01	−0·00
	(0·07)	(0·08)	(0·07)
RF	0·75	5·75	2·54
	(4·15)	(7·12)	(5·86)
MOB	−0·19	2·39	0·73
	(2·99)	(2·51)	(3·06)
FLB	4·62	3·77	4·32
	(4·15)	(5·13)	(4·49)
$FASB$	−1·03	−4·64	−2·32
	(3·47)	(4·10)	(4·06)
NIR	11·39	−6·80	4·89
	(11·60)	(9·81)	(14·01)
NDC	−7·00	7·66	−1·77
	(10·25)	(5·24)	(11·25)

B. *Adjusted-multiplier approach*

Average annual percentage rates of change*

	Periods of Rising[1] International reserves 36 quarters	Periods of Decreasing[2] International reserves 20 quarters	Total period 56 quarters
M	8·34 (3·32)	9·15 (2·57)	8·63 (3·05)
Contribution of			
m^a	2·28 (11·81)	10·46 (12·72)	5·20 (12·86)
B^a	6·07 (12·08)	−1·31 (14·19)	3·43 (13·23)
k	1·25 (1·37)	0·86 (0·55)	1·11 (1·15)
$t + fd^1$	−0·90 (1·45)	−0·43 (1·07)	−0·73 (1·34)
$r + l$	−0·13 (1·71)	0·54 (0·75)	0·11 (1·47)
e	0·01 (0·82)	0·31 (1·12)	0·12 (0·94)
b	−1·41 (7·59)	7·14 (11·43)	1·65 (9·94)
mob	−0·09 (5·55)	3·70 (2·98)	1·26 (5·10)
fd	1·12 (2·68)	1·33 (3·24)	1·20 (2·87)
fas	2·46 (5·41)	−3·04 (3·60)	0·50 (5·50)
ε	0·01 (2·51)	−0·06 (2·65)	−0·00 (2·53)
NIR	16·37 (21·17)	−9·94 (16·39)	6·96 (23·24)
NDC	−10·29 (15·88)	8·63 (6·29)	−3·53 (16·06)

* See corresponding footnote of Table V(A).

(1) 1959/1–1959/2
1960/2–1961/3
1963/4–1965/1
1966/3–1969/3
1970/4–1972/4

(2) 1959/3–1960/1
1961/4–1963/3
1965/2–1966/2
1969/4–1970/3

Footnotes

* The work on this paper has been supported by a grant from the Landeszentralbank Berlin. I am grateful to the Deutsche Bundesbank and the members of its research department for continued statistical support.

1. Brunner and Meltzer (1966) and (1968).
2. Brunner (1973b).
3. Fratianni (1972); Korteweg (1973); Siebke (1973); Willms (1971).
4. Brunner and Meltzer (1971).
5. See the E.C. study *Monetary Policy in the Countries of the European Economic Community—Institutions and Instruments*, chapter on Federal Republic of Germany, pp. 79–133.
6. Besides these traditional private deposit liabilities a special cash deposit requirement for certain types of borrowing abroad by private enterprises was introduced in March 1972. The idea of this measure was to eliminate the interest rate differential *vis-à-vis* forcing countries by forcing the enterprises to hold a fixed fraction of the funds borrowed as interest-free deposits at the Bundesbank. We treat these special deposits as a source of the monetary base.
7. In passing it may also be noted that the endogeneity-exogeneity issue is of no relevance as regards the quality of the extended monetary base in serving as the optimal monetary policy indicator.
8. On this see, for example, Brunner (1973a), p. 14.
9. In the conference version of this paper the excess reserve ratio was described differently, namely, as also depending positively on the Eurodollar market rate, taking into account that German banks are net borrowers in foreign short-term markets. Läufer insisted that this relationship should be negative instead of positive.

   In fact, both of us were wrong. The banks' borrowing from abroad takes place through the supply of deposit liabilities to foreigners of which within my framework is taken care of by a price-setting function (A. 38), defining the German interest rate on foreign deposits. Thus the Eurodollar rate has no place in (A. 28).
10. See also the discussion of *FAL* as a source component.
11. While Fratianni, Siebke and Willms do not state the sign of the partial derivatives or elasticities in question (see their work cited in footnote [3]), Brunner expects the interest elasticity of the currency ratio to be about zero in the case of the U.S. and to be negative in the case of some European countries; see Brunner (1973a), p. 8.
12. Note that for simplifying reasons we do not differentiate the demand for bank securities by foreigners. As a rough approximation equation (4.44) also takes care of this.
13. During the monetary deceleration of 1973 even a negative rate of growth of the money stock was observed, namely, 0·6 in the third quarter of 1973.
14. Its cœfficient of variation was not more than 0·02 for the total period to be compared to 0·28 for m^a.
15. This results from the fact that banks are not forced to report on domestic and foreign deposits, subject to reserve requirements, separately during periods where the Bundesbank requires identical reserve ratios for these deposits.

    In future work we will partition the ratio into two ratios using an estimation procedure already developed although it seems that the combined ratio $t + fd^1$ does not behave very differently from the ratio t.
16. The average required reserve ratio on demand deposits varied between 0·08 and 0·18, on time deposits between 0·06 and 0·14, and on savings deposits between 0·04 and 0·08.
17. It may be noted that one of the periods of monetary acceleration and two of the periods of deceleration were too short to consist of more than the defined opening and terminating phase.

18. See Brunner, K., 'Monetary Management and the Central Banks', mimeographed paper, p. 42–7.

19. Sub-periods of heavily rising or decreasing international reserves have been defined as periods exhibiting positive or negative rates of change in international reserves exceeding DM 5 billion for corresponding quarters. None of these sub-periods had a duration of more than one year.

20. See Willms (1971), p. 24.

21. For a similar line of reasoning see for instance Alexander (1973).

22. But note that this statement does not require that the Bank consciously operated on the base or the money supply.

23. See Willms (1971), p. 23.

24. This does not rule out that domestic policy during certain periods was offset to some degree by international capital flows. Kouri and Porter report an offset coefficient of 0·77 for Germany (Kouri & Porter (1974)). In future work it will have to be checked whether their estimates are reliable. One of the problems with their estimates is that they fully added the 'errors and omissions' of the balance-of-payments statistics to private capital flows.

25. Allowing for a variety of hypotheses on autocorrelation does not lead to significant changes of the parameters in the money supply equations (4.4) to (4.6) as can be seen from the following preliminary estimates:

(4.4a)

$$\ln M = 0·72^* + 0·98^* \ln B^e$$

with $u_t = 0·34^* u_{t-1} + 0·34^* u_{t-2} + \varepsilon_t$ $\bar{R}^2 = 1·00$

(4.5a)

$$\ln M = 0·74^* + 0·98^* \ln B^e + 0·00 \ln d - 0·00 \ln i^e$$

with $u_t = 0·35^* u_{t-1} + 0·33^* u_{t-2} + \varepsilon_t$ $\bar{R}^2 = 1·00$

(4.6a)

$$\ln M = 0·65^* + 0·98^* \ln B^e - 0·02 \ln d + 0·08 \ln i$$

with $u_t = 0·50 u_{t-1} + \varepsilon_t$ $\bar{R}_2 = 1·00$

I am very grateful to Patrick McMahon for having supplied these estimates.

26. For more successful estimates of the interest rate function, see Neumann (1977).

27. See Willms (1971), p. 20.

A Theoretical and Empirical Analysis of the German Money Supply Process— a Comment

ANTHONY. S. COURAKIS

The question I propose to discuss is: in what sense does Professor Neumann's paper enhance our knowledge of the monetary process in the Federal Republic of Germany?

As stated in the introduction the aims of the paper are threefold.

(*a*) To gain insight into the behaviour of the various determinants of the money supply.

(*b*) To examine whether and to what degree the Bundesbank is in control of the money stock.

(*c*) To report some preliminary findings relating to the reduced form money supply equations traced in this paper.

Common to all three is of course the question of definition chosen for the *money supply* and hence the issue of *desirability* of controlling alternative candidates. Yet as the author limits himself to the, in my view by no means readily acceptable, assertion that '. . . in the German case it can be demonstrated that it is (the) collection of assets (classifying as media of exchange) which explains best the movement of the general price level and economic activity' (p. 75), I would not dwell on this issue.

As regards (*a*) above the reader is confronted with a remarkable wealth of information as the author proceeds in highly consistent fashion to analyse the behaviour of the various determinants of the money stock and to record exhaustively their behaviour both for the period as a whole and for various subperiods. Much of the study, however, deals with the other two issues. The results, it is argued, 'point to the conclusion that the extended money multiplier approach is superior to any other analytical approach in serving as a foundation and *device* for money supply management', p. 105.

In so far as this statement is to be interpreted as denoting the fact that the results recorded in this paper suggest the existence of a close association between the extended monetary base and the money stock, defined as above, there can of course be no dispute. Yet for this to serve as a focus for policy prescription it would seem desirable to establish what the author has in my view failed to establish, namely that the regularities recorded describe relationships that derive from conditions similar to those that would prevail if the monetary authority were to follow policies designed to ensure control of the extended monetary base, or that the slope and position of such relationships is independent of the precise pursuits of the monetary authority [1].

Granted the controversy in the U.K. over whether or not the reserve base and consequently the money supply is, given the authorities' policy vis-à-vis interest rates, an exogenous variable, someone accustomed to thinking within the framework in which British monetary policy operates is, inevitably, distinctly aware of the significance that the authorities' conception of policy carries in interpreting past experience. Yet as regards this type of issue little is to be found in Professor Neumann's study. This is not to suggest that the author is oblivious of the problem; for as he puts it: 'Our knowledge of actual impulse behaviour of the Bundesbank, reflected by the movement of the monetary base, is not sufficient (to resolve the issue of whether the Bundesbank actually controlled the money supply or the monetary base in the past); in addition, we need to know precisely [2] what the intended behaviour was' (p. 102). Rather, it is the case that he is willing to proceed with his investigation on the assumption that intentions were such as to justify an analysis, presented on pp. 102–3, that secures the conclusion that the results point to 'a relatively high degree of controllability', p. 103.

Alas, in applied economics one rarely knows anything precisely. Yet as— from his own writings [3]—Professor Neumann is well aware, some evidence is available to the Bundesbank's conception of relevant policy variables and of the process through which changes in such variables affect the economy. Indeed, it is quite clear that for much of the period to which Professor Neumann's study relates, Bundesbank policy has aimed at influencing the asset-holding preferences of market participants in general and of banks in particular, rather than at dictating the volume of high-powered money. Furthermore, the precise framework of action adopted does suggest that the possibility of very high elasticity of substitution between high-powered money and other assets comprised in free liquid reserves cannot be disregarded, while Professor Neumann's finding of almost total absence of excess reserves from bank portfolios does point (with vengeance) in the same direction [4].

Yet high elasticity of substitution between cash and other assets traditionally defined to comprise bank liquidity suggests that at the level of aggregation adopted by Neumann there would seem to be little grounds for distinguishing between cash and other assets readily convertible into cash. The relevant monetary base may then be viewed to comprise not only high-powered money but also bank holdings of assets readily convertible into cash [5]. Past experience then provides valuable information as to how changes in this 'super extended monetary base' affect the behaviour of the money supply while the regularities observed between changes in the extended monetary base and the money stock are no more than a manifestation of the endogenous nature of B^e during this period. To put it differently, a recommendation to control the stock of high-powered money must derive from evidence that during the period to which Professor Neumann's results relate there has been a stable relationship between the money stock and the 'super extended monetary base'; for in the extreme case of perfect substitution between cash and bank holdings of liquid assets OL the holdings of such assets constitute the excess cash reserves of the banking system and will manifest themselves as such if policy were to aim at controlling B^e by reducing the degree of substitution between B^e and OL.

On a different plane, Professor Neumann's study does reveal that the extended monetary base provides a very clear indicator of the combined effect of policies adopted by the authorities, as the behaviour of this aggregate summarizes the responses of all market participants to the various autonomous and policy induced changes to which the German economy has been subject. In so doing it fills a gap that no other single indicator proposed so far has bridged and as such its place in the list of contributions to our knowledge of the German monetary process is well secured.

Footnotes

1. Experience in the U.K. since the 1971 reversal of policy to, allegedly, Friedmanian pursuits provides ample testimony of the fragility of observed 'fundamental regularities' derived from (and in the light of experience, specific to) a particular policy context and yet employed as the basis for policy prescription in another.
2. Emphasis added.
3. Neumann (1972).
4. So also does his observation that 'It is productive for banks to hold excess reserves although this productivity has always been relatively low for German banks because they have in general been able to raise sufficient funds when needed by selling paper through the discount window or in the open market' (p. 83).
5. See also Courakis (1973) and, somewhat differently, Griffiths (1973).

5

The Demand for and Supply of Money in the Federal Republic of Germany: 1965-1974*

STEPHEN F. FROWEN AND PHILIP ARESTIS

Introduction

In recent years a number of empirical studies have estimated demand-for- as well as supply-of-money functions, the latest tendency being to secure integration, treating the money stock as endogenous. This paper attempts to cover both approaches [1].

Among the earlier studies of the demand for money in the Federal Republic of Germany is the paper by König (1968) for the period 1957–66 dealing with the Latané-type of demand-for-money function and the short-run and long-run behaviour of money demand; it also discusses a general distributed lag function for money demand. A subsequent study carried out by Woll (1969) covering the period 1949–66 showed little evidence for the interest hypothesis, whereas a very good fit for measured and permanent income could be observed for different definitions of the money variable. A further study on the demand-for-money function for the years 1950–60 by Roskamp and Laumas (1970) strongly suggests a stable aggregate demand-for-money function, regardless of which definition of money is used; in the latter study, income, wealth and the rate of interest were found to be significant determinants of the demand for money. More recently Hamburger (1974) also found the West German demand for money to be a relatively stable function of income and interest rates, while similar results were obtained by Gebauer (1974), who reports some estimates of the supply-of-money function also, and comes to the conclusion that some endogenous variables, notably some interest rate, should be included in this latter function [2].

We begin by presenting a model of the demand for money which is derived from the distributed lag model by Feige (1967) and by Laidler and Parkin (1970).

The Demand for Money Models

Our demand function for money can be set out in the form of the following four models:

Model 1

$$m_t^* = a_{10} + a_{11}y_t^e + a_{12}r_t \tag{5.1}$$
$$y_t^e = y_{t-1}^e + b(y_t - y_{t-1}^e) \tag{5.2}$$
$$m_t = m_{t-1} + c(m_t^* - m_{t-1}) + u_{1t} \tag{5.3}$$

where

m_t^* = desired per capita real money balances
m_t = actual per capita real money balances
y_t^e = expected (permanent) per capita real income
y_t = per capita real GNP
u_{1t} = error term
r_t = some interest rate

From these equations it follows that:

$$m_t = d_{10} + d_{11}y_t + d_{12}r_t + d_{13}r_{t-1} + d_{14}m_{t-1} + d_{15}m_{t-2} + v_{1t} \tag{5.4} [3]$$

where

$$d_{10} = a_{10}cb \tag{M1.i}$$
$$d_{11} = a_{11}cb \tag{M1.ii}$$
$$d_{12} = a_{12}c \tag{M1.iii}$$
$$d_{13} = - a_{12}c(1 - b) \tag{M1.iv}$$
$$d_{14} = 2 - c - b \tag{M1.v}$$
$$d_{15} = -(1 - c)(1 - b) \tag{M1.vi}$$
$$v_{1t} = u_{1t} - (1 - b)u_{1t-1} \tag{M1.vii}$$

The problem arising in connection with this model is one of identification because equation (5.4) contains six coefficients, while the model from which it is derived has only five parameters.

Model 1 contains several important alternative hypotheses about the nature of the demand-for-money function, depending upon the values of b and c. However, there are real advantages in estimating simpler forms of the model in which b and/or c are assumed equal to unity (see Laidler and Parkin (1970)). We may, therefore, follow the procedure of these authors and estimate the three simplified versions of Model 1, with one important difference: where b is assumed to be equal to 1, and measured rather than permanent income is therefore the relevant variable, Laidler and Parkin imply that the demand for money will adjust almost immediately to an increase in aggregate money income due to a rise in population or in the price level. Deflating lagged money by current prices, however, as done here, lowers the impact response of money demanded with respect to the price level substantially. Nevertheless, it may be appropriate to allow for some intermediate speed of adjustment to price changes and for the possibility that the effect of a change in real income may be different from the effect of a change in prices. Therefore, where permanent income plays no role, the price level is included as a separate explanatory variable. We thus have the following 'simplified' versions of Model 1:

Model 2

$$c = 1 \tag{5.5}$$
$$m_t^* = a_{20} + a_{21} y_t^e + a_{22} r_t \tag{5.5}$$
$$y_t^e = y_{t-1}^e + b_2(y_t - y_{t-1}^e) \tag{5.6}$$
$$m_t = m_t^* + u_{2t} \tag{5.7}$$

From these equations it follows that:

$$m_t = d_{20} + d_{21} y_t + d_{22} r_t + d_{23} r_{t-1} + d_{24} m_{t-1} + v_{2t} \tag{5.8}$$

where

$$d_{20} = a_{20} b \tag{M2.i}$$
$$d_{21} = a_{21} b \tag{M2.ii}$$
$$d_{22} = a_{22} \tag{M2.iii}$$
$$d_{23} = -a_{22}(1 - b) \tag{M2.iv}$$
$$d_{24} = (1 - b) \tag{M2.v}$$
$$v_{2t} = u_{2t} - (1 - b)u_{2t-1} \tag{M2.vi}$$

In this case we have the conventional permanent income hypothesis of the demand for money.

Model 3

$$b = 1$$
$$m_t^* = a_{30} + a_{31} y_t + a_{32} r_t + a_{33} p_t \quad \text{since } y_t^e = y_t \tag{5.9}$$
$$m_t = m_{t-1} + c(m_t^* - m_{t-1}) + u_{3t} \tag{5.10}$$

where p_t is the income deflator (nominal divided by real GNP).

From these equations it follows that:

$$m_t = d_{30} + d_{31} y_t + d_{32} r_t + d_{33} p_t + d_{34} m_{t-1} + v_{3t} \tag{5.11}$$

where

$$d_{30} = a_{30}c \qquad \text{(M3.i)}$$
$$d_{31} = a_{31}c \qquad \text{(M3.ii)}$$
$$d_{32} = a_{32}c \qquad \text{(M3.iii)}$$
$$d_{33} = a_{33}c \qquad \text{(M3.iv)}$$
$$d_{34} = (1 - c) \qquad \text{(M3.v)}$$
$$v_{3t} = u_{3t} \qquad \text{(M3.vi)}$$

In this case the demand for money depends upon measured rather than permanent income and actual cash balances approach equilibrium with a lag.

Model 4

$$b = 1,\ c = 1$$
$$m_t^* = a_{40} + a_{41}y_t + a_{42}r_t + a_{43}p_t \quad \text{since } y_t^e = y_t \qquad (5.12)$$
$$m_t = m_t^* + u_{4t} \qquad (5.13)$$

From these equations it follows that:

$$m_t = d_{40} + d_{41}y_t + d_{42}r_t + d_{43}p_t + v_{4t} \qquad (5.14)$$

where

$$d_{40} = a_{40} \qquad \text{(M4.i)}$$
$$d_{41} = a_{41} \qquad \text{(M4.ii)}$$
$$d_{42} = a_{42} \qquad \text{(M4.iii)}$$
$$d_{43} = a_{43} \qquad \text{(M4.iv)}$$
$$v_{4t} = u_{4t} \qquad \text{(M4.v)}$$

This is a straightforward measured income formulation of the demand for money.

It is apparent that our general model incorporates several important alternative hypotheses about the nature of the demand for money, and that a great deal can be learned from estimating equation (5.4) subject to the constraints (M1.i–M1.vii) upon the values of its coefficients. Estimation of equation (5.4) enables one to test simultaneously these alternative hypotheses about the demand for money. For example, if lagged adjustment to equilibrium is an important consideration, then estimation of equation (5.4) should reveal that the parameter c is less than unity; similarly if adjustment was more or less instantaneous, the estimate of c should not differ significantly from unity. The value of the parameter b should yield information about the importance of the permanent income hypothesis for explaining the demand for money in the Federal Republic of Germany. However, reliance on equation (5.4) only would not be advisable for the simpler cases derived, i.e. Models 2–4.

These models can provide important insights in their own right. Estimation of equations (5.8) and (5.11), for example, provides information on the importance of distinguishing between the operation of a lag in the formation of income expectations on the one hand, and a slow adjustment on the other. Similarly, if it turned out that the simple equation (5.14) was the one to be preferred on statistical grounds, the question of loss of information comprised in ignoring the existence of lags is still of interest. In this study we concentrate on testing the empirical relevance of the simpler special case formulations, i.e. equations (5.8), (5.11) and (5.14), for the Federal Republic of Germany, while ignoring the special problems involved in dealing with functions of the complexity of equation (5.9) [4].

The above Models 2–4 were estimated using the technique of OLS (ordinary least squares) and with seasonally adjusted quarterly data for the Federal Republic of Germany covering the period 1965(I) to 1974(IV). The following two definitions of the money stock were considered:

M_1 = currency and sight deposits of domestic non-banks (quarterly average of monthly observations), seasonally adjusted, DM millions

M_2 = M_1 plus time deposits with maturities of less than four years (quarterly average of monthly observations), seasonally adjusted, DM millions.

Each of the above was tested with r_t equal to:

r_1 = day-to-day money market rate in Frankfurt;

r_2 = money market rate on one month loans in Frankfurt;

r_3 = money market rate on three months loans in Frankfurt;

r_4 = average of the money market rate on three months loans in Frankfurt and the net rate of three months loans in the Eurodollar market (i.e. the rate on three months Eurodollar loans less the three months forward premium between the U.S. $ and the DM);

r_5 = yield on fully-taxed fixed interest securities.

The functions for the dependent variables M_1 and M_2 were estimated in the case of each of the five interest rates for the period mentioned above, taking the data in

(a) absolute terms
(b) logarithms
(c) first differences

Some Empirical Results

The tests carried out were of the simpler forms of the model, embodied in Models 2–4 [5] (i.e. equations (5.8), (5.11), and (5.14)). The results of these tests are as follows:

Model 2 [6]

Model 2 is more sophisticated than Model 4 in that permanent income is introduced though no adjustment lags in the dependent variable are yet assumed. The price level which does not appear significant in Model 4 is not included in this model.

All regressions were highly significant at the 1% level, as revealed by the size of the F statistics, except when the M_2-definition of money is used and the data are in first differences. The percentage of variations explained was in general very high, R^2 being greater than 0·975 for all regressions except, of course, when first differences are used; R^2 then ranges from 0·288 to 0·760. An examination of the t statistics associated with the various coefficients reveals that the lagged dependent variables were highly significant in all cases [7]. Income was significant in explaining variations in all the dependent variables except M_2 (income was less significant where r_5 was taken as the rate of interest, but was still significant at the 5% level).

The rate of interest was highly significant in explaining variations in M_1, regardless of the rate of interest used. The same does not apply to M_2; however, the double-log transformation yields more significant results than the absolute data version of the model.

The lagged rate of interest was not generally significant at the 5% level. The only exception being M_2 in the logarithmic version of the model where r_5 is almost significant at the 5% level.

Judging, now, the *overall* performance of the equations tested for Model 2, we may summarize the two 'best' equations [8] (both are in logarithms [9]) as:

$$m_{1t} = -0·06642 + 0·36764y_t - 0·03371r_{4t}$$
$$(6·36606) \quad (5·51718)$$
$$- 0·01371r_{4t-1} + 0·47499m_{t-1} \tag{i}$$
$$(1·62827) \quad (5·54377)$$
$$R^2 = 0·99227$$

$$m_{2t} = 0·00036 + 0·02943y_t - 0·02471r_{1t}$$
$$(0·32570) \quad (3·09262)$$
$$+ 0·00815r_{1t-1} + 1·03006m_{t-1} \tag{ii}$$
$$(0·99028) \quad (16·60584)$$
$$R^2 = 0·99533$$

The best of the above two equations is obviously the one that utilizes the M_1-definition of money, although one must bear in mind that the lagged interest rate does not have the right sign. One should therefore reserve judgment on the proposition that the permanent income formulation is the proper explanation of the demand-for-money function.

Models 3 and 4

These are, of course, the same models with the important difference that Model 3 provides for the possibility that actual balances approach equilibrium with a lag.

We discuss the simpler model first, i.e. Model 4. In this model measured income is used, and no lag adjustment hypothesis is made. However, the percentage of variation explained by the regression R^2 is in general surprisingly large. It is, in fact, over 0·94 for all regressions, except when the data are transformed into first differences in which case the R^2 ranges between 0·198 and 0·527. Again, the size of the F statistics showed that the regressions for all dependent variables had F statistics which were highly significant at the 1% level, revealing a significant explanatory power, whichever interest rate was used.

The price level appears to be a significant determinant of both M_1 and M_2; in fact, it is insignificant only when M_1 is combined with the average of the three months money market and the Eurodollar rates, and when first differences are used. The yield on fully-taxed fixed-interest securities possibly has some significance in explaining variations in M_2. With this exception, all interest rates only show a reasonable amount of significance in explaining M_1. Even in these cases, the interest elasticity is very small compared with that of income, which is always a significant determinant of variations in both M_1 and M_2 regardless of the rate of interest used.

The 'best' *overall* estimates for Model 4 are summarized below (both equations in logarithms).

$$m_{1t} = -0.51146 + 0.59440y_t - 0.05959r_{4t} + 0.08338p_t \quad \text{(iii)}$$
$$\phantom{m_{1t} = -0.51146 + } (9.25280) \quad (9.39905) \quad (1.50969)$$
$$R^2 = 0.97032$$
$$m_{2t} = -2.75507 + 0.87319y_t - 0.31812r_{5t} + 0.71022p_t \quad \text{(iv)}$$
$$\phantom{m_{2t} = -2.75507 + } (5.50180) \quad (3.63898) \quad (4.19826)$$
$$R^2 = 0.96344$$

Turning now to Model 3 and taking the results as a whole, the striking fact is that in all equations, no matter what definitions of the money stock and the rate of interest are used, the lagged money stock variable was always significant. The individual results tend to follow the pattern of the results of

Model 4, but the coefficients in Model 3 are 'worse' than in Model 4. The price and income variables are mostly insignificant when M_2 is used and the model is in absolute values or in logarithms. The 'best' estimates are summarized below (both are in logarithms).

$$m_{1t} = -0.09965 + 0.29412y_t - 0.04158r_{4t}$$
$$(6.02458) \quad (10.39500)$$
$$+ 0.01167p_t + 0.56781m_{t-1} \qquad \text{(v)}$$
$$(0.37743) \quad (8.73823)$$
$$R^2 = 0.99163$$
$$m_{2t} = -0.63097 - 0.04856y_t - 0.09525r_{5t}$$
$$(0.50384) \quad (2.42923)$$
$$+ 0.18506p_t + 0.96411m_{t-1} \qquad \text{(vi)}$$
$$(2.33014) \quad (12.74435)$$
$$R^2 = 0.99430$$

We note that the combination of the M_1-definition with the r_{4t} rate of interest performs quite satisfactorily in both Models 3 and 4, as well as in Model 2. Indeed, we may claim that M_1 is probably more important in a statistical sense than M_2.

In comparing the results for all three models we note that in terms of the t statistic the only equation that performs 'properly' is the simplest model, i.e. Model 4. The inclusion of the lagged money stock variable, although significant itself, makes some of the variables insignificant—and in the case of the income variable it also changes the sign; furthermore, it implies a rather slow adjustment. However, it is obvious that if we take into consideration other statistical criteria too (beyond the t statistic) all three models provide satisfactory results—at any rate more satisfactory results than those obtained by Laidler and Parkin (1970) in the case of the U.K. economy. The appropriate conclusion is probably that irrespective of definition of the money stock there is a strong negative relationship between some interest rate and the money stock, although the M_1-definition appears to perform slightly better. The lagged interest rate variable in Model 2, on the other hand, adds nothing at all; it only takes the right sign when M_1 is employed, but that is all one can say. In the same model the lagged money stock variable, as in the case of Model 3, implies a slow adjustment, too [10]. One may therefore conclude that lag effects are important in the demand-for-money function, but perhaps not important enough not to justify a simple function of the type of Model 4.

Another important result is the apparent superiority of the r_{4t} definition of the rate of interest in the demand-for-money function—i.e. the average of the money market rate on three months loans in Frankfurt and the net rate of three months loans in the Eurodollar market [11]. Not only is this a short-term rate, it is also supposed to reflect the going rate charged on bank credit (see Gebauer (1974)). The Eurodollar rate can be thought of as a measure of the degree of substitution between domestic and foreign financial assets. This obviously can have implications for an 'open economy' like West Germany, which, during the estimation period, has probably been the economy with the highest degree of liberalization of its international capital movements despite temporary devices aimed at influencing the actual flow of capital. It is scarcely surprising that r_{4t} performs well with the M_1-definition of the money supply only. For if we were to use M_{2t}, instead of M_{1t}, changes in r_{4t} may not, in fact, cause any changes in the demand for money, but may simply lead to changes in the composition of the portfolios of individual holders. For example, an increase in the Eurodollar rate may result in a shift from domestic holdings of time deposits to Eurodollar time deposits of the same maturity, thus changing the composition of individual portfolios only, with the demand for money being unchanged. This argument seems to be especially valid when time deposits (fully covered) are closer substitutes for each other than time and demand deposits.

In summary we can claim that our results so far throw considerable light on three issues of crucial importance in assessing the role of money in the economy. In particular:

(a) *The predictability of the demand-for-money function.* It is obvious from our analysis, and in particular the R^2 values, that this function is predictable enough for the period considered in this study.

(b) *The role of interest rates in the function.* In all six equations we presented above, the interest rate variable plays an important role in determining the demand for money.

(c) *The relative importance of long-term and short-term interest rates.* The superiority of the r_{4t} rate reveals that the short-term rate is relatively more important than the long-term one. Moreover, among short-term interest rates, the Eurodollar rate appears to exert considerable influence.

The Supply of Money and the Simultaneity Problem

We have so far confined ourselves to regressions of the money stock on such variables as the interest rate and income, using various definitions for both the money stock and interest rate variables. However, it is widely accepted that income and the rate of interest are influenced by the money stock, so that the above results are subject to simultaneous equation bias. In order to remove this bias we now postulate a supply-of-money function, treating the money stock as an endogenous variable and taking as exogenous the magnitudes over which the Bundesbank has more direct control [12]. We then integrate our model of the monetary sector with a macro-economic relationship focusing on the 'real' sector; finally, we use appropriate econometric techniques for the estimation of the whole model. Our approach, therefore, is very similar to that of Teigen (1964) and Gibson (1972).

Accordingly, let the money supply function be described by:

$$M_t = m_0 + m_1 r_t + m_2 r_{dt} + m_3 B_t$$

where

M_t = nominal money stock
B_t = Central Bank money stock, i.e. currency in circulation and minimum reserves on domestic liabilities
r_t = some interest rate
r_{dt} = discount rate of the Bundesbank

B_t and r_{dt} are exogenous variables determined by the Deutsche Bundesbank, whereas r_t is treated as an endogenous variable determined by forces of the supply and demand for money. Assume that the following responses are pertinent:

$$\frac{\partial M_t}{\partial r_t} > 0, \quad \frac{\partial M_{2t}}{\partial r_{dt}} < 0, \quad \text{and} \quad \frac{\partial M_t}{\partial B_t} > 0$$

We hypothesize M_t to be positively related to r_t since, *ceteris paribus*, one should expect the banks to expand their earning assets when market interest rates rise, thus increasing the money supply; the same should also happen when the base money increases. However, one should expect the banks to react in the opposite direction when the discount rate goes up [13].

The income determination equation representing the real sector is assumed to be a function of the money stock, autonomous expenditure and lagged income. We thus have

$$Y_t = \alpha_0 + \alpha_1 M_t + \alpha_2 E_t + \alpha_3 Y_{t-1}$$

where E_t is the sum of Government expenditure, investment and exports. This equation can be considered as a reduced-form equation of a model of the real sector such as that described in Teigen (1964). It can, of course, be argued that the treatment of investment as an exogenous element might cause some bias. But we believe that this is not the case in a short-run quarterly model such as ours. In our view changes in monetary conditions affect income in two ways. Firstly, through consumption, and secondly, through investment via changes in the rate of interest. The impact through consumption is quicker than the impact via investment. Changes in the short-term rate which the model accounts for must work through the whole spectrum of interest rates before the impact on investment is felt, and consequently there must be a lag here before investment decisions are influenced which will affect the level of income. For all these reasons, we make Y_t a function of M_{2t} and treat investment as part of E_t.

We now turn our attention to the definitions of the variables B_t, r_t and M_t and argue that B_t should include free liquid reserves, an item which in the past has been of some importance as an instrument of Central Banking in the case of the Federal Republic of Germany. The variable B_t as defined above may be thought of as being determined by the same variables as the money supply, and consequently a strong relationship between the two is inevitable. A more suitable definition for B_t may therefore be one that includes free liquid reserves, and the new definition of this variable we denote as B_t^* [14]. In addition, we also use free liquid reserves as a variable on its own, to be denoted as $(FLR)_t$. As far as the M_t and r_t variables are concerned, we use the M_1-definition and a short-term interest rate. The reason is simple enough: our analysis of the demand-for-money suggests that these definitions perform better than others.

The above two equations were combined with a demand-for-money function, and the system was estimated using two-stage least squares techniques, in order to account for joint determination of the quantity of money demanded and supplied. We note, at this stage, that some of the variables used in this model differ from the ones used earlier when presenting our results for the demand for money. In particular Y_t is current income and E_t current autonomous expenditure; furthermore, the money stock is expressed in nominal terms, since in this case we are interested in explaining the stock of nominal balances provided to the public.

The 'best' estimates are as follows [15]:

$$Y_t = -0.35 + 0.36M_{1t} + 0.28E_t + 0.62Y_{t-1} \quad \text{SEE} = 1.95 \quad (5.15)$$
$$(0.12) \quad (3.02) \qquad (2.75) \qquad (5.75)$$

One Period Ahead Forecast:

    Actual: 256.9000

    Forecast: 260.2186

    Forecast Error: −3.3186

$\chi^2 (1) = 3.00265$ [16]

$$M_{1t}^D = 3.98 + 0.18Y_t - 0.64r_{3t} + 0.72M_{1t-1} \quad \text{SEE} = 0.91 \quad (5.16)$$
$$(3.32) \quad (5.55) \qquad (7.88) \qquad (11.51)$$

One Period Ahead Forecast:

    Actual: 146.7000

    Forecast: 145.4438

    Forecast Error: 1.2562

$\chi^2 (1) = 1.93637$

$$M_{1t}^s = 26.88 + 8.05r_{3t} + 1.24B_t^* - 4.56r_{dt} \quad \text{SEE} = 10.57 \quad (5.17)$$
$$(2.18) \quad (5.05) \qquad (8.62) \qquad (2.23)$$

One Period Ahead Forecast:

  Actual: 146·7000
  Forecast: 122·3652
  Forecast Error: 24·3348
  χ^2 (1) = 5·99001

When $(FLR)_t$ is used, the first equations are not affected, of course, but the M_t^s-function turns out to be

$$M_{1t}^s = 49·65 + 12·32r_{3t} + 0·58(FLR)_t - 7·52r_{dt}$$
$$\quad\quad (2·25) \quad (3·09) \quad\quad (1·10) \quad\quad\quad (1·90)$$

One Period Ahead Forecast:

  Actual: 146·7000
  Forecast: 103·7070
  Forecast Error: 42·9930
  χ^2 (1) = 5·18549

We note that the χ^2 (1) is insignificant in equations (5.15) and (5.16) at the conventional 5% level; however, this statistic is insignificant at the 1% level only in the third equation (for both variants). We also note that allowance has been made for first-order autocorrelation; in one of the three equations the t statistic of p [17] was significant which led us to correct for this weakness by using the transformation suggested by Durbin (1960); all these appear to prove that autocorrelation was not really a problem in this case. We also note the significant coefficients of B_t^* and r_{3t} which imply that the employment of B_t^*, r_{3t} and M_{1t} may be justified on empirical as well as theoretical grounds. However, the results derived by using $(FLR)_t$ as one of the independent variables in the M_t^s-function are insignificant. This may well be due to the fact that, although the Bundesbank succeeded at times in controlling bank lending via changes in free liquid reserves, variations in the stock of money itself often tended to be affected more by international capital movements during periods of fixed exchange rates.

These results are quite acceptable. To begin with we stress that in all equations the post sample parameter stability test clearly shows that the specification of these equations is adequate for prediction. The income equation performs as well as the demand for money which actually shows some improvement when the two-stage least-squares technique is used; in particular, the rate of interest coefficient is improved. The money-supply function, however, provides the most satisfactory and encouraging estimates. The discount rate is significant and of correct sign, a finding in accord with the argument that the Bundesbank can have a strong influence on the money stock when pursuing a conscious discount rate policy. The monetary authorities in Germany can also exert a strong influence on the money stock via changes in the base money which they are assumed to control. The most important result, however, is the strong relationship between r_{3t} and M_{1t}^s; this result highlights the importance of the commercial banking sector in determining the money stock and, if correct, this result is obviously significant for the monetary authorities. The only variable in the supply function they do not control is r_{3t}, and they also have to take into consideration changes in the quantity demanded when operating on the money stock.

Conclusion

The overall conclusion of this study is that a simple demand-for-money function of the type discussed above is justified on empirical grounds. We have also shown that the demand for money and the supply of money can well be estimated simultaneously in the West German case. The estimates we have provided avoid the biases of ordinary least squares and they also overcome some of the problems arising when the money supply is treated as an exogenous variable. Furthermore, the hypothesis that the money supply should be treated endogenously and not exogenously receives strong support from these estimates; what is more, the quantity of money supplied is responsive to some of the same variables which determine the quantity demanded.

Finally, the money-supply function is shown to be well explained by the short-term interest rate, along with other variables; it is this short-term rate which links the supply function to the rest of the model. There is, therefore, a strong link between the monetary sector and the real sector via the money stock, and consequently it is of paramount importance to take into consideration the monetary sector when constructing macroeconomic models. This is not always the case with some of the models reported in the literature.

Footnotes

* The authors are grateful to their discussant, Marcus H. Miller, whose remarks have appreciably influenced the revised version of this paper. They are also indebted to Michael B. J. Frowen, W.Gebauer, George Kouris, Nikolaus K.A. Läufer, Manfred J. M. Neumann, Reinhard Pohl and Manfred Willms for helpful comments and suggestions on the earlier draft of this paper. This work was supported by the Leverhulme Trust Fund.
1. See also Frowen and Arestis (1976a).
2. Interest rates are also found to be significant in the study by Neumann in the volume, see p. 109.
3. This equation is derived as follows: first, substitute equations (5.1) and (5.2) into equation (5.3)—the error term is ignored for simplicity reasons—to get

$$m_t = ca_{10} + ca_{11}by_t + ca_{11}(1 - b)y_{t-1}^e + ca_{12}r_t + (1 - c)m_{t-1} \qquad \text{(i)}$$

Next, lag equations (5.1) and (5.3) one period, substitute the lagged one period equation (5.1) into the equivalent (5.3) equation, and multiply the resulting equation by $(1 - b)$ to yield

$$(1 - b)m_{t-1} = (1 - b)ca_{10} + (1 - b)ca_{11}y^e_{t-1}$$
$$+ (1 - b)ca_{12}r_{t-1} + (1 - b)(1 - c)m_{t-2} \quad \text{(ii)}$$

Finally, subtract equation (ii) from equation (i) to arrive at equation (5.4).

4. We have been unable to find the appropriate computing programme when dealing with this study. (See Footnote 5.)

5. Within the framework of a more extensive study an attempt will be made to estimate Model 1 using a non-linear constraint least squares programme. In this case the problem of distinguishing between expectation and adjustment lags can be tackled.

6. The distributed lag bias arising whenever a lagged dependent variable is used on the right-hand side of the equation is not a problem in our case, as we are dealing with a sufficiently large number of samples ($n = 40$). The bias vanishes asymptotically when the size of the sample increases.

7. We had to make use of two programmes for the estimations of our equations and unfortunately only one of the two provided Durbin-Watson statistics.

8. The criteria used for selecting the 'best' equations are the standard statistical criteria, i.e. expected signs of the variables included in the particular equation, the t statistic, R^2 and the F statistic. For tables of all the results, see Frowen and Arestis (1976 a).

9. The values in brackets are t statistics.

10. This may well be due to the multicolinearity problem which is not dealt with in this paper.

11. See Goodhart and Crockett (1970) and Hamburger (1974). The superiority of the Eurodollar over domestic interest rates in the demand-for-money function has also been demonstrated in a recent study on the world demand for money (see Frowen and Kouris (1977)).

12. The extent of such control obviously depends on the type of exchange rate system in force.

13. The same function can be derived by following Tobin's view that the money stock is determined by both the actions of the banking system and the private sector (see Tobin (1963)). In particular, according to this view, money is created or supplied as a result of the banking system's supply of credit and the non-banks' demand for credit. Money is, thus, created in the credit market at the equilibrium intersection of the demand for and supply of credit. The role of the Central Bank in this formulation of the money-supply determination is to influence the supply side via changes in the base money—the reserve component—and the discount rate. Gebauer (1974), following this kind of theorizing, arrives at a money-supply function which is pretty much the same as the one postulated in this paper.

14. The seasonally adjusted series used in the case of B^*_t, comprised of the extended monetary base plus liquidity reserves, has been kindly placed at our disposal by Reinhard Pohl of the Deutsches Institut für Wirtschaftsforschung, Berlin.

15. Figures in parenthesis refer to t statistics. The quarterly data used for these estimations cover the period 1965(I) to 1974(III), i.e. one quarter is lost due to the fact that we allow for a one period ahead forecast. The SEE notation stands for the standard error of estimate.

16. This is a statistical test for post sample parameter stability, with r degrees of freedom, where r equals the number of observations retained for a post sample parameter stability test.

17. p stands for the autocorrelation parameter.

The Demand for and Supply of Money in the Federal Republic of Germany: 1965–1974—a Comment [1]

MARCUS H. MILLER

I should like to start by discussing aspects of the Feige–Laidler–Parkin model which was used as a basis for the estimation in the first part of the paper. That model was concerned to allow for two different reasons for the lagged adjustment of money to income. The first reason is that the income variable relevant to the demand for money is 'permanent income' and this is assumed to be a distributed-lag function of current income, i.e. it takes some time for permanent income to finish reacting to current income. The other reason is a lag in the adjustment of the demand for money to its 'desired' level, which we refer to as 'lagged adjustment in demand'. It is obviously rather difficult to sort these two reasons out if all you have is two series for income and money. It is, however, true that under the usual assumptions the lagged adjustment in demand does not lead to serially correlated errors, whereas the permanent income theory does [2].

This can be illustrated with a simple version of the demand for money in the following two equations. Assume that the quantity of money demanded is some weighted average of the desired stock of money and the lagged stock of money plus an error term, which is serially uncorrelated.

$$m = cm^* + (1 - c)Lm + u \tag{C5.1}$$

where
$m = $ log of real balances per capita
$L = $ a lag operator

Assuming further that the desired stock of money depends on permanent income with elasticity b, and not upon interest rates, we have

$$m^* = \frac{bx}{1 - L + Lb} \tag{C5.2}$$

where $\quad x = $ log of real income,

and $\quad x^e = $ log of permanent income $= \dfrac{bx}{1 - L + Lb}$ [3]

One can substitute (C5.2) into (C5.1) and multiply through by the denominator $1 - L + Lb$ to get

$$m(1 - L + Lb) = cbx + (1 - c)L(1 - L + Lb)Lm$$
$$+ (1 - L + Lb)u \tag{C5.3}$$

F

But the same multiplication scrambles up the errors as well, generating a moving average error, which implies (first order) serial correlation u it was serially uncorrelated. Laidler and Parkin (1970) referred to the fact that they might have to check for first-order *autocorrelation*. In fact, the error here is a moving average error and does not follow a first-order autoregressive pattern. This is an implication of the 'permanent income' theory which is different from the 'lagged adjustment' theory [4]. The fact that the two reasons for introducing lags have different implications for the error structure may be used to discriminate between them (see Price (1972) for an illustration of this).

The distinction between the two theories was not really attempted on the basis of error structure in the Laidler–Parkin paper, however, a point that has been made before by Dr. Wallis of the London School of Economics. Instead Laidler and Parkin attempted to use a variable not included in equations (C5.1) and (C5.2) above for this task, namely the rate of interest. How it may achieve this end may be seen as follows. If the demand for money depends on the current rate of interest, and if income (both current and permanent) were constant, then the response of money to variations in the rate of interest will give estimates of the lagged adjustment of money demand, as opposed to the lags in the 'permanent income' theory. Thus the coefficients estimated on current and lagged interest rates in the Laidler–Parkin work were of crucial importance in this respect. But the problem was that one needed to include these two different lags of the interest rate in the model and, as in the paper above, it proved difficult to estimate two significant coefficients on successive values of this variable. Thus, the weight of discriminating between these two theories was put upon the interest rate, but the variations in the rate were not sufficient for this task.

I think this has implications for Model 1, which is not fitted in this paper, but may be estimated. The dynamic structure is rather difficult to sort out given the data we have; certainly if the demand for money in Germany has behaved as oddly as it did in the U.K. after 1971, the idea that you can sort out the lags on the basis of fine tests of errors or interest rate coefficients or anything other than something that is brutally obvious is, I think, pretty optimistic! I am not therefore very hopeful about the chances of proceeding with Model 1 and getting better results than Laidler and Parkin obtained for the U.K.

Turning to the models that are reported, I want to consider the reasons given for the inclusion of the price variable as a separate variable on the right-hand side in Models 3 and 4. In these models, where the demand for money is assumed to depend on current income, not permanent income, there the authors include the price level, so instead of equation (C5.2) we have an equation of the form

$$m = bx + dP \text{ where } P \text{ is the log of the price level} \qquad (C5.4)$$

For $d \neq 0$, the demand for real balances is therefore non-homogeneous in the price level, i.e. there is 'money illusion' in the demand-for-money function.

Now, two reasons are given for including the price level in this way: one is to allow for a difference between the real income elasticity and the price elasticity. I do not think that is a good reason because even when $d = 0$, one can estimate the income elasticity freely as b (the price elasticity being equal to 1 by definition); so we can get a difference without having to put P in separately. The more plausible reason for including P is to allow for different speeds of adjustment. But here I would argue that one can vary the estimated speed of response of money to prices without generating 'long-run' money illusion.

To develop this argument, consider the example provided by the practice of deflating lagged money by the price index at various dates. The most common assumption, made in equation (C5.1) above, is that real balances today are a weighted average of some desired level of real balances and real balances last period, so lagged money balances are deflated by the *lagged* price level. Rewriting equation (C5.1) as

$$(M - P) = cm^* + (1 - c)(M - P)L \qquad (C5.5)$$

where M is the log of the money stock and we ignore the error term and the deflation by population, we get a demand for nominal balances as follows:

$$M = cm^* + (1 - c)ML - (1 - c)PL + P \qquad (C5.6)$$

The elasticity of demand for money today with respect to the current price index is therefore equal to 1, which is also the long-run price elasticity.

But if money balances are deflated by the *current* price level, as in the paper being discussed, then we have

$$(M - P) = cm^* + (1 - c)(ML - P) \qquad (C5.7)$$

and so

$$M = cm^* + (1 - c)ML + cP \qquad (C5.8)$$

Thus the short-run price elasticity of demand for M with respect to P is now only c, although *the long-run elasticity is still* 1, as can be confirmed by noting that, when $M = ML$, $M = m^* + P$.

Equations (C5.6) and (C5.8) are the same except for the way in which the price level appears. While in (C5.8) only the current price level is included, with coefficient c, in (C5.6) there is a 'distribution' of past and present prices, with weights summing to c, which, of course, ensures that there is no money illusion. Thus the effect of deflating lagged money by the current price level instead of lagged prices is to *lower* the impact response (of money demanded with respect to the price level) from unity to c, where c is the weight on the 'desired' level of real balances in the adjustment equation and is usually substantially below one.

The above example makes it clear that one may vary the time path of the response of M to P without changing the long-run elasticity. In the paper, Frowen and Arestis have deflated lagged money by current prices, which, as we have seen, implies a low short-run response of M to P; but they also find that current P is significant (at least in Tables 4, 5, 7 and 8 given in Frowen and Arestis (1976)) implying that the short-run price elasticity is higher than this low, constrained value. The preceding discussion suggests that it would be worth investigating the possibility that lagged values of the price level (with coefficients summing to a negative value) have been omitted, before concluding that the long-run price elasticity of demand for money is greater than unity. I personally would be reluctant to reject the hypothesis of a long-run elasticity of unity without more investigation.

Another way of reconciling the positive coefficients estimated for P in Models 3 and 4 (in the levels) with an assumed unit elasticity stems from noting that when these models are estimated in first differences the price variable becomes insignificant, since a constant term was included in the first difference regression, which is the equivalent of a time trend in a regression in the levels of the variables. Thus it is possible that the price index in the level regressions is soaking up the coefficient on some omitted trending variable.

One variable which fills this particular bill is a measure of wealth. Some such measure [5] should presumably be included in Models 3 and 4 which exclude 'permanent income' by construction. Of course many demand-for-money equations estimated for the U.K. do not contain such a measure, but they are in my view the poorer for that.

Footnotes

1. The comments do not deal with the simultaneous model which was added after the conference.
2. This is also something that might be borne in mind when considering what sort of transformations should be performed upon the data.
3. $x^e - x^e L = b(x - x^e L)$ implies $x^e(1 - L + Lb) = bx$ and so $x^e = \dfrac{bx}{1 - L + Lb}$
4. Feige (1967) assumed that the error u was serially uncorrelated whereas Laidler and Parkin assumed that the *transformed* error was well-behaved.
5. Such as the cumulated total of the private sector financial surplus, for example.

6

Price Expectations and Interest Rates in the Federal Republic of Germany

JUERGEN SIEBKE

Introduction

The purpose of this paper is to present some recent estimates of the impact of anticipated inflation on the long-term interest rate [1]. In what follows the main determinants of the rate of interest are first examined, while in the second section results derived on assumptions of Koyck- and Almon-lags [2] are presented.

The Main Determinants of the Interest Rate

Empirical investigation of the fundamental determinants of the long-term rate of interest has in general relied on Keynes' theory of liquidity preference extended to take account of the Fisher effect [3] of the impact of anticipated inflation on nominal interest rates [4].

Acceptance of this point of departure implies confinement of one's analysis to a two-asset, money and bonds, model (Tobin, 1961), as bonds and real assets are treated as perfect substitutes. There is thus only one rate of interest to be explained, that on bonds. By Walras' law we can furthermore dismiss one of these two markets. Dismissing the bond market the rate of interest on bonds is then seen as determined in the money market [5].

Keynes' liquidity preference theory regards the demand for real money balances as a function of the bond rate of interest and the level of real income. Considering the supply of the real money stock as exogenously determined we may solve the equilibrium condition of the money market for the interest rate. Thus, the interest rate is a function of the real money supply and real income. The (negative) impact of variations in the first determinant is called the liquidity-effect or sometimes also the Keynes-effect; the (positive) impact of the second variable is called the income-effect or Wicksell-effect.

This framework does not furnish an explanation for the fact that over relatively long periods nominal interest rates and the price level are positively correlated. The main explanation of this relationship was provided by Fisher's (1896) argument that if future price level movements could be perfectly foreseen, borrowers and lenders would agree on a nominal interest rate that compensates for the anticipated erosion in the purchasing power of money and is thus equal to the real rate of interest plus the anticipated rate of change in prices. Thus the bond rate can be taken to be the sum of the real rate of interest and the anticipated rate of inflation.

Adding the anticipated rate of inflation as a third argument in the demand for money and thus on the right-hand side of the equation for the rate of interest, appears a convenient way for incorporating the Fisher-effect in Keynes' liquidity preference theory. As argued by Sargent (1973), however, this procedure [6] does not present an adequate integration of Keynes' and Fisher's macroeconomic theories and hence one has to interpret the equations employed in the next section to examine the determinants of the nominal interest rate, as inverted demand schedules for money balances rather than as reduced form equations deriving from a larger model.

Specification and Estimation

Two alternative processes of price expectation formation were examined.

Koyck-lag Structure

Under Koyck assumptions the expected rate of change in prices at time t, described by Δp_t^e, is a distributed lagged function of current and past rates of actual changes in prices, Δp_{t-j} ($j = 0, 1, 2, \ldots, \infty$), with geometrically declining weights. In particular

$$\Delta p_t^e = (1 - \lambda) \sum_{j=0}^{\infty} \lambda_j p_{t-j}, \qquad 0 < \lambda < 1 \tag{6.1}$$

where Δ denotes rate of change per unit time.

The specification of (6.1) implies that the sum of the weights equal unity while the mean lag l is given by $l = \lambda/(1 - \lambda)$.

Neglecting the liquidity and income effects we can then express the relationship between the nominal i and real rate of interest r as

$$i_t = r + x\Delta p_t^e \qquad 0 < x < 1 \tag{6.2}$$

and hence, granted (6.1),

$$i_t = (1 - \lambda)r + \lambda i_{t-1} + x(1 - \lambda)\Delta p_t \tag{6.3}$$

Employing the average yield on public bonds as a proxy for i_t, and the cost of living index as the price variable (the percentage change being calculated with reference to the same quarter of the previous year) the following estimates were derived [7] on quarterly data for the period 1960(I) to 1971(II)

$$i_t = 0.493 + 0.889i_{t-1} + 0.116\Delta p_t \qquad (6.4)$$
$$(1.414) \ (16.050) \qquad (2.982)$$

$R^2 = 0.898$, t ratios in brackets

Since the decay coefficient $\lambda = 0.889$ is smaller than one, the empirical result is consistent with the postulated relationship. The regression coefficient for the price variable Δp_t implies a coefficient of the expected rate of inflation $x = 1.045$. This seems to be still compatible with the value of one implied by Fisher's analysis.

The mean lag is 8.8 quarters and hence similar to the findings of Yohe and Karnosky (1969) using the same procedure, or to others applying different frameworks (Feldstein and Eckstein (1970), Feldstein and Chamberlain (1973)). Using monthly data the mean lag increased to 10 quarters. A mean lag of two years and more indicates a relatively long process by which price expectations are formed and transmitted to nominal interest rates.

The simplicity of the Koyck-lag structure vanishes if one integrates the liquidity effect and the income effect. Inserting a third independent variable into equation (6.2), for instance the money stock as a measure for the liquidity effect, would lead to a linear equation of the form of (6.3) that incorporates the current and one period lagged value of this variable. However multicolinearity between these two variables is likely. This is met through the use of constraints implicit in Almon-lag estimation.

Almon-lag Structure

This procedure requires that a specific hypothesis be made regarding the pattern of weights given to the rates of price changes. Since adaptive expectations suggest declining weights that tend to zero the polynomial lag distribution was constrained so that the coefficient of the rate of price changes at the end of the lag to zero.

All estimations have been made with a third-order polynomial distributed lag. In a first step the separated impact of price expectations has been considered. This allows a direct comparison with the result of the preceding section. The findings are very similar to those of Yohe and Karnosky (1969): the mean lag is much shorter.

Using quarterly data the sum of the coefficients reaches its highest value for a total lag of 8 quarters. Extending the length of the lag does not improve the results: the coefficients in the end of the distribution are nearly zero and not statistically significant.

$$i_t = 5.000 + \sum_{j=0}^{7} \alpha_j \Delta p_{t-j} \quad \text{with} \quad \sum \alpha_j = 0.858$$

$$(17.94) \qquad\qquad\qquad\qquad\qquad (8.20)$$

$$\alpha_0 = 0.193 \ (2.54) \qquad\qquad \alpha_4 = 0.094 \ (4.69)$$
$$\alpha_1 = 0.167 \ (8.57) \qquad\qquad \alpha_5 = 0.071 \ (3.78)$$
$$\alpha_2 = 0.141 \ (4.90) \qquad\qquad \alpha_6 = 0.048 \ (1.68)$$
$$\alpha_3 = 0.117 \ (3.86) \qquad\qquad \alpha_7 = 0.025 \ (0.91)$$

$R^2 = 0.802$, t ratios in brackets

The mean lag is 2·3 quarters. For a lag of 10 quarters the value rises only to 2·4 quarters.

Applying monthly data the sum of the coefficients has its highest value for a lag of 30 months. All coefficients are statistically significant.

$$i_t = 4.663 + \sum_{j=0}^{29} \alpha_j \Delta p_{t-j} \quad \text{with} \quad \sum \alpha_j = 0.961, \quad R^2 = 0.739$$

$$(21.03) \qquad\qquad\qquad\qquad\qquad (10.85)$$

Extension of the lag structure revealed that no significant gain is secured from so doing.

Thus, monthly and quarterly data indicate a mean lag of about 2 to 2·5 quarters. This is considerably shorter than the findings applying the Koyck-lag. The sum of the coefficients implies that a permanent 1% increase in the annual rate of inflation would increase the interest rate by 86 basis points and by 96 basis points in the case of quarterly and monthly data respectively. Fisher's approach implies a value of one.

In the expanded model we added the annual rate of change of the real money stock ΔRM and the percentage change of real gross national product $\Delta RGNP$. Both variables are deflated by the GNP deflator. Quarterly data are used in the regressions. Examination of alternative lags again reveal a mean lag of 3 quarters. The coefficient representing the income effect were not always statistically significant and neither were some of the weights of the price index. For a total lag of 10 quarters the estimated equation is:

$$i_t = 5.050 - 0.151\Delta RM_t + 0.076\Delta RGNP_t + \sum_{j=0}^{9} \alpha_j \Delta p_{t-j}$$

$$(6.81) \qquad (4.00) \qquad\qquad (1.74)$$

$\sum \alpha_j = 0.85$, $R^2 = 0.73$, mean lag: 3 quarters

$$\alpha_0 = 0.256 \ (4.29) \qquad\qquad \alpha_5 = 0.043 \ (1.46)$$
$$\alpha_1 = 0.149 \ (5.50) \qquad\qquad \alpha_6 = 0.055 \ (1.98)$$
$$\alpha_2 = 0.083 \ (2.97) \qquad\qquad \alpha_7 = 0.065 \ (2.13)$$
$$\alpha_3 = 0.048 \ (2.45) \qquad\qquad \alpha_8 = 0.065 \ (2.27)$$
$$\alpha_4 = 0.038 \ (1.16) \qquad\qquad \alpha_9 = 0.046 \ (2.23)$$

Using nominal GNP and the nominal money stock as explanatory variables the coefficient for the income effect is statistically significant.

$$i_t = 5.020 - 0.084\Delta M_t + 0.082\Delta GNP + \sum_{j=0}^{7} \alpha_j \Delta p_{t-j}$$

(14·05)   (2·55)   (3·49)

$\sum \alpha_j = 0.805$, $R^2 = 0.87$, mean lag: 3 quarters

(8·94)

This equation implies that the underlying demand function for money is not homogenous of degree one in nominal income and the price level. Again the mean lag is 3 quarters.

In the preceding analysis an attempt was made to examine the importance of the Fisher effect on the behaviour of the long-term rate of interest. The results from both Koyck and Almon lag price expectation formulation processes suggest a significant, less than unity, response of the long-term rate to the rate of change in price level. Furthermore the total price expectation effect on the rate of interest is found to conform to a lag considerably shorter than that traced by Gebauer (1973) whose results show the total price expectations to be transmitted over a period of five years.

Footnotes

1. The results reported can be said to comprise a review of estimates earlier presented by Siebke & Willms (1972, 1973) and Gebauer (1973).
2. Koyck (1954), Almon (1975).
3. Fisher (1896 and 1930).
4. See for example Yohe & Turnovsky (1969).
5. A first attempt towards empirical analysis of the interest rate in a multi-market model is presented in Feldstein & Chamberlain (1973).
6. Employed by Feldstein & Eckstein (1970).
7. It should be stressed that if the disturbance term u_t is introduced into equation (6.2) the classical assumptions about the disturbance must be assumed to be valid for $(u_t - u_{t-1})$.

Price Expectations and Interest Rates in the Federal Republic of Germany— a Comment

MICHAEL PARKIN

This discussion falls into three parts. First, it attempts to clarify the questions that are at issue, second, it comments on the underlying theoretical analysis used by Siebke, and third, it comments on his empirical work and results.

It seems to me, looking at the earlier literature on this subject, that there are two distinct questions that people have asked, and I am not clear which of these two Siebke is primarily interested in. One question has been: is the Fisher hypothesis true, or conversely, can we refute the Fisher hypothesis? The second question has *assumed* the Fisher hypothesis to be true and asked: What are the weights in the relationship between the anticipated rate of inflation on the one hand, and the actual rate on the other? These two distinct questions are of course very interesting in and of themselves. The first is interesting because if it turns out that we cannot refute the Fisher hypothesis then we have a proxy for, or some would say a direct measure of, the expected rate of inflation. The second question is important because we might want to study the dynamic interaction between the actual and expected rates of inflation and the ways in which they interact with other real and monetary variables.

Let me now consider briefly some of Siebke's theoretical propositions. They are not absolutely essential to the empirical work which his paper presents, but I disagree with him on one or two points of detail which ought to be brought out and be discussed. First, he begins by making all the assumptions needed to reduce the world to one which has only two assets. He then argues that if bonds and real assets are perfect substitutes their yields will be equal, which is true, provided we are talking about *real* yields. However, he goes on to talk *as if* he does not mean equality of real yields for he goes on to introduce the Fisher effect as if it was something different from the effect that arises automatically as a result and consequence of the assumption that real assets and bonds are perfect substitutes. If they are, indeed, perfect substitutes, then their real rates of interest will be equal and the nominal rate on bonds will differ from the rate on real assets by the anticipated rate of inflation. It is this that gives rise to the Fisher hypothesis. The assumption of perfect substitutability implies the relation between the real and nominal rate. That is not made clear, at least to me, in the first few pages of the paper.

I cannot accept what he further argues, namely, that it is appropriate that the anticipated rate of inflation be added as an additional argument to the demand function for real balances. If we are making the assumption that bonds and real assets are perfect substitutes, then the anticipated rate of inflation is already in the demand for real balances once we put the nominal bond rate of interest in the equation. It may be decomposed into a real rate of interest and an anticipated rate of inflation with the additional maintained hypothesis that the coefficients on each will be equal. That is an alternative way of stating that real assets and bonds are perfect substitutes for each other.

Let us now move on to some empirical considerations which follow immediately from this point. One way in which the Fisher hypothesis may be tested directly is in the manner suggested and carried out by Gupta (1970) specifying the demand for real money $(M/P)^d$ as,

$$\frac{M^d}{P} = \alpha + \beta y + \gamma r_n + \varepsilon$$

where
$y = $ real income
$r_n = $ nominal rate of interest
$\varepsilon = $ residual
α, β, γ parameters

If this equation turns out to be a reasonable specification of the demand-for-money function possessing the usually required statistical properties then we could ask the question: is it true that the demand for money is equal to:

$$\frac{M^d}{P} = a + by + cr_r + d(r_n - r_r) + \varepsilon$$

where r_r is the real rate of interest and the difference between r_n and r_r is the anticipated rate of inflation with $a = \alpha$, $b = \beta$, $c = \gamma$ and $d = \gamma$? If it turns out that the hypothesis that $c = d = \gamma$ cannot be rejected then neither can the Fisher hypothesis be rejected. If that test has been performed and it has turned out in support of the Fisher hypothesis, then it is possible to use $r_n - r_r$ as a measure of the expected rate of inflation, and together with the past values of the actual rate of inflation to compute the weights that relate the anticipated rate of inflation to the previous actual rate.

Let me move on now to discussion of Siebke's estimation of that relationship. He estimates an equation in which the nominal rate of interest is the dependent variable and the previous actual rate of inflation (either using a Koyck- or Almon-lag), with and without other variables from the demand-for-money function as independent variables. Now in the specifications which use all the variables from the demand-for-money function including the money stock what he has done, essentially, is to estimate the demand-for-money function in a rather unusual way. You can start off with M as some function of the usual list of explanatory variables and 'solve' it for any variable in the equation that you choose and then estimate the coefficients. The coefficients of the demand-for-money function would be obtained by reversing the algebra and returning to an equation with M on the left-hand side. I am not enough of an econometrician to know the properties of all the alternative parameter estimates, but there has got to be a right way to estimate the demand-for-money function, and my instinctive preference is for estimating it in the way that is suggested by theory, namely with the demand for money on the left-hand side and the things that determine the demand for money on the right-hand side. To estimate an interest rate equation we need an explicit *reduced form equation* that shows how the interest rate is being determined in the markets for debt and goods with the simultaneous clearing of those markets. So I am not convinced that estimating the demand-for-money function with the interest rate as the dependent variable is appropriate. I am much happier with the procedure of running the nominal rate on a distributed lag function of the rate of inflation, because that, combined with the assumption that the real rate is a constant plus a random disturbance, is a reduced form that we could generate under appropriate assumptions. I am not entirely happy, however, even with that procedure for reasons developed by Sargent (1972).

Now three small econometric points: first, I was surprised that for the variants of the model where there is more than one variable in the interest rate equation it was claimed that the Koyck technique could not be used; it could have been, provided the non-linear overidentified restrictions on the parameters and the transformed error structure were taken into account. Second, I find it distressing that the explicit moving average error in the specification is assumed away. Third, there is a recently-developed set of techniques for estimating distributed lag functions by Dhrymes which has, I think, helped us to overcome many of the problems we had with the Koyck procedure that Siebke is using. Two problems arise with the Koyck transformation: one is that we wind up with a moving average error term and the other is that we have covariance between the error term and one of the explanatory variables. The Dhrymes techniques, which are now increasingly operational with programmes available in many universities, enables us to overcome both those problems.

I would now like to make two points on Siebke's empirical work of more economic substance. First he tells us that he would expect the weights relative inflation to the nominal interest rate to decline. On theoretical considerations there is room for doubt about this. Work done over the last few years on expectations and on the relation between expected and previous actual values of variables indicates that we should not have a strong *prior* about the shape of the weight distribution. Geometrically-declining weights are optimal in the sense that if a set of weights which have that pattern are used the expectation on the average is equal to the actual out-turn only if the series that is being forecast has a very simple stochastic structure. David Rose (now at the University of British Columbia) presented a paper at the Budapest meetings of the Econometric Society in 1972 which shows that there is a generalized error learning analogue for any stochastic process and the analogue is one in which expectations are revised not in the light of the last error, but in the light of *all* errors. That reduces to a general distributed lag function, the precise form of which could be derived analytically from an ARIMA analysis of the series being forecast.

Secondly, I want to turn to a proposition that is made quite early on in the paper. It is stated fairly boldly that since price expectations cannot be observed we have to make some indirect hypothesis about them. I believe that price expectations can be observed, and I think quite a lot of work has been done to observe them. Apart from the fact that they can be observed by looking at the appropriate differences in interest rates, they can be observed by asking people questions, and a great deal of question asking has been done in Germany, Britain, the United States of America and several other places. There are three papers, Carlson and Parkin (1973), DeMenil (1973) and Knöbl (1973), all of which transform qualitative 'up', 'down', 'no change' expectations about prices into quantitative expected rate of inflation series. So there is a directly-observed inflation series available for Germany. It turns out, according to Knöbl's studies, that it performs reasonably well in exercises similar to that which Siebke is doing, that is, there is a fairly good relationship between the directly observed expected rate of inflation and the gap between a real and nominal rate.

Finally, when one talks about inflation expectations one usually fails to specify that time horizon over which the expectation is being formed—I plead guilty in many contexts. There seem to me to be a lot of interesting questions about the relationship between expected inflation rates over different lead times and the previous history of prices. Many decisions are made with a forecast horizon of a month or so and many of a year. For these different purposes we need different expectations of the rate of inflation. At some stage someone should examine the time structure of inflation expectations.

7

An Econometric Model of the Financial Sector of the Federal Republic of Germany*

HEINZ KÖNIG, WERNER GAAB AND JÜRGEN WOLTERS

The model aims to explain changes in the holdings of a range of financial assets and liabilities by the nonbank private sector, commercial banks and the Government sector. In principle, it is based upon the stock adjustment theory of portfolio behaviour as used by de Leeuw (1963, 1968), Goldfeld (1966), Silber (1970), Norton (1970), Helliwell (1969) and others. It is generally argued that the desired stock of any asset depends on the holder's wealth, the actual and/or the expected yield on the respective assets and alternative assets. Uncertain expectations of asset holders and/or transaction costs in buying and selling assets are assumed to result in a delay in adjusting actual asset holdings to the desired levels.

The first section presents the structural equations and definitional relationships of the model and, in addition, some remarks on special features of the model. The second part contains the results of three kinds of dynamic simulations—a deterministic simulation and stochastic simulations with uncorrelated and autocorrelated error terms—as well as *ex post* forecasts for 1972.

Specification of the Model

Structural Equations and Definitions

The model consists of 19 structural equations and nine identities. Because some of the equations are non-linear in endogenous variables structural equations are estimated by two stage least squares as suggested by Goldfeld and Quandt (1968). First stage estimation is based upon 16 principal components of all predetermined variables, explaining 98·7% of the generalized variance and guaranteeing a sufficient number of degrees of freedom for the computation of regressions [1]. The time span of estimation is from the third quarter of 1960 to the fourth quarter of 1971. With the exception of private wealth all data are seasonally unadjusted. Unless otherwise indicated all values are in billions of current DM; data for stocks are the end-month values for the last month of each quarter. The interest rate variables are percentages, an interest rate of 5% is 5·00. Reserve ratios and value variables in ratio form are proportions. Figures in parentheses below regression co-efficients are t-values. $\bar{R}^2$ is the square of the correlation coefficient corrected for degrees of freedom, $DW1$ is the Durbin–Watson statistic for first order autocorrelation, and $DW4$ is the statistic for fourth order autocorrelation [2].

Currency holdings

$$\Delta BGP = 3{\cdot}271 + \underset{(6{\cdot}7)}{1{\cdot}209S_1} + \underset{(9{\cdot}9)}{1{\cdot}375S_2} + \underset{(8{\cdot}3)}{1{\cdot}243S_3}$$
$$- \underset{(10{\cdot}5)}{0{\cdot}456BGP_{-1}} + \underset{(10{\cdot}6)}{0{\cdot}131\,YV} - \underset{(5{\cdot}8)}{0{\cdot}268RTE_{-1}} \qquad (7.1)$$
$$\bar{R}^2 = 0{\cdot}788,\ DW1 = 1{\cdot}8,\ DW4 = 2{\cdot}0$$

Holdings of demand deposits

$$\Delta SEP = -1{\cdot}306 - \underset{(4{\cdot}1)}{3{\cdot}430S_1} - \underset{(1{\cdot}9)}{0{\cdot}681S_2} - \underset{(4{\cdot}1)}{1{\cdot}800S_3}$$
$$- \underset{(5{\cdot}1)}{0{\cdot}476SEP_{-1}} + \underset{(5{\cdot}5)}{0{\cdot}210\,YBSP} - \underset{(3{\cdot}3)}{0{\cdot}561RTE} \qquad (7.2)$$
$$\bar{R}^2 = 0{\cdot}927,\ DW1 = 1{\cdot}8,\ DW4 = 2{\cdot}1$$

Holdings of short-term time deposits

$$\Delta \ln TEPK = -1{\cdot}818 - \underset{(2{\cdot}4)}{0{\cdot}219S_1} - \underset{(5{\cdot}7)}{0{\cdot}346S_2} - \underset{(6{\cdot}4)}{0{\cdot}346S_3}$$
$$+ \underset{(2{\cdot}1)}{0{\cdot}280D_1} - \underset{(4{\cdot}7)}{0{\cdot}415 \ln TEPK_{-1}} - \underset{(3{\cdot}3)}{0{\cdot}395\,\Delta \ln TEPK_{-1}}$$
$$+ \underset{(3{\cdot}2)}{0{\cdot}766 \ln YBSP} + \underset{(5{\cdot}5)}{1{\cdot}074 \ln RTE} - \underset{(4{\cdot}0)}{0{\cdot}782 \ln RKK_{-1}}$$
$$- \underset{(3{\cdot}0)}{0{\cdot}421 \ln REURO3} \qquad (7.3)$$
$$\bar{R}^2 = 0{\cdot}855,\ DW1 = 2{\cdot}2\ DW4 = 1{\cdot}4$$

Holdings of long-term time deposits

$$\Delta \ln TEPL = -0{\cdot}490 + \underset{(2{\cdot}2)}{0{\cdot}026S_1} - \underset{(0{\cdot}7)}{0{\cdot}009S_2} - \underset{(0{\cdot}8)}{0{\cdot}010S_3}$$
$$- \underset{(5{\cdot}1)}{0{\cdot}126D_2} - \underset{(2{\cdot}6)}{0{\cdot}167 \ln TEPL_{-1}} + \underset{(3{\cdot}0)}{0{\cdot}315 \ln VP}$$
$$+ \underset{(2{\cdot}7)}{0{\cdot}104 \ln RTE} - \underset{(1{\cdot}9)}{0{\cdot}190 \ln RSCHULU} \qquad (7.4)$$
$$\bar{R}^2 = 0{\cdot}483,\ DW1 = 1{\cdot}8,\ DW4 = 1{\cdot}8$$

Holdings of savings deposits

$$\Delta SPE = -6{\cdot}066 + 1{\cdot}947 S_1 - 0{\cdot}312 S_2 + 0{\cdot}257 S_3$$
$$(8{\cdot}3) \qquad (0{\cdot}9) \qquad (1{\cdot}2)$$
$$- 0{\cdot}073 SPE_{-1} + 0{\cdot}255 \Delta SPE_{-1} + 0{\cdot}273 VP$$
$$(3{\cdot}1) \qquad (1{\cdot}6) \qquad (3{\cdot}9)$$
$$+ 1{\cdot}045 RSPE - 0{\cdot}875 RANL_{-1} - 0{\cdot}146 \Delta P/P$$
$$(2{\cdot}1) \qquad (2{\cdot}5) \qquad (2{\cdot}6) \tag{7.5}$$
$$\bar{R}^2 = 0{\cdot}900, \; DW1 = 1{\cdot}7, \; DW4 = 2{\cdot}3$$

Private holdings of Government securities and bank bonds

$$\Delta(WPP + SCHULU) = -5{\cdot}029 + 0{\cdot}301 S_1 - 0{\cdot}608 S_2$$
$$(1{\cdot}2) \qquad (2{\cdot}4)$$
$$+ 0{\cdot}095 S_3 - 0{\cdot}183(WPP + SCHULU)_{-1}$$
$$(0{\cdot}4) \qquad (3{\cdot}9)$$
$$+ 0{\cdot}578 \Delta(WPP + SCHULU)_{-1}$$
$$(4{\cdot}5)$$
$$+ 0{\cdot}238 VP + 0{\cdot}337 RSCHULU$$
$$(3{\cdot}9) \qquad (1{\cdot}7)$$
$$- 0{\cdot}450 RSPE_{-1} - 0{\cdot}558 RUSBL$$
$$(1{\cdot}7) \qquad (2{\cdot}2) \tag{7.6a}$$
$$\bar{R}^2 = 0{\cdot}690, \; DW1 = 2{\cdot}0, \; DW4 = 2{\cdot}4$$
$$RANL = -0{\cdot}536 + 1{\cdot}082 RSCHULU$$
$$(32{\cdot}9) \tag{7.6b}$$
$$\bar{R}^2 = 0{\cdot}960, \; DW1 = 1{\cdot}8, \; DW4 = 1{\cdot}9$$

Short-term loans to the nonbank private sector

$$\Delta KKP = -2{\cdot}982 + 0{\cdot}404 S_1 + 1{\cdot}933 S_2 - 0{\cdot}506 S_3$$
$$(0{\cdot}5) \qquad (3{\cdot}6) \qquad (0{\cdot}9)$$
$$+ 5{\cdot}841 D_1 - 0{\cdot}228 KKP_{-1} + 0{\cdot}175 YBSP$$
$$(4{\cdot}5) \qquad (3{\cdot}4) \qquad (3{\cdot}7)$$
$$+ 0{\cdot}185(IPGES - APGES - GUNV)$$
$$(2{\cdot}4)$$
$$- 0{\cdot}701(RKK - RTE)$$
$$(2{\cdot}7) \tag{7.7}$$
$$\bar{R}^2 = 0{\cdot}774, \; DW1 = 1{\cdot}4, \; DW4 = 1{\cdot}9$$

Long-term loans to the nonbank private sector

$$\Delta KLP = -2{\cdot}830 + 0{\cdot}205 \Delta KLP_{-1} + 0{\cdot}618 ANLPN$$
$$(2{\cdot}3) \qquad (10{\cdot}0)$$
$$- 0{\cdot}592(RKL - RKL_{-4}) + 0{\cdot}982 \Delta RTE$$
$$(4{\cdot}5) \qquad (2{\cdot}8) \tag{7.8}$$
$$\bar{R}^2 = 0{\cdot}863, \; DW1 = 2{\cdot}1, \; DW4 = 1{\cdot}4$$

Mortgage loans to the nonbank private sector
$$\Delta KLPW = -0.012 - 1.029\Delta S_1 - 0.705\Delta S_2 - 0.385\Delta S_3$$
$$(9.6) \qquad (8.8) \qquad (5.7)$$
$$+ 0.770\Delta KLPW_{-1} + 0.107 IPWOHNN$$
$$(8.4) \qquad\qquad (3.8)$$
$$- 0.115(RKL - RKL_{-4})$$
$$(3.5) \tag{7.9}$$
$$\bar{R}^2 = 0.875,\ DW1 = 2.2,\ DW4 = 1.8$$

Commercial bank holdings of open market papers
$$\Delta OM = 3.533 - 0.411 OM_1 + 0.058(E - MR)$$
$$(5.1) \qquad\qquad (4.8)$$
$$- 0.192 KK + 0.876 RUSA_{-1}$$
$$(4.9) \qquad\quad (4.5)$$
$$- 0.807(REURO3 + SWAP)$$
$$(6.2) \tag{7.10}$$
$$\bar{R}^2 = 0.561,\ DW1 = 1.6,\ DW4 = 2.0$$

Commercial bank holdings of Government securities
$$\Delta WPB = -0.748 + 0.272 S_1 + 0.112 S_2 + 0.339 S_3$$
$$(2.9) \qquad (1.2) \qquad (3.7)$$
$$- 0.401 WPB_{-1} + 0.039(E - MR) - 0.078 KK$$
$$(7.2) \qquad\qquad (8.7) \qquad\qquad (7.3)$$
$$+ 6.750 KAOB/ANL + 0.169 RANL**(8)$$
$$(3.6) \qquad\qquad (2.1)$$
$$- 0.240\ RKL$$
$$(2.7) \tag{7.11}$$
$$\bar{R}^2 = 0.763,\ DW1 = 1.9,\ DW4 = 1.8$$

Commercial bank borrowing from the Bundesbank
$$\Delta RFK = 0.310 + 6.502 D_1 - 6.967 RFK_{-1}/KONT_{-1}$$
$$(5.3) \qquad (4.5)$$
$$- 0.274\Delta(E - MR - K) - 2.284 RDISL$$
$$(5.2) \qquad\qquad\qquad (4.8)$$
$$+ 1.966 RUSA + 0.608(REURO3 + SWAP)_{-1}$$
$$(4.6) \qquad\quad (3.4) \tag{7.12}$$
$$\bar{R}^2 = 0.728,\ DW1 = 2.2,\ DW4 = 1.5$$

Supply of bank bonds
$$\Delta SCHULU^A = 4.293 - 0.052 S_1 - 0.548 S_2 - 0.427 S_3$$
$$(0.3) \qquad (3.2) \qquad (2.5)$$
$$- 1.110 D_1 - 0.341 SCHULU^A_{-1} - 0.082(E - MR)$$
$$(2.6) \qquad (4.9) \qquad\qquad (4.8)$$
$$+ 0.148 KL + 1.115(RKL - RSCHULU)$$
$$(5.5) \qquad\quad (2.8)$$

$$- 0.659RKL_{-1}$$
$$(3.4) \tag{7.13}$$
$$\bar{R}^2 = 0.698, \ DW1 = 1.5, \ DW4 = 1.7$$

Commercial bank holdings of net foreign assets
$$\Delta DEVKB = 3.558 + 4.235S_1 + 1.650S_2 + 1.783S_3$$
$$(7.7) \qquad (2.5) \qquad (3.5)$$
$$- 0.791DEVKB_{-1} + 0.666\Delta DEVKB_{-1}$$
$$(6.1) \qquad\qquad (4.4)$$
$$+ 0.119(E - MR) - 0.460KK$$
$$(5.7) \qquad\qquad (6.0)$$
$$- 0.597RDISL_{-1} + 0.486\ (REURO3 + SWAP)$$
$$(1.6) \qquad\qquad (2.0) \tag{7.14}$$
$$\bar{R}^2 = 0.771, \ DW1 = 2.0, \ DW4 = 2.0$$

Short-term loan rate
$$RKK = 2.253 - 0.707S_1 - 0.127S_2 - 0.226S_3$$
$$(3.7) \qquad (0.7) \qquad (1.2)$$
$$+ 0.608RKK_{-1} + 0.387RDISL$$
$$(9.0) \qquad\qquad (4.0)$$
$$- 11.197(UER + OM + KONT - RFK)/(E - MR)_{-1}$$
$$(2.2) \tag{7.15}$$
$$\bar{R}^2 = 0.941, \ DW1 = 1.8, \ DW4 = 1.5$$

Long-term loan rate
$$RKL = -0.433 + 0.121S_1 + 0.225S_2 + 0.227S_3$$
$$(0.9) \qquad (1.7) \qquad (1.9)$$
$$+ 0.748RKL_{-1} - 0.298RKL_{-2} + 0.311RKK$$
$$(5.0) \qquad\qquad (2.8) \qquad\qquad (5.2)$$
$$+ 2.454KL/(E - MR)_{-1}$$
$$(2.1) \tag{7.16}$$
$$\bar{R}^2 = 0.945, \ DW1 = 2.1, \ DW4 = 1.8$$

Yield on time deposits
$$RTE = -0.886 + 0.742RTE_{-1} - 0.190RTE_{-2}$$
$$(5.3) \qquad\qquad (1.7)$$
$$+ 0.385D_3.RKK + 0.496D_4.RDISL$$
$$(6.1) \qquad\qquad (4.9) \tag{7.17}$$
$$\bar{R}^2 = 0.968, \ DW1 = 1.7, \ DW4 = 1.9$$

Yield on savings deposits
$$RSPE = 0.317 + 0.399RSPE_{-1} + 0.237RKL$$
$$(6.5) \qquad\qquad (6.0)$$
$$+ 0.084RDISL_{-1}$$
$$(2.5) \tag{7.18}$$
$$\bar{R}^2 = 0.954, \ DW1 = 2.2, \ DW4 = 1.8$$

Monetary base identity
$$BGP + MR + UER = GOLD - DEVKB + OMZB + WPZB$$
$$- EPBU - NPOSST + RFK + REST \quad (7.19)$$

Required reserve idendity
$$MR = RSSE.(SEP + SEST) + RSTE.(TEPK + TEPL)$$
$$+ RSSPE.SPE \quad\quad\quad\quad\quad\quad (7.20)$$

Open market papers identity
$$OM + OMZB = OMG \quad\quad\quad\quad\quad\quad\quad (7.21)$$

Market equilibrium condition of Government securities and bank bonds
$$(WPP + SCHULU) + WPB + WPZB = WP + SCHULU^A \quad (7.22)$$

Further identities
$$WP + KKST + KLST - SEST - TEST - NPOSST = GESV \quad (7.23)$$
$$E = SEP + SEST + TEPK + TEPL + TEST + SPE \quad (7.24)$$
$$KK = KKP + KKST \quad\quad\quad\quad\quad\quad\quad\quad (7.25)$$
$$KL = KLP + KLPW + KLST \quad\quad\quad\quad\quad (7.26)$$
$$K = KK + KL \quad\quad\quad\quad\quad\quad\quad\quad\quad (7.27)$$

List of Variables

* denotes an exogenous variable

$*ANL$ = Government bonds with maturity of four years and more, billions of current DM

$*APGES$ = total depreciation of the domestic private sector, billions of current DM

BGP = currency holdings of the nonbank private sector, billions of current DM

$*D_1$ = dummy variable, 1 for 1969(IV), 0 elsewhere

$*D_2$ = dummy variable, 1 for 1969(IV) to 1971(IV), 0 elsewhere

$*D_3$ = dummy variable, 1 for 1967(II) to 1971(IV), 0 elsewhere

$*D_4$ = dummy variable, 1 for 1960(III) to 1967(I), 0 elsewhere

$DEVKB$ = commercial bank net holdings of short-term foreign assets, billions of current DM

E = total deposits of the nonbank domestic sector, billions of current DM

$*EPBU$ = demand deposits of the nonbank domestic private sector at the Bundesbank, billions of current DM

$*GOLD$ = gold stock of the Bundesbank, billions of current DM

$*GUNV$ = retained earnings, billions of current DM

$*IANLPN$ = private net fixed investment, billions of current DM

$*IPGES$ = total private investment, billions of current DM

*IPWOHNN = private net investment in residential construction, billions of current DM

K = total loans of commercial banks to the nonbank domestic sector, billions of current DM

*KAOB = Government bonds with maturity up to four years, billions of current DM

KK = short-term loans of commercial banks to the nonbank domestic sector, billions of current DM

KKP = short-term loans of commercial banks to the nonbank domestic private sector, billions of current DM

*KKST = short-term loans of commercial banks to the Government sector, billions of current DM

KL = long-term loans (incl. mortgage loans) of commercial banks to the nonbank domestic sector, billions of current DM

KLP = long-term loans of commercial banks to the nonbank domestic private sector, billions of current DM

KLPW = mortgage loans of commercial banks to the nonbank domestic private sector, billions of current DM

*KLST = long-term loans of commercial banks to the Government sector, billions of current DM

*KONT = rediscount quotas of commercial banks, billions of current DM

MR = required reserves of commercial banks, billions of current DM

NPOSST = net position of Government with the Bundesbank, billions of current DM

OM = commercial bank holdings of open market papers, billions of current DM

*OMG = outstanding volume of open market papers (including holdings of the Bundesbank), billions of current DM

OMZB = Bundesbank holdings of open market papers, billions of current DM

*P = implicit deflator of gross national product, 1962 = 100

*$\Delta P/P$ = $100 \, (P_t - P_{t-4})/P_{t-4}$

RANL = yield on long-term Government securities, per cent

$$RANL**(8) = 2 \, RANL - \tfrac{1}{8} \sum_{i=1}^{8} RANL_{-i}$$

*RDISL = weighted average of discount and Lombard rate of the Bundesbank, per cent

*REURO3 = 3-month Eurodollar-rate, per cent

RFK = commercial bank borrowing (discounts and advances) from the Bundesbank, billions of current DM

RKK	= interest rate on short-term loans, per cent
RKL	= interest rate on long-term loans, per cent
RSCHULU	= yield on bank bonds, per cent
RSPE	= interest rate on savings deposits, per cent
*RSSE	= average reserve ratio required against demand deposits, proportion
*RSSPE	= average reserve ratio required against savings deposits, proportion
*RSTE	= average reserve ratio required against time deposits, proportion
RTE	= interest rate on time deposits, per cent
*RUSA	= selling rate of the Bundesbank for open market papers, per cent
*RUSBL	= yield on long-term U.S. Government securities, per cent
*S_i	= quarterly seasonal dummy variables, $i = 1, 2, 3$
SCHULU	= private holdings of bank bonds (stock outstanding minus holdings of commercial banks), billions of current DM
SEP	= demand deposits of the domestic nonbank private sector, billions of current DM
*SEST	= demand deposits of the Government sector, billions of = current DM
SPE	= savings deposits of the domestic nonbank sector, billions of current DM
*SWAP	= forward rate against U.S.-dollars (report (+), deport (−)), per cent
TEPK	= short-term time deposits of the domestic nonbank private sector, billions of current DM
TEPL	= long-term time deposits of the domestic nonbank private sector, billions of current DM
*TEST	= time deposits of the Government sector, billions of current DM
UER	= excess reserves of commercial banks (incl. vault cash), billions of current DM
*VP	= weighted average of seasonally adjusted disposable personal income (YVS)

$$= 0 \cdot 20186 \sum_{j=0}^{20} (0 \cdot 8)^j \mathrm{YVS}_{-j},$$

billions of current DM

*WP	= outstanding volume of Government securities, billions of current DM
WPB	= commercial bank holdings of Government securities, billions of current DM

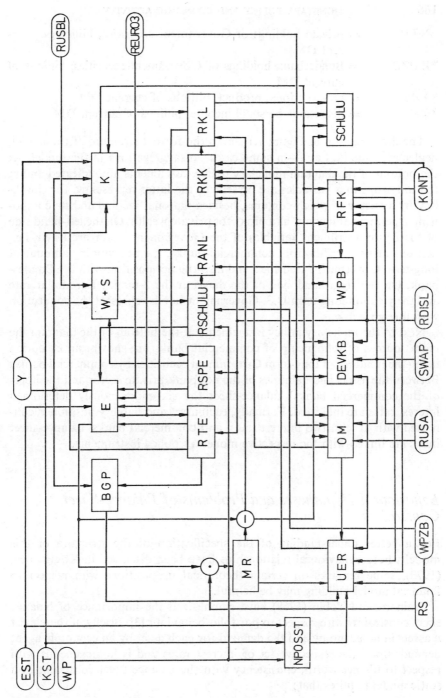

Figure 7.1. Flow diagram

WPP   = private holdings of Government securities, billions of current DM

*WPZB = Bundesbank holdings of Government securities, billions of current DM

*YBSP = gross national product, billions of current DM

*YV   = disposable personal income, billions of current DM

The flow diagram in Figure 7.1 shows the formal structure of the model, neglecting time lags and—in some cases—disaggregations in the model. At the bottom of the diagram monetary policy instruments are indicated and at the top exogenous variables are presented, the latter represented for simplicity by a vector *Y* which contains, besides national income and its components, 'permanent income' as a proxy for private wealth. On the left-hand side of the figure instrument variables of the Government sector are listed, i.e., deposits at and credits from commercial banks, the outstanding amount of long-term Government securities, and also the net position with the Bundesbank. On the right-hand side of the diagram the 3-month Eurodollar rate and the yield on long-term U.S.-Government bonds represent the connection with foreign markets.

Next to the monetary policy instruments at the bottom of the diagram the main sources of refinancing of commercial banks are shown, an exception being the holdings of long-term Government securities by commercial banks. Between the assets and liabilities of the nonbank private sector and the items of the commercial banks' balance-sheet the six endogenously determined interest rates are indicated. Formally, each asset and liability position is connected with at least two interest rates, and commercial banks' balance-sheet items are linked with the respective monetary policy instruments.

Behavioural Hypotheses and Problems of Balance-Sheet Constraints

For a better understanding of the specification of the structure of this model whose behavioural relationships have been discussed in König *et al.* (1973), some remarks on certain theoretical propositions with respect to financial model building may be helpful.

Brainard and Tobin (1968) have emphasized the importance of balance sheet constraints with respect to portfolio behaviour [3]. Briefly, if there exist *n* assets in an economy and the demand for each asset by an economic agent depends upon the respective set of interest rates and is homogeneous with respect to his net worth, consistency with the balance sheet constraint in a static model requires that:

(a) the column sum of coefficients with respect to wealth (i.e. the constants) should be equal to unity;

(b) the column sum with respect to a specific interest rate should be equal to zero;

(c) the row sum of all interest rate coefficients should also be equal to zero and

(d) the matrix of interest rate coefficients should be symmetrical.

In addition in a dynamic model in which responses of actual to desired levels are described by a partial adjustment process, all columns of the adjustment coefficient matrix must have the same sum [4].

Although we do not know of a large-scale empirically-tested model which meets all these constraints [5], there is no question that in the case of rational portfolio behaviour these restrictions have to be considered as desirable theoretical properties of financial models. In empirical work, however, there may arise some difficulties. In the present case, for instance, balance-sheet constraints (a) and (b) have not been imposed because some important assets are still not included. These are, for the private nonbank sector, mainly real capital, industrial bonds held by commercial banks, and claims (and liabilities) against foreign countries. With respect to the banking sector (besides minor items like real assets) common stocks of so-called dominated companies and participations, common stocks and industrial bonds held by banks and long-term foreign balances are the most important balance-sheet items not covered in the model.

Secondly, apart from the exclusion of some important assets, some difficulties did arise with regard to an adequate definition of the balance-sheet constraint of the private nonbank sector. Data on private net worth are not available and, therefore, permanent income has been used as a proxy, following the approach of de Leeuw (1968), p. 468. Experiments on the assumption that private asset, demand is homogeneous with respect to this variable, however, have been unsatisfactory. This corresponds with results reported by Goldfeld (1969) for the United States.

Furthermore, with respect to the column adding-up constraints we may add an argument discussed extensively by Ando and Modigliani. Both authors argue that 'paying careful attention to the adding-up constraint is not the question of estimation, but the a priori specifications of the individual equations' [6]. The adding-up constraint implies that a specific variable in an equation must appear at least in one more equation. 'The explicit attention to the adding-up constraint helps us in specifying the underlying behavioural hypothesis for all equations, because otherwise, the residual equation may look very unreasonable, meaning then that at least some of the other equations must also be unreasonable' [7]. On the other hand, if in the decision process one particular item is treated as a genuine residual, 'so long as one is careful not to specify the remaining equations to make the residual equation outrageous, from the statistical point of view, estimating the system treating one of the items as the residual is likely to be less subject to serious biases' [8].

Thirdly, even though we estimate only demand equations for a subgroup of all financial assets, theory tells us that we must, of course, deal with all interest rates. That means we have to look for interest rate effects corresponding to those assets whose demand equations are not explicitly estimated and, in addition, we should impose zero-sum constraints of interest rate coefficients on each estimated equation.

Concerning the rates of return that should be included as relevant for omitted assets, experiments have been performed with the earning-price ratio of common stocks and the rate of inflation as a proxy for the opportunity costs of holding nominal assets by the private sector and with various foreign interest rates as indicators of rates of return on foreign assets. In a strict theoretical sense, to guarantee symmetry implies then the inclusion of at least nine interest rates in each demand equation or—if the row-zero condition is imposed—eight interest rate differentials. Other non-rate variables than net worth may also be important, for instance, national income as proxy for transaction demand of money. These affect asset demands by altering the variance-covariance matrix of expected returns and, hence, all interest rate coefficients and the constants if demand is supposed to be homogeneous with respect to net worth. Needless to say, this raises further complications. To deal with those in a theoretically proper manner requires not only the inclusion of all non-rate variables but also the products of each non-rate variable times each interest rate. To fulfil all those requirements seemed to be an unmanageable task in a quarterly time series model.

In view of the resulting statistical problems in estimating such a model we proceeded in a more pragmatic way. As far as the demand equations are concerned the typical specification is as follows:

(a) Besides the 'own' interest rate each equation contains at least one other rate for a competing asset, an exception being only the demand equations for currency, demand deposits and mortgage loans.

(b) A specific interest rate appears at least in two equations.

(c) Non-rate variables are selected according to their dominant influence.

In order to guarantee the row-zero-sum condition of interest rates coefficients, interest rate differentials have been used as explanatory variables, i.e., the difference between the 'own' rate and the respective rates of other assets. Multicollinearity on the one hand, and the fact that these differences are much more dominated by error terms than the corresponding levels, resulted in most cases in poor statistical significance levels of regression coefficients. Consequently, the following procedure was adopted: interest rates of assets which are highly multicollinear due to institutional arrangements and for which on *a priori* grounds it could be assumed that the corresponding asset must not be considered as an essential alternative of portfolio decisions are excluded in the respective equation. For example, due to the so-called *Haben-Zinsabkommen*, according to which the interest rates on time deposits and savings deposits are determined by some kind of a mark-up equation from the discount rate during the first half of the sample period, the interest rate on time deposits is excluded in the demand equation for savings deposits because it is generally believed that private households as holders of the overwhelming part of savings deposits do not invest in time deposits during the sample period [9]. On the other hand, the interest rate on savings deposits does not appear in the time deposit equations because, in fact, during this period only firms held time deposits and savings deposits are not considered as an important alternative.

Specification of some of the structural equations will look very familiar to the monetary theorist. Therefore, in order to save space, we will focus attention on some special features which are essential with respect to the working of the model.

Firstly, the basic hypothesis about commercial bank behaviour is that banks are willing to accept all short-term credit demand at the going short-term loan-rate. This is based upon the fact that German banks in general consider the supply of loans as the most important part of their activity. The resulting process of credit supply has been most thoroughly described by Lutz (1970). For instance, if an increase in credit demand is assumed, commercial banks will realize this demand by additional borrowing at the Bundesbank, by repatriation of short-term foreign assets and/or by selling open market paper to the Bundesbank if excess reserves are not available or are too small to cover the loss of Central Bank money. Due to the decrease in liquid assets and/or the increase in borrowing of commercial banks from the Bundesbank, banks will gradually raise the short-term loan rate in order to reduce the demand for credits. Thus, the short-term loan rate is not directly related to credit demand but only indirectly through the changes in the liquidity position of banks.

Secondly, concerning the market for long-term securities there are two particular aspects which require comment. On the supply side, there are two types of securities: Government bonds whose supply is considered to be determined exogenously and bank bonds whose supply depends *inter alia* upon their yield. Demand for securities is also composed of two components: the demand by the nonbank private sector for which both types are considered to be homogeneous, and the demand by commercial banks for

Government securities. An increase in the supply of Government securities, for instance, which leaves the total outstanding debt of the Government unaltered, i.e., a structural change in types of debt, thus induces a rise in their yield and, hence, a reallocation of private portfolios in favour of those securities. On the other hand, an increase in the yield will cause banks to reduce the supply of bonds. Secondary effects are induced by the increase in the net position of the Government. This will result in a reduction of excess reserves and, therefore, initiate an increase in the short-term loan rate.

Finally, with respect to the supply of deposits, the very simple structural equations for the respective yields try to take into account two particular aspects of deposit rate setting. During the first half of the sample period deposit rates are estimated, according to institutional arrangements, as a function of the discount rate. With respect to the yield on savings deposits the discount rate serves even in the second part of the sample period as a guideline. These institutional relationships are modified upon the assumption of profit maximization of banks leading thus to a model of deposit rate setting similar to those used by Weber (1966) and Goldfeld and Jaffee (1970).

Simulation and Prediction Results

Introductory Remarks

In this section we are concerned with the degree to which the simulated time series of the endogenous variables conform to the actual time paths and the accuracy of *ex post* forecasts for 1972.

The question to what extent simulations are a meaningful tool for the validation of econometric models is still under debate. Those who recommend the use of simulations consider it not only as an instrument for analysing the dynamic properties of models, particularly of large-scale nonlinear models, but also as an appropriate tool to test the validity of models [10]. Critics, however, have argued that both in linear and nonlinear models simulation gives no additional information in regard to the validity of a model. According to Howrey and Kelejian (1971), for example, simulation may be used only for exploring the dynamic properties of models but not for their validation. In the case of linear models nonstochastic simulation yields a disturbance term, i.e., the difference between any element of the actual endogenous variable and its corresponding simulated value, that is both autocorrelated and heteroskedastic, while stochastic simulation implies a relationship between the observed values and the simulated values of endogenous variables similar to that of a model of errors of measurement. In nonlinear models, simulated values can be expected to diverge systematically from the corresponding historical values. Therefore, simulation may not be viewed as a proper tool for testing the validity of a model. It may, however, serve as an approximation for studying the dynamic properties of nonlinear models 'because of the difficulties involved in obtaining analytical solutions to a system of nonlinear equations' [11].

With respect to this kind of simulation, it is generally believed that the dynamic properties of nonlinear models should not be studied in terms of nonstochastic simulations because the solutions obtained when the disturbance terms of the structural equations are neglected may yield different patterns from the solutions that include these disturbances. The variability of endogenous variables is not only the result of variations in the exogenous variables but also of variations in the disturbances series. Furthermore, stochastic simulations give the possibility of evaluating the confidence limits of predicted values. On the other hand, stochastic simulations of large-scale models are very computer-time-consuming which sometimes restricts research effort.

In the following sections three types of simulations are presented to allow for a comparison of their properties: a deterministic simulation, and stochastic simulations with uncorrelated and autocorrelated disturbances respectively.

Solution of the model is based upon the Gauss–Seidel method. All types of simulations over the sample period have the actual values of lagged endogenous variables for 1960(III) as initial conditions. In the subsequent periods lagged endogenous variables enter the model with their estimated values and only exogenous variables are used with their actual values. Both uncorrelated and autocorrelated disturbances for the stochastic simulations are generated according to the method suggested by McCarthy (1972). These multivariate normally distributed pseudo-random numbers have for a large number of observations the same properties in respect to the variance-covariance matrix as those of the structural disturbances of the model. Each type of stochastic simulation has been repeated 100 times, the initial conditions being always the same.

Simulations for the Sample Period

Figures 7.2–7.11 contain graphical comparisons of the predicted time series based upon a deterministic simulation, and the observed values over the period 1960(III)–1971(IV) for selected variables. In each chart actual values are shown as a solid line and predicted values as a dashed line. Figures 7.2–7.4 show results for variables primarily related to the behaviour of the nonbank private sector, Figures 7.5–7.8 are variables of the banking system and Figures 7.9–7.11 present the results for three interest rates.

Private holdings of currency (Figure 7.2) and demand deposits (Figure 7.3) may be considered as trend-variables, the latter with a distinct seasonal pattern. Private holdings of short-term time deposits are characterized by

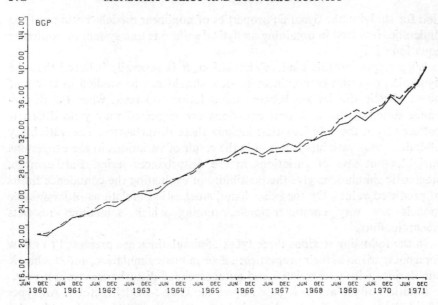

Figure 7.2. Currency holdings

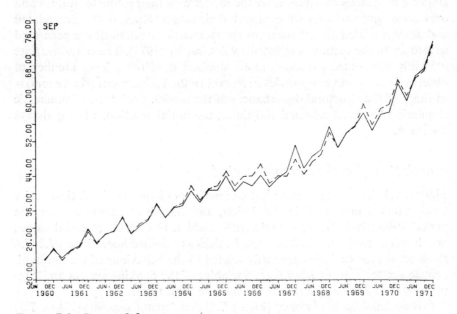

Figure 7.3. Demand deposits

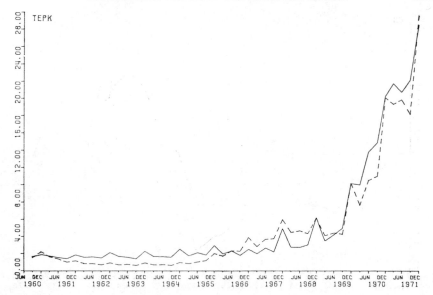

Figure 7.4. Short-term deposits

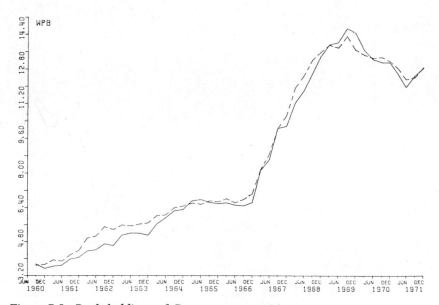

Figure 7.5. Bank holdings of Government securities

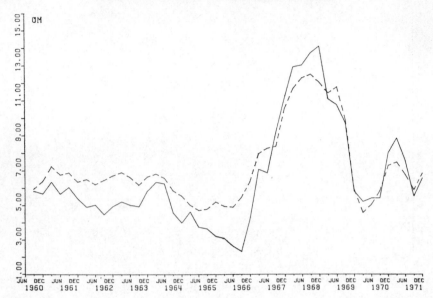

Figure 7.6. Bank holding of money market paper

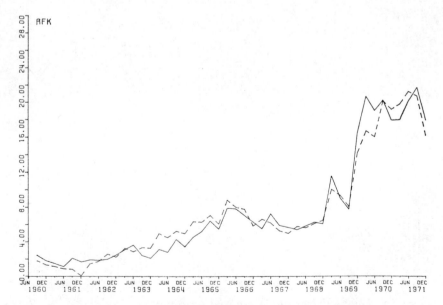

Figure 7.7. Banks borrowing from Bundesbank

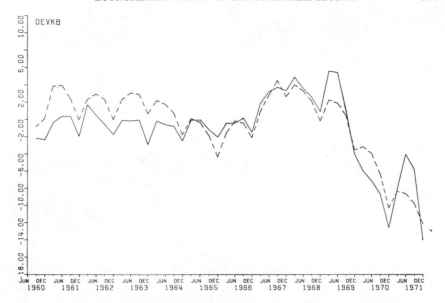

Figure 7.8. Bank holdings of short-term foreign assets

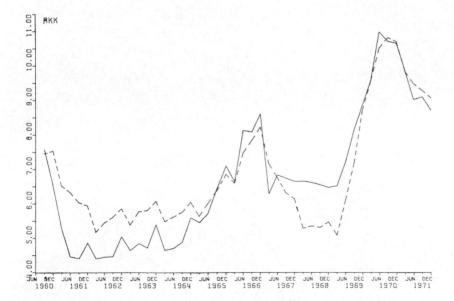

Figure 7.9. Interest rate on short-term loans

G

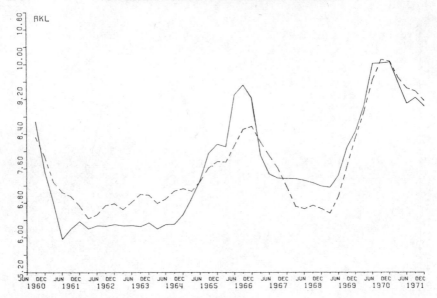

Figure 7.10. Interest rate on long-term loans

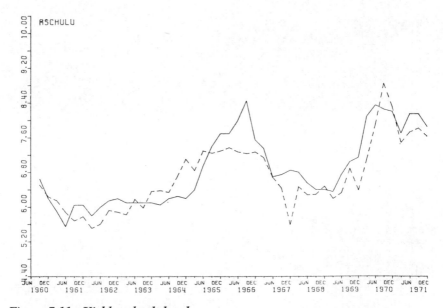

Figure 7.11. Yield on bank bonds

little variation during the first part of the sample period until 1966 and by a high rate of increase since 1967 owing to the abolition of legal maximum rates on time deposits. Whereas the percentage errors, i.e., the difference between actual and simulated values in relation to the corresponding actual value, for currency and demand deposits are very low—the highest being 2·6% for currency and 6·4% for demand deposits—those for time deposits are comparatively large. During the first part of the period with a low level of time deposits the underestimation results in errors up to 60%, declining to a maximum error of 25% later on [12].

In general simulated values of variables of the banking sector disclose a similar pattern. With the exception of commercial bank borrowing at the Bundesbank (Figure 7.7) simulated values are overestimated in the beginning of the period but approximate satisfactorily to the development during the time of rapid increases and/or fluctuations. Relative errors, therefore, are large in the beginning and decline subsequently to a maximum of 6·3% for commercial bank holdings of Government securities (Figure 7.5); 20·6% for holdings of open market papers (Figure 7.6); 20·5% for borrowing and about 115% in 1971(II) for commercial bank holdings of foreign assets (Figure 7.8).

Simulations of both the short-term and long-term loan rate yield similar results. Variables are overestimated for the period of low interest rates at the beginning of the 1960s. The peaks in 1966(IV) and 1966(III) and the subsequent decline are underestimated while there is a good approximation of the rise of interest rates in the 1970s. On the whole, the simulated series of the yield on bank bonds shows a similar picture but, in contrast to both loan rates, there is no systematic overestimation at the beginning of the sample period.

These considerations in respect of the 'goodness of fit' are confirmed by the results presented in Table 7.1. Columns 2, 5 and 8 contain the root of the dimensionless mean square error for the deterministic simulation, the mean stochastic simulation with uncorrelated errors and the mean stochastic simulation with autocorrelated errors respectively [13]. Columns labelled 'Intercept' and 'Slope' present the regression coefficients of a linear regression of actual on simulated values for the sample period. In view of the arguments by Howrey and Kelejian (1971) there are no statistical tests listed. The reader is reminded that these results may be used primarily for a comparison of the properties of the three types of simulations but not to test the validity of the model.

Firstly, in terms of RMSE the approximation of actual values by simulated values is comparatively high for holdings of currency, demand deposits and savings deposits, private and commercial bank holdings of long-term securities and both short-term and long-term loans to the private sector. Within the group of interest rates the yield on savings deposits, long-term securities and long-term loan rate is better predicted than the yield on time deposits and the short-term loan rate. The dimensionless mean square errors are comparatively large for all variables which are important in respect to the refinancing of the banking system, especially for commercial bank holdings of foreign assets and excess reserves. Notice, however, that in the context of the model excess reserves are determined by a definitional equation and, hence, pick up all the errors of the relevant structural equations. Secondly, a glance at the table shows that in terms of *RMSE* both the deterministic simulation and the stochastic simulation with autocorrelated disturbances have the same properties. The stochastic simulation with uncorrelated disturbances yields not only larger mean square errors but also regression coefficients which are in some cases very different from those of both other methods.

The variability of results of stochastic simulations is characterized by Figure 7.12 which contains charts for the standardized frequency distributions of selected variables. The distributions are based on 100 independent replications of stochastic simulations with autocorrelated disturbances [14]. In each

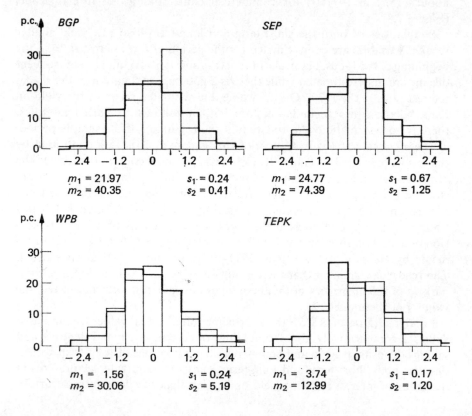

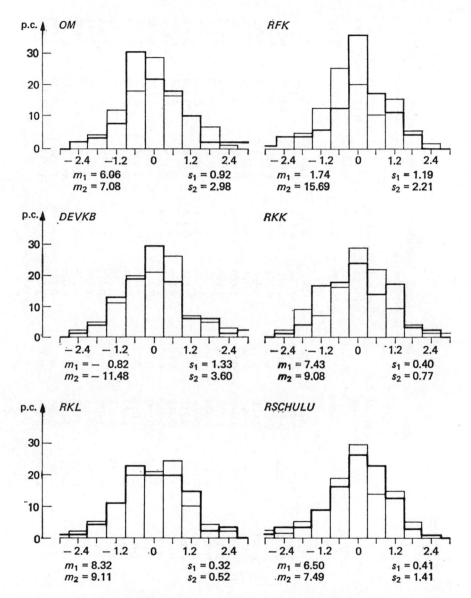

Figure 7.12. Standardized frequency distributions of selected endogenous variables, stochastic simulations with autocorrelated error terms

Table 7.1 Dynamic simulations, 1960(III)–1971(IV)

Variable	Deterministic simulation			Mean stochastic simulation (uncorrelated)			Mean stochastic simulation (autocorrelated)		
	RMSE	Regression of actual on simulated values		RMSE	Regression of actual on simulated values		RMSE	Regression of actual on simulated values	
		Intercept	Slope		Intercept	Slope		Intercept	Slope
(1)	(2)	(3)	(4)	(5)	(6)	(7)	(8)	(9)	(10)
BGP	0·014	0·235	0·989	0·016	0·724	0·970	0·013	0·257	0·989
SEP	0·024	0·208	0·991	0·025	0·832	0·973	0·024	0·175	0·992
TEPK	0·160	0·307	1·034	0·225	0·043	1·182	0·151	0·133	1·037
TEPL	0·081	2·136	0·921	0·148	−1·346	1·175	0·079	2·599	0·905
SPE	0·019	−1·000	0·992	0·048	−7·074	1·093	0·017	−0·927	0·994
WPP + SCHULU	0·020	0·516	0·996	0·031	1·420	0·956	0·020	0·439	0·997
WPB	0·042	−0·473	1·030	0·080	−1·109	1·171	0·041	−0·472	1·031
*SCHULU*ᴬ	0·026	0·117	1·000	0·032	0·393	0·974	0·026	0·053	1·001
RSCHULU	0·066	0·579	0·939	0·120	2·246	0·621	0·066	0·589	0·935
RANL	0·068	0·498	0·953	0·128	2·174	0·627	0·068	0·479	0·954
KKP	0·035	5·018	0·944	0·035	4·594	0·945	0·035	4·851	0·946
RKK	0·119	−0·463	1·043	0·134	−0·305	1·066	0·117	−0·356	1·028
KLP	0·042	−1·964	0·990	0·050	−2·414	0·985	0·040	−1·829	0·990
KLPW	0·047	3·163	1·006	0·035	3·016	0·993	0·044	2·787	1·008
RKL	0·067	−0·790	1·097	0·067	−0·777	1·093	0·066	−0·652	1·078
OM	0·175	−2·544	1·268	0·280	0·376	1·061	0·172	−2·536	1·271
RFK	0·128	−0·186	1·029	0·132	−0·412	1·011	0·131	−0·217	1·038
UER	1·253	2·308	0·155	2·062	1·855	0·128	1·288	2·322	0·141
DEVKB	0·515	−0·708	0·879	0·704	0·270	0·684	0·525	−0·697	0·890
RTE	0·137	0·141	1·004	0·179	0·034	1·100	0·136	0·148	0·999
RSPE	0·055	−0·287	0·065	0·054	−0·241	1·054	0·054	−0·243	1·054
OMZB	0·221	1·486	0·818	0·352	2·206	0·520	0·217	1·468	0·818

chart the thin line represents the distribution for 1960(III), the heavy line for 1971(IV). Means and standard deviations are given by m_1, m_2 and s_1, s_2 respectively. Standard deviations at the end of the period are much larger than those at the beginning. Furthermore, casual observation already reveals that, in general, there exists a tendency of skewness. This is confirmed by tests on normal distribution. In both periods less than 30% of empirical distributions of all endogenous variables are not significantly different from normal distribution at a 1% level [15]. The general tendency for the distributions not to be normal is caused by the nonlinearities of the model. Reduced form disturbances are nonlinear transformations of normally distributed errors of structural equations. Moreover, the charts show that in both periods at least 60% of simulated values are concentrated roughly in a two-sided one standard deviation interval around the mean.

Finally, a comparison of predicted values of endogenous variables based upon a deterministic simulation with the results of the above stochastic simulation supports the argument that the former approximates fairly well the mean values of the latter. With the exception of the predicted value of commercial bank borrowing for the period 1971(IV) all other forecasts by deterministic simulation are within a two-sided interval of two standard deviations around the mean value of stochastic simulations with autocorrelated disturbances.

Ex post *forecasts for 1972*

For the most of 1972 monetary policy was, roughly speaking, mainly characterized by efforts of the monetary authorities to reduce international interest rate differentials, especially between the Eurodollar market and the home market, and by measures to control the monetary expansion caused by extraordinary capital inflows from abroad. While foreign reserves of the Central Bank declined in December 1971 by about DM 5·5 billion, they had already increased again by 9·2 billions in the first two months of 1972. Subsequently, after a period of normalization the 'sterling-crisis' and, in turn, the weakness of the dollar swept foreign reserves in again in considerable amounts. For the first time since the liberalization of international capital movements in the late 1950s the monetary authorities tried to support the use of traditional policy instruments by newly-introduced legal regulations for private nonbank borrowing from abroad and by administrative interventions with respect to the selling of domestic securities to foreigners. Starting on 1 March 1972, private nonbanks were obliged to hold 40% (after 1 July 50%) of their borrowings from abroad without any interest payments at the Bundesbank (*Bardepotpflicht*). Private nonbank capital imports, induced by low foreign interest rates, declined very sharply owing to this increase in the costs of borrowing. Furthermore, after the beginning of July 1972, the selling of domestic open market paper and long-term securities to foreigners had to be formally approved by the Bundesbank. According to the reports of the Bundesbank [16] this reduced transactions with foreigners from about DM 10 billion during the first two quarters of 1972 to less than 0·1 billion until October.

The need for nonbank borrowers to hold non-interest bearing deposits from foreign credits at the Bundesbank as well as the need for legal approval of security sales to foreigners are not simple restrictions with respect to the functioning of the capital markets more or less in accord with previous experience. They probably influenced behavioural relationships and, therefore, an explicit treatment of possible structural changes would be desirable. This, however, is impossible due to missing data.

Table 7.2 reports the results of *ex post* forecasts. Column 3 contains the percentage prediction errors of 'naive' forecasts assuming that the yearly rate of change of each quarter in 1972 equals the yearly rate of change of the corresponding quarter in 1971 [17] .Columns 4–6 and 7–9 show the percentage prediction errors for a deterministic simulation and for the mean values of 100 replications of stochastic simulations with autocorrelated disturbances. The labelling of columns by quarter i at the top means that the corresponding prediction starts in each case the i-th quarter before the forecast quarter. For instance, quarter 1 means that forecasts use as lagged endogenous variables actual values of the previous period. Four-quarter forecasts are, therefore, simulations implying a time horizon of one year for the forecaster.

A glance at Table 7.2 reveals that the predictions of the model are in general superior to naive forecasts. Root mean square errors for all variables in Table 7.2 over the whole forecasting period are 0·243 for naive forecasts and 0·112 for four-quarter predictions by deterministic simulation. Root mean square errors of naive forecasts for individual variables for the forecasting period are only in five cases smaller than the corresponding of four-quarter deterministic predictions, the important cases being private holdings of long-term time deposits, the yield on bank bonds and commercial bank holdings of foreign assets.

The comparatively large prediction errors of the model for the yield on long-term securities may be attributed at least partly to the particular developments in the monetary sector mentioned above. For example, the large increase of foreign demand for long-term securities at the beginning of 1972 is not reflected in a corresponding rate of growth of (domestic) private wealth. Hence, there will be a tendency to overestimate the yield on long-term securities. On the other hand, the reduction of transactions with foreigners caused by the interventions of the Bundesbank will lead to an opposite effect. Moreover, prediction errors are influenced by speculative international capital

Table 7.2 *Prediction errors (per cent) for alternative forecasting types*
(− denotes over-estimation, + denotes underestimation)

Variable	Time	Naive	Deterministic			Stochastic		
			quarter			quarter		
			1	2	4	1	2	4
(1)	(2)	(3)	(4)	(5)	(6)	(7)	(8)	(9)
BGP	1972 (1)	6·1	−0·2	−0·2	−0·3	−0·1	−0·2	−0·3
	(2)	6·3	1·5	1·5	1·1	1·6	1·6	1·1
	(3)	4·1	−0·6	0·4	0·4	−0·6	0·4	0·3
	(4)	3·8	1·8	1·3	1·6	1·8	1·3	+1·6
SEP	1972 (1)	3·7	0·3	0·7	0·8	0·3	0·6	0·7
	(2)	0·3	2·3	2·3	2·3	2·2	2·2	2·2
	(3)	−2·0	1·1	2·5	2·4	1·0	2·3	2·2
	(4)	−0·6	0·6	0·9	1·4	0·5	0·9	1·3
TEPK	1972 (1)	−95·3	−5·8	−8·6	3·8	−7·2	−8·1	3·1
	(2)	−19·3	5·6	1·2	4·8	4·6	0·1	5·8
	(3)	−29·2	14·5	12·9	8·3	12·1	10·8	7·4
	(4)	−24·5	−14·5	−6·0	−6·4	−13·2	−6·3	−6·9
TEPL	1972 (1)	16·9	6·0	8·1	12·6	6·2	8·2	12·0
	(2)	7·0	−3·8	7·4	10·2	−4·5	7·2	9·4
	(3)	11·4	3·0	2·1	15·8	2·7	1·3	15·7
	(4)	10·6	4·4	7·6	20·2	4·3	7·1	19·8
SPE	1972 (1)	1·2	0·0	0·5	0·2	0·0	0·5	0·1
	(2)	1·3	0·5	1·2	1·4	0·5	1·2	1·3
	(3)	1·4	−0·3	−0·6	1·5	−0·3	−0·7	1·4
	(4)	0·3	−0·7	−1·5	0·5	−0·7	−1·5	0·4
WPP+ SCHULU	1972 (1)	3·3	4·1	4·6	4·2	4·1	4·6	4·2
	(2)	8·0	2·5	7·1	7·4	2·5	7·1	7·5
	(3)	9·4	0·6	3·7	7·5	0·7	3·8	7·5
	(4)	7·6	0·5	1·3	6·0	0·5	1·3	6·1
WPB	1972 (1)	16·2	1·6	0·1	1·5	1·7	0·1	1·4
	(2)	15·3	−2·9	−6·2	−6·7	−3·3	−6·6	−7·2
	(3)	6·5	1·9	−5·7	−10·1	1·7	−6·2	−10·5
	(4)	−0·2	−3·3	−2·6	−11·2	−3·1	−2·7	−11·6
SCHULU[A]	1972 (1)	3·1	5·9	6·3	5·9	5·8	6·2	5·6
	(2)	8·7	2·9	8·7	9·1	2·9	8·6	9·0
	(3)	8·2	1·1	4·2	8·7	1·2	4·2	8·7
	(4)	7·9	0·2	1·4	6·6	0·2	1·4	6·6
RSCHULU	1972 (1)	3·7	−15·6	−19·4	−20·8	−15·4	−19·1	−20·2
	(2)	1·8	33·6	9·6	9·5	34·7	10·6	10·4
	(3)	0·6	23·1	11·1	−6·5	23·3	11·7	−6·6
	(4)	11·6	26·5	26·1	9·2	26·5	26·2	9·3
KKP	1972 (1)	5·8	0·7	2·1	2·8	0·7	2·1	2·8
	(2)	8·6	4·3	4·5	6·1	4·3	4·6	6·2
	(3)	4·7	0·6	3·9	4·8	0·5	3·8	4·7
	(4)	2·1	3·6	4·0	6·5	3·6	4·0	6·5

Variable	Time	Naive	Deterministic			Stochastic		
			quarter			quarter		
			1	2	4	1	2	4
(1)	(2)	(3)	(4)	(5)	(6)	(7)	(8)	(9)
RKK	1972 (1)	−23·6	9·9	7·2	6·1	10·0	7·7	6·2
	(2)	1·5	−4·1	5·5	3·1	−4·0	5·7	3·3
	(3)	−1·7	3·0	−1·1	4·7	3·0	−1·0	5·0
	(4)	15·6	0·7	3·9	4·1	0·2	3·4	3·6
KLP	1972 (1)	1·6	−0·1	−0·2	0·5	−0·2	−0·3	0·4
	(2)	1·6	0·1	−0·0	0·9	0·2	0·0	0·9
	(3)	−0·3	1·4	1·6	1·4	1·3	1·6	1·3
	(4)	−0·0	1·4	2·9	3·0	1·4	2·9	2·9
KLPW	1972 (1)	2·6	−0·2	−0·1	−0·2	−0·2	−0·1	−0·2
	(2)	3·1	−0·0	−0·3	0·0	0·0	−0·4	−0·0
	(3)	2·7	−0·3	−0·3	−0·6	−0·3	−0·2	−0·6
	(4)	3·2	1·1	0·6	0·0	1·1	0·6	0·0
RKL	1972 (1)	−16·2	2·7	1·3	0·3	3·1	2·3	1·1
	(2)	0·2	−3·6	1·1	−0·8	−3·5	1·5	−0·2
	(3)	−1·7	2·2	−1·7	1·3	2·4	−1·4	1·7
	(4)	8·1	3·1	5·5	4·7	2·9	5·4	4·7
OM	1972 (1)	−131·6	−1·2	−5·8	−8·7	0·3	−3·7	−8·0
	(2)	−59·4	8·1	11·8	1·4	4·9	9·4	−1·4
	(3)	0·3	−4·7	−16·7	−11·6	−3·9	−18·6	−12·0
	(4)	−32·9	−10·8	−14·6	−16·1	−10·1	−13·6	−17·2
RFK	1972 (1)	15·0	−5·1	−9·3	−2·5	−5·8	−9·8	−2·5
	(2)	−34·9	2·8	−10·3	−7·4	4·6	−9·7	−6·8
	(3)	−16·4	5·9	9·8	−5·2	5·7	10·3	−5·6
	(4)	3·8	34·4	42·1	29·1	33·8	41·4	28·2
DEVKB	1972 (1)	−25·7	126·5	88·6	71·2	126·7	91·1	73·6
	(2)	−37·5	−37·6	52·4	35·0	−37·4	52·7	34·7
	(3)	−25·5	57·2	4·9	30·1	55·4	2·7	28·1
	(4)	−16·5	−3·0	31·4	−10·2	−3·3	29·8	−12·4
RTE	1972 (1)	−21·5	−1·9	−4·0	−2·5	−1·7	−2·4	−1·7
	(2)	12·7	−4·0	0·5	−1·0	−3·5	1·1	0·2
	(3)	−8·8	6·1	0·6	6·0	5·1	0·0	6·3
	(4)	21·7	21·7	26·7	28·1	21·7	26·2	27·8
RSPE	1972 (1)	−19·7	6·8	6·8	6·0	6·9	7·3	6·2
	(2)	−0·4	0·1	5·1	4·5	−0·2	4·9	4·5
	(3)	−0·6	5·6	4·0	7·0	5·4	3·7	6·9
	(4)	−0·3	3·4	6·8	7·3	3·9	7·2	7·7

movements and by the counteracting policies of monetary authorities. Commercial bank holdings of foreign assets, i.e., their net liabilities, are systematically under-estimated during the periods of exchange speculation (first and third quarter). The marked underestimation of the interest rate on time deposits for the last quarter of 1972 may be partly the result of structural change of private borrowing in favour of domestic credits caused by the *Bardepotpflicht*.

Both deterministic and stochastic simulations yield almost identical results. Percentage prediction errors show small but not systematic differences. As one would expect, forecasts starting one quarter before the forecasting period approximate actual values in general better than those assuming a longer time horizon of the forecaster. For deterministic simulation prediction errors of one-quarter (four-quarter) forecasts are less than 2% in 41 (30)%, between 2 and 5% in 29 (20)% and between 5 and 10% in 14 (30)% of all cases. In view of the particular developments mentioned at the beginning of this paragraph forecasts may be considered to be satisfactory.

Footnotes

* Abridged version.
1. In contrast to Kloek & Mennes (1960) only the same set of principal components is used. Predetermined variables in individual equations are neglected as proposed by Dhrymes (1970), pp. 264–72.
   Eigenvalues and eigenvectors of the correlation matrix of predetermined variables are computed with the subroutine Eigen, IBM Applications Program, H 20-0205-3, White Plains, 1968, pp. 164–5. Regressions are performed with a modified version of Regre, IBM Applications Program, *ibid.*, p. 407.
2. K. F. Wallis (1972).
3. See also Parkin (1970a) & (1970b), Ladenson (1971), Clinton (1973) and Ladenson; (1973).
4. M. L. Ladenson (1973), p. 1005.
5. In fact, there are only a few empirical studies which deal for a small number of assets explicit with these constraints. See, for instance, Courakis (1975) & (1974), Feige (1964), Gramlich & Kalchbrenner (1969), Gramlich & Hulett (1972), Parkin (1970a) and (1970b), White (1975).
6. Ando & Modigliani (1972), p. 31.
7. Ando & Modigliani (1972), p. 31.
8. Ando & Modigliani (1972), p. 33.
9. This attitude has changed since 1972 with the increasing rate of inflation. This is indicated in the recent flow of funds statistics of the Bundesbank which contain for the first time data on household holdings of time deposits.
10. For example, Boughton & Naylor (1971), p. 363.
11. Howrey & Kelejian (1971), p. 309.
12. It has been argued that a structural change exists in regard to the development of time deposits due to the abolition of legal maximum rates. Tests with separate demand and supply functions for sub-periods have as yet been unsuccessful.
13. The root of the dimensionless mean square error is defined as follows:

$$RMSE = (\sum_i (A_i - P_i)^2 / \sum_i A_i^2)^{1/2}$$

with A_t: actual value and P_t: predicted value by simulation in period i, $i = 1, \ldots$, T.

14. Lack of space prevents reproduction of the results of the stochastic simulations with uncorrelated error terms. Furthermore, results of Table 7.1 suggest that simulations with autocorrelated disturbances yield a better approximation of actual values.

15. For normality test see Gebhardt (1966).

16. See *Deutsche Bundesbank Monthly Report*, December 1972, p. 6.

17. The predicted value is:

$$x^*(t + 4) = x(t) + \frac{x(t) - x(t - 4)}{|x(t - 4)|} x(t)$$

An Econometric Model of the Financial Sector of the Federal Republic of Germany—a Comment

GORDON FISHER

I came to this paper ignorant of the institutional background of the financial sector of the Federal Republic of Germany and about the availability of financial statistics for this country, so it is clearly difficult for me to be confidently critical or constructive about a piece of work which builds on these two essential elements. Having studied the paper in detail and listened to Professor König's remarks, however, I must now gratefully acknowledge to being much less ignorant than I was at the outset. I particularly liked the way in which the institutional background and the availability of data were used to argue the case for excluding certain supply equations from the model, and the case for a special treatment of the market for long-term securities. Too often what is presented in support of a particular econometric structure is couched in terms which are not clearly related to institutional features or data availability, and this tends to hide the real truth of what has been done and why. The paper and König's presentation were particularly helpful in this respect.

My own interest in models of the financial sector stems from a more fundamental interest in the transmission mechanism of monetary policy. In contemporary models of Western economies, it is not unusual to characterize the transmission mechanism by wealth, credit availability and cost of capital effects on the real sector; and among these, wealth effects have been demonstrated to be of strategic importance, particularly (in recent years) the inflationary aspects of wealth-holding. König, Gaab and Wolters (KGW for short) deal only with the financial sector, so the transmission mechanism is as yet unspecified and will remain so until a real sector has been grafted on to their model. This absence of a real sector and the accompanying transmission mechanism tends to cloud various weaknesses in their model. Take, for example, the demand for currency equation. This is made a function, *inter alia*, of nominal disposable personal income, a not unusual formulation. However, given that the demand for currency is primarily a transactions demand, it would seem sensible to make this equation consistent with the consumption function, when such a function is introduced within a real sector. To the extent that the consumption function would depend on permanent income, then one would expect the demand for currency equation to depend on the same variable. Yet even here a weakness of the model would be masked, for KGW argue for the use of permanent income *as a proxy for wealth*, on the ground of data availability, not as a variable in its own right. Moreover, a direct measure of wealth would throw up the need for its endogenous generation within the model and thereby highlight the need for proper consideration of the equity market and of accounting constraints on asset holding equations, both of which are lacking in the present model. An empirical treatment of these considerations plus a wealth-dependent consumption function would then allow wealth to play its full and proper role in the transmission mechanism. On the other side of the coin, a wealth-dependent currency demand equation would be an important source of real feed-back effects on the financial sector.

More generally, the absence of a real sector, and hence of endogenous feedback to the supply side of the financial sector, would seem to limit the range of behaviour that may be captured in the KGW specification. For example, what would otherwise be endogenous arguments determining the Central Bank's reactions to real sector developments must be treated as exogenous or the reactions themselves left unexplained and thereby made exogenous. The same would obviously apply in respect of anti-inflation policy. Thus given a regime of fixed exchange rates and the openness of the West German economy, the money supply can only be determined domestically by neutralizing international financial flows so as to maintain domestic monetary policy objectives. This has, of course, long been recognized as technically impossible in anything but the short run. And full recognition of this behavioural interplay requires an endogenous treatment not only of the money supply itself but also of the arguments determining that supply (Willms (1971), Porter (1972)).

As indicated, KGW introduce permanent income as a proxy for wealth on the ground of data availability. Yet the same could be said of early attempts to incorporate wealth into financial models of the U.S., a difficulty which was eventually overcome by the construction of an appropriate wealth series by the model-builders themselves. Econometric model-building, as I am sure KGW are aware, is not only about using readily available series; it is also about the tedious job of constructing series which are not immediately available but which are necessary for a proper evaluation of the theory upon which the model is based. I hope this will not detract from what KGW have already achieved; indeed, it is intended more in the way of encouragement to undertake further research than as criticism of what has been developed so far.

One consequence of using a proxy for wealth is that proper adding-up restrictions cannot be made to apply. We may interpret this as a specification error, except to the extent that we recognize and impose a further restriction which defines wealth in terms of the empirical estimates of permanent income. If we do not recognize this additional restriction we obfuscate the full implications of what we are doing. The use of permanent income in place of wealth undoubtedly gets round the practical problem of data availability, but it also throws up the need for an additional restraint on the system which cannot be imposed for the very reasons that lead us to the notion of permanent income in the first place. But this subtle point aside, KGW are right, in my opinion, to emphasize the importance of restrictions on wealth-holding equations, and they are careful to explain the practical and other reasons why such restrictions are not imposed. I think a few comments are called for here.

In considering restrictions it is important, in my view, to distinguish between constraints that should apply to ensure that adding-up criteria are satisfied, and constraints which are implied by virtue of assumptions about behaviour. I shall call the former adding-up constraints and the latter behavioural constraints. On p. 167 KGW list five constraints in all: (a) and (b) are adding-up constraints; (c) and (d) are behavioural constraints, and there is an additional behavioural constraint arising out of the assumed dynamic adjustment process. I have some difficulty understanding the need for (c), for if the symmetry restriction (d) and the adding-up constraints apply, it is surely the case that (c) follows as a logical consequence of the other three (i.e. (a) (b) and (d). On the contrary, (a) (b) and (c) do not imply (d), so in this sense (d) is an additional restriction, even though it makes (c) redundant.

Turning now to the reason for distinguishing adding-up from behavioural restrictions, it is this: the former *may* be satisfied automatically in an unconstrained estimation of every asset-holding equation, but in general, behavioural restrictions *must be imposed and tested*. Leaving aside the symmetry restrictions for the moment, KGW quote Ando and Modigliani to the effect that adding-up constraints are not 'the question of estimation but (of) the *a priori* specifications of the individual equations'. To the extent that adding-up restrictions are automatically satisfied, this is undoubtedly correct. Thus if we have linear wealth-holding equations each containing the same explanatory variables and, say, 2SLS is applied to every equation, then it must be the case that the adding-up restrictions on coefficients will be satisfied. No restrictions need be applied. Moreover it is then immaterial whether we estimate all equations, or estimate all but one and leave the final equation to be determined as a residual. But if each equation does not contain the same explanatory variables, it will not generally be true that the adding-up constraints will automatically apply: they will have to be imposed in much the same way as the symmetry restrictions would need to be imposed. Ando & Modigliani suggest that a convenient way of handling this problem is to estimate all but one equation and derive the remaining one to satisfy the adding-up criteria, and that this residual equation should be carefully selected so as not to make it outrageous from a specification point of view.

Practically speaking, this is a reasonable procedure, but it is nevertheless arbitrary; it would appear that the adding-up constraints could equally well be satisfied by estimating all equations subject to the required coefficient restrictions which ensure that the sum of wealth-holding is precisely equal to total wealth. If this is correct, then in this case the adding-up restrictions are no different from behavioural restrictions and, since the latter are in principle testable, so are the former, whence one has, via the tests, a statistical device for checking whether the restrictions are acceptable to the data, and hence whether the specifications are also acceptable. While this approach would seem less arbitrary than that suggested by Ando & Modigliani, it turns out that the two are equivalent, at least in a special sense. The reason for this (though KGW fail to note it) is that the adding-up requirements will not be satisfied unless it is also recognized that the sum of the errors across all equations must be zero. This linear dependence in the errors ensures singularity of the covariance matrix. Thus, if we take account of covariation between equations (as we ought to on the ground of efficient use of information), then we run into the difficulty of calculating the inverse of a singular matrix. If we handle this problem by use of a generalized inverse, then it turns out that restricted least squares is invariant to the choice of generalized inverse and hence to the choice of the residual asset. Presumably the same result also applies to more general linear estimation methods. On these matters see Sparks (1974) and Powell (1969).

Of course, if we admit to non-linear asset equations, additional difficulties arise. It is not then generally possible to impose the adding-up restrictions, unless some linear equations are also admitted. Unfortunately, these place undue strain on the linear part of the system and thereby raise awkward questions about the interpretation to be placed on the estimates.

I hope this protracted discussion of constraints clarifies the Ando-Modigliani view in the context that KGW chose to state it. It is, I fear, a little less straightforward than KGW seem to imply. Indeed, it is difficult to evaluate the consequences of not imposing adding-up restrictions at this stage, even with simulations, since an incomplete model is not fully checkable. When the coverage of the financial sector is complete and a real sector added, an evaluation of this kind will not only become feasible, but also crucial, at least in principle. This is because the greatest interest centres on the 'ultimate' effects of financial sector developments on real economic magnitudes, and since wealth would then be a most important transmitting variable, a crudeness in the estimation of financial stimuli may exacerbate the behaviour of aggregate expenditures by failure to confine effects by appropriate restrictions.

Turning now to other features of the model, I was surprised by the general absence of inflationary effects. In the wealth-holding equations, for example, only holdings of savings deposits feature a term in the rate of change of prices. Similarly, there are no anticipated inflationary effects in the long-term loan rate equation; equally surprising, there are no anticipated exchange rate effects either. These omissions call for comment. The long-term loan rate is generated, *inter alia*, by the current value of the short rate and the once- and twice-lagged long rate. This structure would seem to be in marked contrast to the long-rate equations in contemporary U.S. models, where a considerable amount of good structural modelling has been done. For example, in the MPS model, the long-rate is explained by a long distributed lag of the short rate, the expected rate of change in prices and a term reflecting recent instability in the short rate, the last-mentioned feature causing a significant asymmetry between expansionary and contractionary monetary policies. It should be emphasized that, if there are differences between these corresponding equations in the MPS and the KGW models—and there are— they are not essentially to be found in the relations between the long and the short rates. In the KGW model, for example, equation (7.16) may be rewritten (with B as the backward shift operator) as

$$(1 - 0.748B + 0.298B^2)r_L = \lambda + \theta x + 0.311r_S,$$

where r_L is the long rate, r_S the short rate, λ represents a set of quarterly constants and x the ratio of long-term loans to the lagged value of total deposits less required reserves. Abstracting from consideration of variation in x, it is clear that a finite moving average on r_L is related to the current value of r_S. Since the moving average part is in this case invertible, it follows that r_L may also be expressed as an *infinite*, stable lag distribution on the short rate, r_S. If we approximate this infinite lag distribution by a long finite lag in r_S, it is readily seen that the long-rate equations in the MPS and KGW models conform to the extent of the restrictions and the approximation described. Where they are different is in the remaining terms. In particular, having carried out the inversion on the KGW equation, there will be an infinite lag on x and this must be compared, in the MPS model, with the expected rate of increase in prices and the recent instability in the short rate; and of these two I would regard the latter as a rather special (U.S.) feature.

Now as indicated above, I would expect a long-term loan rate for the Federal Republic of Germany to be influenced by the expected exchange rate and the expected rate of increase in prices (in the U.S. I would expect only the latter, since the U.S. is in the nature of a closed economy compared with West Germany). In particular, an expected increase in the DM relative to the U.S. $ will encourage trading in favour of the former and thereby also encourage an increase in deposits (from 'abroad'); and this increase will, after some delay, lead to a decrease in the long rate, until the demand for loans is itself affected. On the other hand, an anticipated rise in the domestic rate of inflation will, *ceteris paribus*, increase the demand for (long-term) loans to the extent that the funds provided may be used to avoid the effects of price increases when they come. Briefly—and crudely—this is the story the KGW long-rate equation tells us. Thus, structural considerations aside, what KGW appear to have done is to cut through a great deal of sophisticated and tedious calculation by routing expected exchange rate and inflationary effects through the ratio x of loans to lagged deposits minus reserves [1]. This ratio measures the *outcome* of decisions (in so far as they are relevant) about loans and deposits which are *caused* by expected movements in prices and the exchange rate. What is missing is the appropriate structural link from these expectations variables to the ratio x.

I should like to encourage KGW to pursue this point further in their future research, for two reasons. Firstly, it would seem desirable, from a purely structural viewpoint, that the links described should be explored in order to effect a more complete causal theory of behaviour. Secondly, it would appear from the simulations that the rate equations in general, and the long rate in particular, are less satisfactory than, for example, the wealth-holding equations, from the point of view of their ability to capture observed time-paths.

Another area where I would anticipate the expected exchange rate playing a role is in respect of short-term capital flows from abroad. I see this as an important and interesting feature of the West German economy. But again I am unhappy about the structural features of the KGW model in this respect, principally because expected exchange rate effects are evidently by-passed. In the model, capital flows from abroad have an initial impact on the short rate which then gets passed on to the long rate and thence to the savings deposit rate. Presumably capital flows are controlled primarily via the discount rate, except to the extent that there may be offsetting effects via the supply of bank bonds, the commercial banks' holdings of foreign assets and the general effects that total deposits have on the rest of the system. In addition, control is also effected by a range of (changing) administrative rules, and these, together with data limitations, work against a structural formulation and evaluation of this process. Again, data problems permitting, I would encourage further research in this field, particularly in respect of the structural modelling of capital flows and their management via expected exchange rate effects.

Footnote

1. If equation (7.16) is re-written $\gamma(B)r_L = \lambda + \theta x + \beta r_s$ where $\gamma(B)$ represents the second-order polynomial in B, then $r_L = \alpha + \theta\gamma^{-1}(B)x + \beta\gamma^{-1}(B)r_s$, α being the appropriate constant. If further $\gamma^{-1}(B) = \delta(B)$ and we regard $\delta(B)x = x^*$ as an expectation term, then we may think of expected exchange rate and inflationary effects being routed via *expectations* on x, namely x^*.

8

Further Evidence on the Relative Importance of Fiscal and Monetary Actions in the Federal Republic of Germany*

NIKOLAUS K. A. LÄUFER

The Work of Andersen and Jordan

In a study for the United States Andersen and Jordan (referred to as A & J) found the response of economic activity to measures of monetary policy to be larger, more reliable and faster than the corresponding response to measures of fiscal policy [1]. Economic activity was measured by nominal GNP. The narrow money stock and the extended monetary base were used as alternative indicators of monetary policy, while fiscal policy was represented either by the high employment surplus or by its components, full employment expenditures and full employment tax receipts of the Government.

The narrow money stock is composed of currency and demand deposits. The monetary base may be defined from the user's side by summing currency, banks' actual reserves at the Central Bank and vault cash of banks. The extended monetary base is obtained by further adding (cumulated) past changes of legally required reserves. The high employment budget surplus is an estimate of the Government budget surplus defined in the framework of national income analysis for a more or less arbitrary level of high employment economic activity. As an indicator of changes in direction and strength of discretionary fiscal policy, the concept of a high employment budget attempts to eliminate the influence of current changes in GNP on the budget position by measuring Government expenditures and receipts at a level of GNP consistent with full or high employment [2].

The tests performed by A & J are based on estimates of coefficients and statistics in an equation of the following distributed lag type:

$$Y_t = a + bt + \sum_{i=0}^{l_m} m_i I_{t-i}^m + \sum_{j=0}^{l_f} f_j I_{t-j}^f + u_t \qquad (8.1)$$

where

$Y_t =$ nominal GNP in period t
    (measure of economic activity)
  $t =$ measure of trend if not an index of the time period
$I^m_{t-j} =$ indicator of monetary policy in period $t - j$
$I^f_{t-j} =$ indicator of fiscal policy in period $t - j$
  $u_t =$ stochastic error term

$m_0(f_0)$ is a measure of the impact of monetary (fiscal) policy, while $m_1, m_2, \ldots (f_1, f_2, \ldots)$ are measures or weights of lagged effects. $l_m(l_f)$ represents the maximal length of the lag of monetary (fiscal) policy.

The total ($=$ impact $+$ lagged) effects of monetary (fiscal) policy are given by the total sum of coefficients, i.e.

$$\sum_{i=0}^{l_m} m_i \text{ and } \sum_{j=0}^{l_f} f_j$$

The hypotheses of A & J relate to the difference in *size* of (estimated) sums of coefficients, to the differences in *reliability* of statistical estimates and to the difference in *time* necessary for lagged effects of both types of policy to show up. Reliability is measured by t-ratios, which indicate the degree of significance that may be attached to estimated coefficients. The difference in time may either be measured by the difference in average lag or by the difference in total lag [3].

The Interpretation of the Andersen and Jordan Equation

Equation (8.1) does not represent a specific theory or a specific model. It should be interpreted as either a final form equation or as an interim form, if not as a reduced form equation [4]. It defines a class of models or theories whose elements have final, interim or reduced forms containing at least an equation of the type represented by equation (8.1). Since the error term u_t may be interpreted to contain linear combinations of additional predetermined and/or exogenous variables, the models of this class are not necessarily limited to the exogenous variables

$$I^m_t, I^m_{t-1}, \ldots \text{ and } I^f_t, I^f_{t-1}, \ldots.$$

From these considerations it is obvious that equation (8.1) does not imply a specific concept of the transmission mechanism [5] for impulses of monetary and fiscal policy [6].

An expansion of the extended monetary base while the fiscal indicator remains constant is the consequence of (*i*) *pure* open market policy [7], (*ii*) lowering the rates of legally required reserves and (*iii*) a change in financing a given *constant* budget deficit by using Central Bank credit instead of selling

Government securities. With a given *constant* monetary base, financing an increase of the Government budget deficit (pure fiscal policy) may mean financing by displacing private demand for finance capital. This way of financing has been termed 'crowding-out' [8]. Crowding-out of borrowing for private expenditures can cause negative partial and even negative total effects of *pure* fiscal policy [9]; i.e. it may cause single negative f_j-coefficient and even cause a negative sum total of those coefficients. The crowding-out interpretation is particularly important in discussing statistical results. It is obvious from these considerations that positive m_i-coefficients and f_j-coefficients of either sign are capable of an economic interpretation.

Appropriate Measures of Fiscal and Monetary Policy

There are various shortcomings of the full employment Government budget surplus FES as an indicator of fiscal policy. The concept is difficult to estimate and it is based on a series of doubtful assumptions with respect to growth of real income, inflation and the distribution of income. The main defect stems from the upward trend in full-employment tax receipts FET, which is a consequence of growth in full-employment GNP. Due to this trend the FES changes even where Government expenditures and tax rates remain unchanged. Thus, normal growth of real income, reinforced by inflation according to the GNP deflator, introduces an upward movement of the FES without any discretionary change in fiscal policy. Especially during periods of inflation, the irregular behaviour of the GNP deflator, applied for converting real GNP into nominal GNP, would introduce a strongly fluctuating endogenous dependence into the FES observations. Therefore, we have used the intitial stimulus (IS) concept instead of the FES as a fiscal policy indicator [10].

The IS-concept attempts to include exclusively those movements in the budget, which are caused by discretionary acts of fiscal policy. We consider as discretionary on the expenditure side all variations in total Government expenditures and on the revenue side all initial [11] variations in tax receipts due to changes in tax rates, the tax base and/or the terms of payments. In this concept changes in tax receipts due to changes in economic activity (income growth) or prices (inflation) are omitted.

An unbiased indicator of monetary policy should take account only of those movements in the stock of money which are the exclusive result of actions of monetary policy. Policy-induced changes in the quantity of money are due either to Central Bank controlled movements in the monetary base or to variations in the money multiplier in consequence of changes in legally required reserve ratios. The money stock as an indicator of monetary policy includes both these factors, but it is also influenced by the behaviour of banks and the non-bank public. The *ordinary* monetary base does not include the impact of the required reserves policy. Therefore, as an indicator of monetary policy, it is incomplete. Yet, the concept of the *extended* base permits the disadvantages of both these indicators to be avoided. By adding the so-called 'liberated reserves' [12] to the ordinary monetary base one obtains the *extended* base. The extended base thus is a summary indicator of all acts of monetary policy which are important from an aggregative point of view [13]. From these considerations it follows that the quantity of money is the worst, the ordinary monetary base is a better and the extended monetary base is the best among the three indicators of monetary policy.

Aspects of Trend-Removal

For the purpose of stabilization policy in a growing economy one is interested in *cyclical* relations between measures of policy and economic activity and not in relations between *trend* components of these measures. One is looking for the effects of an acceleration or a deceleration in the rate of growth of policy variables on the rate of growth in economic activity. Therefore, some attention should be given to the method of eliminating trend from the variables to be correlated.

If there is *linear* trend in all variables, its influence is correctly captured by the term bt of equation (8.1). In this case, using first differences of variables is a successful method of trend elimination. But if the trend is nonlinear, first differences are an inappropriate method and eventually introduce bias in favour of monetary policy. Actually, this may be observed in the F.R.G. where the trend in economic activity is better correlated with measures of monetary policy than with measures of fiscal policy. If this nonlinear trend is *exponential*, then the use of growth rates of variables is a successful method of trend elimination. In addition, for the F.R.G. during the period 1960 to 1970 first differences of quarterly GNP and quarterly money stock still showed a significant upward trend [14]. This indicates a nonlinear trend which may be approximated exponentially. Thus, in the case of the F.R.G. first differences are not a sufficient method to eliminate trend and the use of growth rates seems to be an improvement. Growth rates have the additional advantages of reducing heteroskedaticity of the residuals and of reducing multicollinearity among the variables.

Empirical Results

In the tabular survey, Table 8.1, we have summarized the technical details of the procedure underlying our empirical results. We may emphasize that no

Table 8.1. Tabular survey and comparison of method

Authors	Andersen & Jordan	Läufer
Country	U.S.A.	F.R.G.
Period	1952(I)–1968(II)	1960(I)–1970(IV)
Optimality criteria	?	minimum standard error of regression equation
Lag technique	Almon Lags	Almon Lags
Degree of polynomials	4	4
Constraining of polynomials	one and two end point restrictions	no end point restrictions
Length of the lag distribution	variable, but *a priori* equal for fiscal and monetary policy	variable, but *not a priori* equal for fiscal policy, monetary policy and foreign impulses
Data-form	seasonally adjusted quarterly data	seasonally adjusted quarterly data + seasonal dummies
Transformation of variables	first differences (growth rates unpublished)	growth rates (first differences rejected)
Indicator of economy activity	GNP (nominal)	GNP (nominal)
Indicator of fiscal policy	(a) full employment budget surplus (b) full employment gov. expenditures alone (c) full employment gov. expenditures and tax receipts as separate variables	initial stimulus
Indicator of monetary policy	preferred: money stock less preferred: extended monetary base	extended monetary base (rejected: money stock)
Indicator of foreign impulses	neglected	exports

end point restrictions were imposed on the polynomials which we applied in order to restrict the estimates of distributed lag coefficients. We have searched the lag space from zero up to 16 lagged periods (quarters) allowing the lag length to be different for each of the three variables (fiscal and monetary policy indicators, exports). This required the calculation of close to 5000 regressions [15]. Applying the minimum standard error criterion does not lead to clear-cut results as there are several *relative* minima for the standard error. But an interesting border line exists dividing the lag space into two separate subspaces.

In the first subspace the total time used by the fiscal policy variable to work out its effects on GNP is below two years (less than 8 quarters). Monetary policy does not require more than two and a half years (requires less than 11 quarters), while foreign impulses (exports) do not require more than two years (require less than 9 quarters). The second subspace is defined by a time requirement of two years and more (8 and more quarters) for fiscal policy, more than two and a half years (11 and more quarters) for monetary policy and more than two years (9 and more quarters) for foreign impulses (exports).

In the first subspace the optimal regression [16], according to the minimum standard error (equation (8.1) in Table 8.2) all hypotheses of A & L may be

Table 8.2. Policy comparison—Regressions of relative changes in GNP on relative changes in indicators of monetary policy, fiscal policy and of foreign impulses (Initial stimulus F as fiscal policy indicator, extended base B as monetary policy indicator, exports Ex as indicator of foreign impulses; growth rates g)

Equation (8.1)

CONST.	-0.65		7. VAR.	$g(Ex)$	
	(-0.53)		4th-degree polynomial no end point restrictions		
2. VAR.	0.56 ⎫				
	(0.92) ⎪				
3. VAR.	-0.15 ⎬ seasonal		PERIOD	COEFF.	BETA-COEFF.
	(-0.25) ⎪ dummies		$t-0$	0.17	0.35
4. VAR.	0.16 ⎪			(1.68)	
	(0.27) ⎭		$t-1$	0.09	0.19
				(0.98)	
5. VAR.	$g(F)$		$t-2$	0.02	0.03
No polynomial restrictions				(0.21)	
			$t-3$	0.02	0.04
PERIOD	COEFF.	BETA-COEFF.		(0.25)	
$t-0$	0.22^*	0.55	$t-4$	0.10	0.21
	(2.85)			(1.47)	
Sum of	0.22^*	0.55	$t-5$	0.16	0.33
Coeff.	(2.85)			(1.60)	
			$t-6$	0.01	0.02
				(0.10)	
6. VAR.	$g(B)$		Sum of	0.56	1.17
No polynomial restrictions			Coeff.	(1.95)	
PERIOD	COEFF.	BETA-COEFF.	R^*R ADJ.	0.26	
$t-0$	-0.03	-0.04	R^*R	0.53	
	(-0.19)		F	1.97	
$t-1$	0.13	0.16	F_1/F_2	$13/23$	
	(0.71)		SE	0.012392	
$t-2$	-0.02	-0.03	DW	1.43	
	(-0.14)		N	37	
$t-3$	0.29^*	0.37			
	(2.04)				
Sum of	0.36	0.46			
Coeff.	(0.94)				

Lag space for F, B and Ex: 0–6 lagged quarters, or F: 0–6, B: 0–9, Ex: 0–7 lagged quarters.
In the lag spaces indicated the regression has minimal standard error.

refuted. The effects of monetary policy are not larger, nor more reliable, nor faster. Instead, fiscal policy has an instantaneous effect which is highly significant, while monetary policy does not show a significant single effect before the third lagged period, and the total effect of fiscal policy as measured by the sum of beta coefficients [17] is higher (by 20%) than the total effect of monetary policy, while it is slightly lower (by a third) if ordinary instead of the beta coefficients are compared [18, 19]. In the second subspace we have a monetarist world with significant crowding-out effects of fiscal policy and a confirmation of A & J's hypotheses [20].

In addition, the whole lag space has been investigated by considering a row of successively larger lag spaces at first with a maximum of 6, then 7 up to a maximum of 16 lags for each of the three variables F, B, Ex. Using the minimum standard error criterion an optimal regression was determined for each of the successive lag spaces considered. Only the results for the shortest and longest lag spaces are presented.

It is interesting to note that any regression, which is optimal for a given lag space, loses the property of optimality when the lag space is sufficiently extended. Thus, for the alternative lag spaces considered, the best regression (*optimum optimorum*) is obtained when the lag space has reached its largest extensions.

The fiscal coefficients in this case oscillate from significant positive to significant negative values back to significant positive values. In the present context such an oscillatory behaviour is hard to explain or understand by means of economic theory and seems to be a statistical artefact. With no theoretical reason for oscillatory true coefficients the oscillations may indicate an overstated lag length.

It is well known [21] that a specification error is committed whenever the lag length is overstated by a number of periods larger than the degree of the polynomial (less the number of end point restrictions). If the true lag is zero, then with no end point restrictions and a 4th-degree polynomial a specification error is committed as soon as a lag length of more than four quarters is assumed.

In the optimal regressions of the alternative lag spaces considered, negative fiscal coefficients do not appear before there is a (maximal) lag length of more than six quarters of the fiscal policy variable. Thus, negative fiscal policy coefficients of an oscillatory nature do not appear before a technical possibility of committing a specification error by overstating the lag length, exists. In addition, the oscillatory nature of fiscal coefficients was present in all regressions fitted except, of course, in equation (8.1) where fiscal policy appears with no lag. Therefore, the interpretation of oscillatory coefficients in equation (8.2), Table 8.3, as a sign of misspecification may also be applied to the other equations excluding the first.

Table 8.3. Policy comparison—Regressions of relative changes in GNP on relative changes in indicators of monetary policy, fiscal policy and of foreign impulses (Initial stimulus F as fiscal indicator, extended base B as monetary policy indicator, exports as indicator of foreign impulses; growth rates g)

Equation (8.2)

CONST.	−0·17	
	(−0·23)	
2. VAR.	0·52	
	(3·20)	
3. VAR.	−0·07	seasonal
	(−0·45)	dummies
4. VAR.	−0·06	
	(−0·44)	

5. VAR. $g(F)$
4th-degree polynomial no end point restrictions

PERIOD	COEFF.	BETA-COEFF.
t–0	0·23	0·56
	(9·97)	
t–1	0·17	0·43
	(12·05)	
t–2	0·10	0·24
	(5·72)	
t–3	0·01	0·02
	(0·44)	
t–4	−0·08	−0·19
	(−5·48)	
t–5	−0·15	−0·37
	(−10·79)	
t–6	−0·20	−0·50
	(−12·55)	
t–7	−0·23	−0·57
	(−12·47)	
t–8	−0·23	−0·57
	(−12·21)	
t–9	−0·21	−0·51
	(−12·12)	
t–10	−0·16	−0·40
	(−11·63)	
t–11	−0·10	−0·25
	(−8·03)	
t–12	−0·03	−0·08
	(−2·14)	
t–13	0·03	0·07
	(1·27)	
t–14	0·07	0·17
	(2·86)	
t–15	0·07	0·17
	(3·33)	
t–16	0·01	0·04
	(0·76)	
Sum of Coeff.	−0·71	−1·76
	(−6·22)	

6. VAR. $g(B)$
4th-degree polynomial no end point restrictions

PERIOD	COEFF.	BETA-COEFF.
t–0	0·24	0·31
	(2·28)	
t–1	0·25	0·32
	(3·39)	
t–2	0·25	0·32
	(3·75)	
t–3	0·33	0·42
	(5·03)	
t–4	0·48	0·61
	(7·32)	
t–5	0·58	0·74
	(9·48)	
t–6	0·42	0·54
	(6·19)	
t–7	−0·31	−0·40
	(−5·67)	
Sum of Coeff.	2·23	2·86
	(5·31)	

7. VAR. $g(Ex)$
No polynomial restrictions

PERIOD	COEFF.	BETA-COEFF.
t–0	−0·01	−0·02
	(−0·36)	
t–1	−0·19	−0·40
	(−5·73)	
t–2	−0·05	−0·11
	(−1·07)	
t–3	−0·12	−0·25
	(−3·49)	
t–4	0·19	0·39
	(7·46)	
Sum of Coeff.	−0·18	−0·38
	(−1·88)	

R^*R ADJ	0·98
R^*R	0·99
F	59·52
F_1/F_2	18/8
SE	0·0023613
DW	2·11
N	27

Lag space for F, B and Ex: 0–16 lagged quarters.
In the lag spaces indicated the regression has minimal standard error.

Such specification errors lead to biased and inconsistent estimates and invalid tests. Therefore, in the regressions presented, whenever the fiscal policy variable appears with negative coefficients, it is very likely that this is not a sign of crowding-out of private by fiscal expenditure but merely the consequences of a specification error committed by overstating the lag length.

Conclusions

It is obvious that we need further information in order to make a correct decision about the lag space to be considered. This *a priori* information might come from as yet unavailable knowledge about the underlying economic structure. But for the moment it appears that in the German case the A & J tests do not lead to firm conclusions unless a price is paid in the form of additional *a priori* restrictions. If one assumes with the author that the effects of fiscal policy work out in less than two years, while those of monetary policy do not require more than two and a half years and those of foreign impulses (exports) do not require more than two years, then the regression results reject the A & J hypotheses [22]. Instead, we find that in the F.R.G. the effects of fiscal policy on economic activity are about equally strong and at the same time they are faster and more reliable than those of monetary policy.

Appendix

(A guide to the tables and to the sources of data)

A Guide to the Tables

The following explanations hold for all tables of this paper.

$g(\ )$	= growth rate
B	= extended monetary base (monetary policy indicator)
F	= initial stimulus (fiscal policy indicator)
Ex	= exports (indicator of foreign impulses)

t-ratios are stated in brackets below the coefficients.

$R*R$ ADJ.	= coefficient of determination adjusted for degrees of freedom
$R*R$	= coefficient of determination unadjusted
F	= F-statistic of the F-test
F_1 and	
F_2	= degrees of freedom associated with the F-statistic
F_1/F_2	= degrees of freedom for the t-test

SE = standard error

DW = Durbin-Watson's d-statistic to test (first order) autocorrelation

N = sample size

*   = t-value is significant at a level of significance of at least 95%
          (two-sided hypothesis)

Sources of Data

The data for the initial stimulus (IS), the extended monetary base and the quantity of money are those of Neumann (1973).

I gratefully acknowledge the seasonal adjustment of the monetary series by the German Institute for Economic Research (DIW), Berlin.

The seasonally adjusted data for quarterly GNP and exports were taken from the following publications of this institute. DIW: 'Vierteljährliche volkswirtschaftliche Gesamtrechnung, Bundesrepublik Deutschland, Saisonbereinigte Daten 1950–1965', and DIW: 'Vierteljährliche volkswirtschaftliche Gesamtrechnung, Bundesrepublik Deutschland einschl. Saarland und Berlin, Saisonbereinigte Daten 1960–1971', Berlin, July 1971.

Footnotes

* This is an extension of the analysis presented in Läufer (1975).

1. See Andersen & Jordan (1968), de Leeuw & Kalchbrenner (1969) and the reply of Andersen & Jordan (1969). See also Corrigan (1970b) and Keran (1969, 1970a).

Keran's first article extends the test-period for the U.S. chosen by A & J and uses quarterly data for the years 1919–1969. In the second article Keran arrives at results for Canada, Japan and the Federal Republic of Germany (F.R.G.) confirming those for the U.S. Since Keran is proceeding strictly along the lines of A & J, our method and its justification form an implicit criticism of Keran's procedure as far as the F.R.G. is concerned. A critical summary of the results of various studies for the U.S. including the results of large-scale econometric models is given in Fisher & Sheppard (1972).

2. Details of the full employment Government budget surplus concept are given in Oakland (1969) and Corrigan (1970a, 1970b).

3. The total lag is measured by $l_m(l_f)$. The average time-lag is defined as the weighted average of the number of time periods by which lagged effects are delayed, the weights or coefficients of lagged effects being assumed to be positive.

4. It has been seriously doubted that it is justified to call equation (8.1) a reduced form equation (Fisher & Sheppard (1972), pp. 98–101).

5. A survey of alternative concepts of the transmission mechanism of monetary impulses is given by Brunner (1971), pp. 26–35. A particularly clear representation of the monetarist concept of the transmission mechanism may be found in Friedman & Meiselman (1964), esp. pp. 215–22.

6. This non-commitment seems to form a particular advantage of the A & J approach to a test of the relative importance of monetary and fiscal policy actions. However, this point of view loses much of its attractiveness if examined more thoroughly as is done by Fisher & Sheppard (1972), pp. 98–101. In their analysis for Germany Frowen & Arestis (1976b) have committed themselves to a structure with a Keynesian transmission mechanism.

7. Open market policy here is to be understood in the broad sense, including rediscounts, loans on collateral, etc. Pure open market policy is given if there is a change in the monetary base while the Government budget deficit and the required reserve ratios remain constant.

8. See Culbertson (1968), p. 463, and Spencer & Yohe (1970).

9. Pure fiscal policy is given when there is a change in the Government budget deficit while the extended monetary base remains constant.

10. See Oakland (1969) and Corrigan (1970a, 1970b). Following the lines of Corrigan and Oakland, Neumann has constructed indicators of fiscal policy in the F.R.G., for the years 1959–1970.

11. In this paper *initial* changes in tax receipts ΔT_i are changes during the first quarter after an alteration of the tax laws. The initial stimulus IS may be formally defined by $F_t = E_t - TC_t$, which is the difference between Government expenditure E, and cumulated *initial* changes of tax receipts.

$$TC_t = \sum_{i=0}^{t} \Delta T_i$$

An act of discretionary fiscal policy, as understood in the text, refers to $\Delta F_t = \Delta E_t - \Delta T_t$ or to $g(F_t) = g(E_t - TC_t)$. Using the example of a tax system, where only income is taxed, the meaning of T_i, the initial tax change may further be clarified. Let t be the tax rate and Y_i the income (GNP). Then, according to the IS-concept, ΔT_i is defined as

$$\Delta T_i = Y_i \Delta t$$

in contrast to

$$(Y_i + \Delta Y_i)(t + \Delta t) - Y_i t = \Delta(Y_i t) = Y_i \Delta t + t \Delta Y_i + \Delta Y \Delta t$$

$t \Delta Y_i$ is precisely that part of the additional tax receipts, which is included by the FES but excluded by the IS-concept, since it is not directly related to acts of discretionary fiscal policy. $\Delta Y \Delta t$ is neglected by both concepts.

As it turns out the results change only slightly by using E instead of F.

12. See Neumann, Ch. 4 in this volume.

13. We are assuming throughout that the Central Bank can control the monetary base. The reader should not necessarily interpret this assumption as a practice which he is invited to adhere to. The following result applies where the authorities act 'as if' they had control.

14. Regressing first differences of Y, of the stock of money M, of the fiscal indicator F, and of the extended base B^e on time, we obtain the following t-ratios for the positive trend coefficients:

	DY	DM	DF	DB^e
t	$3 \cdot 09^a$	$1 \cdot 70^b$	$1 \cdot 48$	$0 \cdot 48$

degrees of freedom: 41

(*a*) significant at a $0 \cdot 5 \%$ level (one-tail test)

(*b*) significant at a 5% level (one-tail test)

15. If the distributed lag of a variable does not extend to more than four (lagged) periods the application of a 4th-degree polynomial (without end point restrictions) would either be nonfeasible (in case of less than four lagged periods) or without effect (in case of exactly four lagged periods). Thus in all cases (combinations) where the lag length of a variable was below five periods, ordinary least squares were applied without polynomial restrictions for that variable. According to this rule the search of the three-dimensional lag space was not limited to combinations (triples) of lags of at least four periods but was extended to any combination of at least zero (!) lagged periods.

16. As it turns out in the optimal regression of the first subspaces only the coefficients of the export variable are constrained by a polynomial while those of the monetary policy variable (extended monetary base) are left unconstrained.

17. Beta coefficients are regression coefficients of standardized variables. Standardized variables are variables with a mean value zero and standard deviation one. Any variable may be standardized by subtracting the mean value and dividing the difference by the standard deviation of the variable. Thus standardized variables are variables of identical variability as measured by the standard deviation. Any difference in the size of the beta coefficients is not related to the difference in variability (as measured by the standard deviation).

18. Since the reader may doubt the relevance of beta coefficients for this comparison we may add that we even doubt the relevance of the difference in total effects question. In actual policy making, any difference in size of these effects may be compensated for by an appropriate choice in the size of the policy variable (growth rate of the policy indicator). Before we know more about the relative social costs of adjusting policy variable we cannot attach much significance to the question of difference in size of the policy effects as measured by the size of coefficients. This is different when the question of speed and reliability is considered.

19. In an earlier unpublished paper and in spite of several differences in method and for a subspace similar to the first one we arrived at basically the same empirical results. In that paper endpoint restrictions were applied while seasonal dummies were omitted. This indicates that Dhrymes (1971) (pp. 232–234) is overstating his case against endpoint restrictions, which is also obvious from the fact that in his examples he uses 2nd-degree polynomials. With 4th-degree polynomials he would not be able to observe such dramatic numerical changes due to alterations in endpoint restrictions on which he reports.

For an extension of Dhrymes's argument against endpoint restrictions in the present context see Schmidt & Waud (1973).

20. Additional calculations have shown that the tax component of our fiscal indicator is of negligible importance since almost identical results are obtained by substituting Government expenditures (as applied in constructing the fiscal indicator) for the fiscal indicator. These results may be related to those of Frowen & Arestis (1976b). The sums of their dynamic multiplier are 0·885 for monetary and 1·17 for fiscal policy. Unfortunately, their estimates cannot be tested statistically. For the time profile of their policy multipliers see their table.

21. See Schmidt & Waud (1973), p. 13.

22. For Great Britain (1958(I)–1967(III)) the hypotheses of A & J also appear not to be confirmed. Thus we read: 'The results of the regressions presented would, if they were accepted as valid reduced forms, perhaps suggest that it is fiscal measures (at least in the representation they have been given) rather than monetary measures which are the more powerful and certainly the quicker-acting'. Artis & Nobay (1972), p. 87.

Contrary evidence has also been presented for the U.S. Waud (1974) found that when the question of the relative importance of fiscal and monetary policy is examined on a more disaggregated level, where the possibility of reversed causation and the problem of single-equation least squares bias is reduced, 'fiscal influences and monetary influences on economic activity are both significant and appear equally important'.

Further Evidence on the Relative Importance of Fiscal and Monetary Actions in the Federal Republic of Germany—a Comment

K. M. HENNINGS*

Monetary policy has always played a prominent role in any attempt to influence the course of the West German economy. This is as much due to the institutional framework of the financial sector and the particular role of the Bundesbank as the monetary authority in it as to the fact that the Bundesbank enjoys an independence from even high-level Government interference which is quite unknown to other central banks. Moreover, fiscal policy presents a problem in a decentralized federal state in which independence of public spending decisions is jealously guarded, and all the more so as the parliamentary process is rather slow. Nevertheless, fiscal policy has been used, and increasingly so in the 1960s when adherence to the regime of fixed exchange rates threatened the efficacy of monetary policy.

In view of all this the West German experience with monetary and fiscal policy in the 1960s provides a good test case for the evaluation of their relative efficiency. Yet there have been few attempts to discuss the problem with econometric methods [1]. Keran (1970) made an attempt to replicate the results obtained by Andersen and Jordan (1968) for the United States economy, but his approach was much too crude to yield satisfactory results. The same must be said of an earlier attempt by Roskamp and Laumas (1967) to replicate the results obtained by Friedman and Meiselman (1964) for the United States. More recently Willms (1974) suggested that the A & J results were true for West Germany as well. He was mainly concerned with another problem, the evaluation of alternative indicators of monetary policy, but he included variables representing fiscal policy in his regressions and thus in fact estimated for West Germany the equations A & J had estimated for the United States. His findings were that if either the extended monetary base or the money supply represented monetary policy, the relevant coefficients had the expected signs and were all significant: while those of the variables

* The Editors have revised these comments in the light of a response from Nikolaus Läufer (see, for example, footnote [8]).

H

representing fiscal policy were either insignificant or had the wrong sign, or were both insignificant and wrongly signed. Willms did not explicitly draw the conclusion that monetary policy was more efficient than fiscal policy in the period he studied (1958–1969). But he did argue, as A & J had done, that 'the impact of Government expenditure on gross national product is mainly a "crowding out" effect, i.e. Government spending merely displaces private spending' [2]; and he left no doubt that monetary policy, if judged by the right indicator, would be more efficient. However, Willms had to resort to a rather unconvincing argument in order to explain the perverse signs he obtained for the variable representing tax receipts. Moreover, his analysis suffers from technical drawbacks. He used the Almon (1965) lag technique, but restricted the coefficients to lie on a second degree polynomial as well as using endpoint restrictions. This meant that he over-restricted his coefficients, and to this extent misspecified his equations (on this, see Schmidt and Waud (1973)). The perverse signs he found are therefore more likely than not statistical artefacts, and one cannot rely on his findings.

Läufer now presents new evidence from which he concludes that fiscal policy is at least as efficient as monetary policy, and if anything more rapid and more reliable as a policy instrument. His study takes account of criticism that has been advanced against exercises of this kind, and uses a different set of variables to represent the stance of monetary and fiscal policies than his predecessors did. Indeed from a technical point of view it is the most competent analysis presented so far of this particular problem in the context of the West German economy [3]. However, I am not convinced that there is enough evidence to draw the conclusion Läufer has drawn. In the remainder of this note I set out the reasons for my doubts.

Läufer is conscious of the fact that the Almon-lag technique does not provide safeguards against misspecification in the form of inappropriate lag lengths. He therefore searches for relative minima in the standard error within each prespecified maximum lag length, and is exceedingly careful when he comes to compare the 'optimal' equations thus obtained. Nevertheless, he dismisses all but one (the first) of the equations he has estimated because he suspects that they are misspecified. It is therefore on the basis of this preferred estimated equation that Läufer concludes, albeit cautiously and with some hedging, that in the West German economy 'the effects of fiscal policy on economic activity are about as strong and at the same time faster and more reliable than those of monetary policy'. But is this preferred equation so much better an estimate than the rest that it can bear the burden of the proof ? It seems to me that the answer should be in the negative. Neither the standard error nor the Durbin–Watson statistic associated with that equation is such as to assure one that this equation is free from specification error. Moreover, the regression coefficients for the monetary policy variable show the same oscillatory behaviour which, if certain conditions set out in his paper are satisfied, Läufer takes as an indicator of misspecification in his other equations, even though they are not restricted estimates and therefore are not subject to the specification error which Läufer suspects mars his other equations. So one should have doubts. Indeed I will attempt to argue that there is the possibility of another type of specification error which, if present, affects all of Läufer's regression equations.

In the course of his argument Läufer refers to 'a priori information (which) might come from as yet unavailable knowledge about underlying economic structure' of the West German economy. This is unnecessarily agnostic. We know a certain amount about the role of one of the variables he includes in his regressions, and this knowledge about the role of exports in the West German economy can be used here to show that something is amiss. It is well known that in West Germany growth cycles have always been related to export demand. Growth has been export-led, and at the same time exports have been a powerful initiating force making for cyclical movements. More specifically, a rise in export demand has typically set into motion an accelerator-type process which transmitted a rise in exports into a rise first in investment and then in consumption, and which generated a growth cycle on the way. This is well illustrated in Table C8.1.

How well do regressions of growth rates of GNP on to past and present growth rates of exports measure such postulated relationships [4]? Table C8.2 presents some regression results [5]. There is some evidence of the

Table C8.1. Some data on growth cycles in the West German economy, 1959–1970

	Growth rate of real GNP	Percentage contribution to the growth rate of final demand by		
		Exports	Investments	Private consumption
1959	7·0	25	31	31
1960	8·8	24	33	32
1961	5·4	9	23	51
1962	4·2	9	21	50
1963	3·4	22	14	43
1964	6·6	20	37	38
1965	5·7	16	23	45
1966	2·9	28	8	48
1967	−0·3	42	0	33
1968	7·2	26	21	29
1969	8·1	22	26	39
1970	2·9	16	35	36

Source: Calculated from various issues of Wirtschaft und Statistik.

Table C8.2. Estimates and some test statistics resulting from regressing quarterly growth rates of GNP on past and present quarterly growth rates of exports

	1	2	3	4	5	6	7	8	9
Constant	4·96	3·67	3·10	3·63	2·96	1·99	1·44	1·27	1·23
t	4·09	3·95	3·44	3·95	4·09	4·26	4·22	3·84	3·68
$t-1$		0·38	0·38	−0·07	−0·51	−0·31	−0·12	−0·20	−0·10
$t-2$			−0·67	−1·05	−0·88	−1·29	−1·15	−1·13	−0·99
$t-3$				−1·71	−1·47	−1·07	−1·20	−1·15	−1·01
$t-4$					0·77	0·95	0·93	0·89	0·62
$t-5$						1·53	1·63	1·50	1·52
$t-6$							0·35	0·26	0·05
$t-7$								−0·08	0·04
$t-8$									−0·67
SE	1·54	1·58	1·59	1·56	1·53	1·52	1·56	1·61	1·65
R^2 ADJ	0·27	0·25	0·24	0·29	0·31	0·32	0·31	0·27	0·22
DW	2·11	2·08	2·11	1·92	2·06	2·08	2·08	2·07	2·11

presence of negative coefficients of the kind one would expect if indeed exports generate (growth) cycles. The standard error is minimized by an equation which includes lags of up to 5 quarters on exports; the effect on impact (4.26) is subsequently offset in part by negative coefficients over the next three quarters to give a cumulative effect of 1·59 after one year. The cumulative effect after all lags have worked their way out is 4·07, and this is superimposed on a trend of 1·99% growth as measured by the constant terms. (Läufer, in contrast, obtains all *positive* weights, summing to only 0·56, see Table 8.1, equation (8.1)).

Given the omission of other exogenous influences from this regression we do not want to put too much weight on these results. They do, however, suggest that a cyclical response to exogenous stocks is a possibility which should not be ignored. The same reasoning suggests that there is no need to dismiss the oscillating sign pattern of equation (8.2) as a statistical artefact, as Läufer does. The marked differences between the very quick response to fiscal influences and distributed lag response to overseas influences in the preferred equation is, in my view, more in need of explanation. It could be that multicollinearity has distorted the proper lagged pattern for these variables. The above discussion is postulated on the existence of an accelerator strong enough to generate cycles. An accelerator need not generate cycles if it is sufficiently small but I doubt whether a model incorporating a realistic accelerator mechanism is consistent with the non-cyclical responses measured by Läufer's preferred equation.

As is customary in exercises of this kind, Läufer does not specify a structural model from which his regression equations can be derived. Nor did A & J, but it has since been shown that their equation (which is formulated in first differences) can in fact be derived from a fairly conventional macroeconomic model whose starting point is the *ex-post* identity of GNP with various categories of spending (Fisher & Sheppard (1972) pp. 99–101). A similar model can be used to derive equations which come near to those Läufer has estimated [6]. But because Läufer expresses his equations in terms of growth rates their coefficients can no longer be expressed in terms of the structural parameters of the model alone.

I understand that Läufer would express his 'structural' equations as additive in the logarithms, but the GNP identity which must be part of the under-

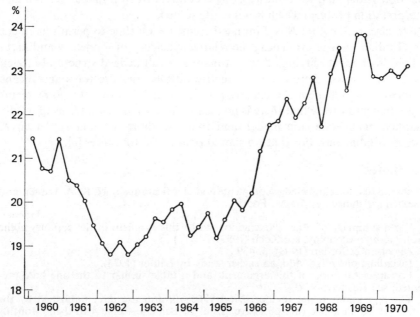

Figure C8.1. Ratio of exports to Gross National Product, West Germany, 1960–1970 (original data seasonally adjusted)

lying model is additive in the levels of the variables. An approximation to such an identity which is linear in the logs will only be valid for particular ratios of the variables concerned, but both fiscal policy actions and exports have varied relative to GNP.

Figure C8.1 shows that variation in the ratio of exports to GNP, and it should be noted that the variation is not just cyclical variation. If one follows Mintz (1969) in the dating of growth cycles, then 1961–2 were downswings, but so were 1966 and 1967. Such considerations lead us to doubt whether one should expect *constant-coefficients* on first differences of the logs of the chosen exogenous variables adequately to portray the effects they have on GNP over the range of variations observed in the sample.

To sum up, I have suggested that there are reasons to suspect that the equations Läufer has estimated are misspecified. I also suggest that their formulation in terms of growth rates is not without problems [7]. I therefore doubt whether the regression coefficients obtained can be taken at face value, and suspect that the question as to the relative efficiency of monetary and fiscal policies in the West German economy has not been settled conclusively. All these doubts are ultimately variations upon one theme: that it is necessary to specify explicitly the structural model from which the estimated regression equation is derived, for otherwise one is confronted by an identification and interpretation problem which is not easily solved.

Exercises of the kind A & J initiated seemed for a time to permit us to cut the Gordian knot of evaluating the relative efficiency of monetary and fiscal policies without specifying, if not estimating, a full-fledged structural model. As Läufer shows, there are econometric pitfalls, and the ways and means adopted to avoid them are equally problematic. His work therefore seems to me to demonstrate that there is no escape from thinking in terms of a fully specified macroeconomic model, and that the short-cut à la Andersen & Jordan is fallacious. For that we should be grateful to Läufer [8].

Footnotes*

* I should like to acknowledge comments and clarifications by N. K. A. Läufer, and research assistance by Mrs M. Foot.

1. For a summary of other work addressed to this problem in the context of the West German economy, see Koch (1959).
2. Andersen & Jordan (1968), p. 439.
3. Including, one might add, an earlier study by Läufer (1973).
4. For an elaboration of this argument, and a table similar to the one here presented, see Kasper (1972)
5. The regressions relate to the period 1963–70, and use data published by the Deutsche Bundesbank (in successive issues of Beihefte Reihe 4 to their Monthly Reports). Ordinary least squares have been used. Dr. Läufer kindly made part of his data available: though there are differences in detail, they yield results similar to those presented here. It should be noted, however, that when Läufer's data are used the standard error is minimized by a regression with a longer lag on exports than when the Bundesbank data are used.
6. The main difference is that Läufer allows for different lag lengths in different variables, while the model proposed in Fisher & Sheppard (1972) does not.
7. There are other problems as well. Can it be assumed that exports are independent of the extended monetary base, the variable used to represent monetary policy actions? The monetary theory of the balance of payments would suggest that the answer is in the negative. Or what is the point of including seasonal dummies in the regression, when all the data are already seasonally adjusted? Or again, how can Läufer's finding be explained that it does not make a difference whether one uses the difference between (initial) Government spending changes and (initial) tax revenue changes, or only the former (see footnote [9] of his paper)? Is one to conclude that tax changes do not affect the course of economic activity in West Germany?
8. While Läufer disagrees with the principal points made by the discussant, he does agree that further work investigating structural models is necessary.

9

Monetary Independence under Fixed Exchange Rates: the Case of West Germany 1958-1972*

MICHAEL BEENSTOCK

Introduction

In an open economy such at that of the Federal Republic of Germany internal and external monetary equilibrium are in principle inextricably interwoven. Monetary flows through the balance of payments are a determinant of domestic monetary conditions and are in turn affected by disturbances and pressures within the domestic money market itself. For example, an attempt by the Deutsche Bundesbank to pursue a restrictive monetary policy would tend to exert upward pressure on domestic interest rates, thereby attracting offsetting inward capital movements from abroad. In principle, there could be a 100% offset, in which case domestic monetary policy would be impotent. This would happen if international capital movements were perfectly elastic with respect to changes in international interest rate differentials. Under these circumstances, attempts by the authorities to alter domestic interest rates would be offset by capital movements. Alternatively, the authorities could only hold the differential open at the expense of accumulating reserves in exceedingly large proportions. However, if capital movements are less than perfectly elastic an independent monetary policy would in principle be possible. Just how inelastic such capital movements are in the West German case is an empirical issue, and an important theme of the present investigation is an attempt to shed light on this parameter.

   It will be argued that the elasticity of international capital movements is a function of subjective uncertainty about future exchange rates and of the investors' aversion to risk. The greater the subjective evaluation of exchange risk and the greater the degree of risk aversion, the more inelastic are capital flows likely to be. In the case of West Germany it would seem that these factors are sufficiently important to insulate the domestic economy from the majority of world monetary influences.

Exchange risk may either be borne in the forward market by speculators who hold open positions, or it may be borne directly in the spot market in the form of uncovered arbitrage. In the former case, uncertainty and risk aversion would be reflected in the elasticity of supply of forward exchange by speculators. When speculators are highly uncertain and risk averse this elasticity would tend to be small. Thus when interest rates alter, the effect of covered interest arbitrage on the balance of payments could be relatively insensitive to movements in international interest rate differentials if the speculative supply of forward exchange were inelastic. If the exchange risk is borne in the spot market, uncertainty and risk aversion would be correspondingly reflected in the elasticity of the *uncovered* arbitrage schedule.

An additional vital aspect of the foreign exchange market is the role and determination of exchange rate expectations. This would be particularly important in the case of West Germany where speculation over the Deutschmark (DM) at times dominated the foreign exchange markets. Shifts in expectations would be represented by shifts in the speculative supply of forward exchange or by speculation in the spot market itself. It will be argued that the modelling of exchange rate expectations requires very careful treatment, for not only are the stability properties of the foreign exchange market affected by the determinants of speculation (see Britton (1970)), but also short-term balance of payments forecasting is as sensitive to exchange rate expectations as it is to interest rates and related monetary factors. Modelling exchange rate expectations is extremely difficult and the methodological and statistical suggestions of this study are perhaps more tentative than is usually the case in economics. Nevertheless, it will be suggested that a practical basis for exchange rate expectations is the 'rational' approach where speculators are hypothesized to forecast price movements on the basis of economic theory itself.

Finally, an attempt is made to analyse the importance of long-term interest rates and long-term capital movements in the West German balance of payments. It will be argued that capital account models cannot be represented by short-term capital movements alone, and in the West German case it would appear that long-term flows are statistically more important than short-term capital flows with regard to the interest rate policies of the Bundesbank.

This study is solely concerned with the issue of monetary independence in the context of capital account transactions. There is, of course, the parallel issue of monetary independence in the context of current account transactions. Thus in principle a monetary expansion overseas would tend to generate a current account inflow thereby affecting the domestic monetary sector. Here the transmission process takes place via the international substitution of traded goods rather than traded financial assets. This transmission mechanism is not discussed here.

In the following section we describe a general equilibrium model of spot and forward market determination in the context of domestic monetary equilibrium. For presentational purposes we abstract from the theoretical linkages between these markets and their associated real markets, e.g. traded goods, etc. From this section we derive a three equation empirical model for estimation purposes that consists of an equation for the forward exchange rate, an equation for short-term capital flows and an equation for long-term capital flows. A brief discussion follows on the modelling of exchange rate expectations, and then the estimates are presented. Lastly, some tentative policy implications of the study are drawn.

Spot and Forward Rate Determination

What follows is not specific to the determination of exchange rates and interest rates in West Germany alone. The purpose of this rudimentary model is to identify the principle theoretical linkages between exchange rates and interest rates in a general equilibrium setting. However, the swap rate is included in the analysis in acknowledgement of the Bundesbank's intermittent use of the swap rate as an instrument of policy [1].

The total currency flow or the change in the reserves $\dot{R}$ is equal to the sum of the current and capital account balances. The current account balance, assuming that the Marshall–Lerner conditions are fulfilled, will vary inversely with the exchange rate S. In what follows, domestic currency is priced in foreign currency units, i.e. domestic currency appreciates with S. Ignoring constants the current account surplus can therefore be written as:

$$-t_1 S - t_2 RP \tag{9.1}$$

where RP is the ratio of domestic prices to foreign prices.

The capital account will depend on arbitrage movements, both covered and uncovered. It will also depend on the flows generated by cover provided by the Bundesbank in terms of swap facilities. Portfolio considerations imply that capital flows will depend on changes in objective and subjective market yields. Thus covered inflows A_1 will depend on changes in the covered differential (appropriately linearized):

$$A_1 = a_1 (\dot{F} - \dot{S} + \dot{RD} - \dot{RF}) \tag{9.2}$$

where F is the forward rate and RD and RF are domestic and foreign interest rates, respectively. Uncovered inflows A_2 will depend on changes in the expected return on uncovered portfolios:

$$A_2 = a_2 (\dot{S}^e - \dot{S} + \dot{RD} - \dot{RF}) \tag{9.3}$$

where S^e is the expected spot rate. Finally flows generated by swap facilities will be determined by the change in the covered differential adjusted for the swap rate SW

$$A_3 = a_3(\dot{SW} - \dot{S} + \dot{RD} - \dot{RF}) \tag{9.4}$$

The change in the reserves can therefore be written (see Basevi (1973), p. 112) as:

$$\dot{R} = -t_1 S + a_1 \dot{F} + a_3 \dot{SW} + a_2 \dot{S}^e - (a_1 + a_2 + a_3)$$
$$(\dot{S} - \dot{RD} + \dot{RF}) - t_2 RP \tag{9.5}$$

When the exchange rate is fixed, $\dot{S}$ is equal to zero. Conversely, when the exchange rate is floating $\dot{R}$ is equal to zero.

The demand for forward exchange will depend on the arbitrage and speculative components as well as the Bundesbank's own position in the official forward market. The arbitrage component will be the integral of equation (9.2) with the sign reversed since covered spot purchases of DM must be matched by forward sales. The speculative component E will depend on the difference between the expected spot rate and the actual forward rate:

$$E = -e(F - S^e) \tag{9.6}$$

Thus as the spot rate is expected to rise relative to the forward rate the demand for forward DM rises because expected speculative profits increase [2].

In principle, an increase in the swap rate will cause some substitution to the official forward market from the unofficial swap market, thereby raising the official forward rate. It is difficult to specify the precise nature of this substitution effect because in practice the swap facility is not accessible to all market participants. Accordingly, equation (9.7), which determines the forward rate (9.2), includes an argument in terms of the swap rate which recognizes this effect:

$$GF = -a_1(F - S + RD - RF) - e(F - S^e) + cSW \tag{9.7}$$

where GF is the authorities' net position out of forward DM.

The money supply will depend on the level of reserves and the accumulation of domestic credit expansion X. In equilibrium the demand for money will equal supply:

$$R + X = -m_1 RD - m_2 S \tag{9.8}$$

i.e., the demand for money varies inversely with the domestic rate of interest and the exchange rate. The inverse relationship with the exchange rate is explained through the transactions demand for money; as the exchange rate appreciates, this has a deflationary effect on the economy, thereby lowering the transactions demand for money.

Equations (9.5), (9.7) and (9.8) determine the spot rate, the forward rate and domestic interest rates respectively. Alternatively, if the spot rate is fixed, equation (9.5) determines the balance of payments. The exogenous variables are foreign interest rates, the swap rate, the ratio of domestic to foreign prices, the authorities' forward position and the accumulation of domestic credit expansion. With a floating rate the system can be written as:

$$
\begin{bmatrix} -(aD + t_1) & a_1 D & aD \\ a_1 & -(a_1 + e) & -a_1 \\ -m_2 & 0 & -m_1 \end{bmatrix} \begin{bmatrix} S \\ F \\ RD \end{bmatrix} =
$$

$$
= \begin{bmatrix} -a_2 D & -a_3 D & aD & t_2 & 0 & 0 & 0 \\ -c & -e & -a_1 & 0 & 1 & 0 & 0 \\ 0 & 0 & 0 & 0 & 0 & 0 & 1 \end{bmatrix} \begin{bmatrix} SW \\ S^e \\ RF \\ RP \\ GF \\ R \\ X \end{bmatrix} \quad (9.9)
$$

where D is the differential operator d/dt and $a = a_1 + a_2 + a_3$. The determinant of the system is:

$$
\text{Det} = [a_1^2 - a(a_1 + e)](m_2 + m_1)D - m_1 t_1(a_1 + e) \quad (9.10)
$$

which has a single stable root

$$
\lambda = \frac{m_1 t_1(a_1 + e)}{(m_2 + m_1)[a_1^2 - a(a_1 + e)]} < 0
$$

since: $a_1^2 - a(a_1 + e) < 0$

The Model

The empirical interest of this study focuses on the capital account in the context of an analysis of forward market activity. Therefore no attempt is made to investigate the empirical structure of the West German monetary sector. Hopefully, however, it would be possible to feed the model to be described into existing models of the West German domestic monetary system. Similarly, no attempt is made to investigate the determinants of the West German current account, but see Beenstock and Minford (1976). However, it should be clear that given econometric models of both the current and capital accounts which are functions of the spot rate it would be possible to simulate the foreign exchange market under floating exchange rates or to analyse the effects of alternative intervention strategies in the spot and forward markets or even the domestic money markets. Equally important in this context would be an analysis of the dynamic stability of the foreign exchange market.

The forward market equation is derived directly from equation (9.7) which when solved for the forward rate yields:

$$F = \frac{1}{a_1 + e}[a_1(S + RF - RD) + eS^e + cSW - GF] \qquad (9.11)$$

An interesting feature of this equation is that the official forward position GF econometrically identifies all the parameters in the equation. Most importantly it identifies a_1 and e separately, the elasticities of covered interest arbitrage and forward speculation, which are crucial to the investigation of monetary independence. Unfortunately, West German data on GF are not available nor was SW specified as an explanatory variable. Consequently the equation that was estimated was of the form:

$$F = \frac{1}{a_1 + e}[a_1(S + RF - RD) + eS^e] \qquad (9.12)$$

The 3-month DM/$ forward rate was selected as the representative forward rate although in practice there is an entire term structure of forward rates. RD [3] was proxied by the 3-month Frankfurt money market rate and RF by the Eurodollar deposit rate [4] of the comparable maturity. Both F and S were expressed as percentage deviations from the official parity of the DM grossed up at annual rates to render them comparable with the interest rates. Thus if F^1 and S^1 are the actual forward and spot rates [5] and π is the official parity the cost of forward cover CFC as an annual percentage may be approximated as:

$$CFC = \left(\frac{F^1 - S^1}{S^1}\right)400 \simeq \left(\frac{F^1 - \pi}{\pi}\right)400 - \left(\frac{S^1 - \pi}{\pi}\right)400 \equiv F - S$$

Next we come to the equation for short-term capital flows STC. Equation (9.2) suggests that covered flows will depend on the change in the covered interest rate differential CD and uncovered flows will depend on the change in the expected differential. Therefore:

$$STC = a_1\Delta F + a_2\Delta S^e + (a_1 + a_2)\Delta(RD - RF - S) \qquad (9.13)$$

Therefore, while in practice it is not possible to identify a_1 from equation (9.12) it is in principle possible to identify it via equation (9.13). And armed with estimates of a_1 in this way it is then possible to identify e the elasticity of the speculation schedule.

STC is defined as 'private short-term capital flows' as presented in the *Deutsche Bundesbank Monthly Report* and are measured in millions of DM. The private short-term capital transactions series includes trade credit on both exports and imports. A given stock of trade credit would finance a given flow of trade so that levels of trade are likely to be related to stocks of assets, in which case changes in trade values would generate capital flows. The proportion of the current balance CB that would be financed through West German credits would depend on relative borrowing costs covered. For example, the value of export credit will equal the value of exports XV multiplied by the relative cost of credit to foreigners

$$XV\left(\frac{RF}{RD + CFC}\right)$$

and import credit will equal the value of imports MV multiplied by relative borrowing costs

$$MV\left(\frac{RD}{RF - CFC}\right)$$

so that the flow of trade credit is:

$$Z = \Delta\left[MV\left(\frac{RD}{RF - CFC}\right) - XV\left(\frac{RF}{RD + CFC}\right)\right] = \Delta(CB.CD) \qquad (9.14)$$

Therefore Z should be specified as an additional explanatory variable in equation (9.13). However, some of the effects of this trade credit term might be accounted for by some of the existing explanatory variables in that equation.

The results reported in this study were estimated by ordinary least squares. Equations (9.12) and (9.13), however, may be expected to be affected by simultaneous equations bias. For example, a random increase in F would tend to increase $(S - RD)$ for the improvement in the forward rate would generate inward arbitrage putting upward pressure on the spot rate and downward pressure on domestic interest rates. Therefore estimates of $a_1/(a_1 + e)$ might be affected by positive simultaneous equations bias. In the context of equation (9.13) a random increase in STC would tend to increase S, reduce RD and reduce F in which case OLS estimates would tend to be biased downwards. Most probably the endogeneity of the spot rate would be the main cause of simultaneity since domestic interest rates are likely to be dominated by domestic factors. Nevertheless, it is clear that appropriate care will be required in evaluating the results [6].

The third and final equation of this simple model relates to the determination of 'private long-term transactions' LTC as defined in the *Deutsche Bundesbank Monthly Report*. Here, too, we adopt the stock adjustment model which underlies the analysis of this study. Therefore, the equation for LTC is similar to the equation for short-term capital transactions with the exception that there is no long-term forward exchange market. Instead all exchange risks have to be incurred directly in the spot market. The other difference is of course the specification of long-term interest rates. RDL, the domestic long-term rate is represented by the long-term bond rate published in the *OECD Main Economic Indicators*. The competing overseas interest rate, RFL, is proxied by the U.S. long-term Government bond rate published in the

IMF's International Financial Statistics. Thus the equation for long-term capital flows is:

$$LTC = h_1\Delta(RDL - RFL) + h_2\Delta S^e - h_3\Delta S \qquad (9.15)$$

This completes the specification of the empirical model to be estimated. However, to render it in estimable form it is necessary to proxy the expected spot rate S^e by some appropriate generating function.

The Expected Spot Rate

In forming their expectations it would be meaningful for speculators to ask themselves the following question. Given this conditional (i.e. conditional on S^e) solution for S and given that speculators' own expectations would affect the future course of S—what is the logical relationship between S_{t+1} with past values of the spot rate and other relevant exogenous variables? In other words, assuming a model of the foreign market and assuming that each speculator in turn assumes the speculative fraternity to deploy a similar underlying model of the foreign exchange market it would follow that:

$$S^e_{t+1} = E(S_{t+1}) \qquad (9.16)$$

i.e. the expected spot rate is the 'rational' solution of an economic model— where $E(S_{t+1})$ is the expected value of the future spot rate as implied by the model.

Since economic forecasters produce econometric forecasts of exchange rate developments it is reasonable to assume that professional speculators who earn their livelihoods on the basis of being proved right would attempt to base their views on as much relevant information as possible and adopt similar 'economistic' methodologies.

In the present context 'rational' expectations, following Muth (1961), would reflect the observation that the current account is likely to depend on relative prices at home and abroad with a distributed lag (*see* Beenstock and Minford (1976)) in which case past values of relative price movements are an important source of information for future exchange market developments. Similarly, any other elements of autoregressiveness or distributed lags where the past provides a rationally based guide to future exchange market developments would contend for inclusion in a rational expectations function.

The rational expectations approach has a basis in economic theory whereas the main contenders of adaptive expectations and mixed regressive-extrapolative expectations do not have any such rationale. Therefore in the present study the tendency has been to lean towards the rational model, and the main sources of relevant historic information are relative prices, domestic economic activity and world economic developments.

The discussion thus far has related to conditions of floating exchange rates. Over the observation period the West German monetary authorities in fact operated an adjustable peg. The underlying rational theory has therefore to be modified. When the exchange rate is pegged it would seem that speculators have to consider two related questions. The first relates to what underlying exchange rate developments would have been in the absence of official intervention. This gives speculators some guide as to how the authorities might alter the peg. The second relates to the question of when the authorities will in fact adjust the peg to its appropriate level. The factors determining the answer to the 'what' question are broadly the same as those that lie behind the determination of expectations when the exchange rate is floating. The factors determining the 'when' issue are likely to be represented by some pressure variable. For example, if the cumulative current account imbalance or the reserve change has been rising the authorities might be expected to recognize the existence of a 'fundamental' disequilibrium and subsequently alter the exchange rate. Indeed the more the cumulative imbalance, the greater the probability that the authorities will alter the exchange rate.

If, for example, the current balance CB is taken to proxy the 'pressure' variable, and relative prices RP proxy the underlying determinants of expectations, we may write:

$$S^e = \sum_{i=1}^{J} w_i CB_{t-1} + \sum_{i=1}^{K} v_i RP_{t-i} \qquad (9.17)$$

Because the current balance will itself depend on relative prices in a dynamic fashion, the rational speculator would reflect this information in his choice of weights. This would be particularly important in the aftermath of an exchange rate adjustment where the current balance might move in a destabilizing direction because of lagged adjustments—the J-curve phenomenon. Thus for given relative prices that would warrant, say, a 10% appreciation, the probability is that the authorities will appreciate the rate increases the greater the cumulative current balance surplus. Alternatively, for a given index of 'pressure' the expected spot rate would vary directly with the degree of relative price imbalance.

Estimation Methods

Given the dynamic specification of the expectations function and the possibility of protracted stock adjustment processes, particularly with regard to long-term capital transactions, a dynamic estimation method is required. In addition there is likely to be simultaneity between short-term capital flows and the forward rate in particular, in which case simultaneous estimation methods would be required.

An attempt was made to treat the simultaneity problem by a selection of instrumental variables. However, no satisfactory results were obtained and the main body of the results were estimated without regard to simultaneity.

Two methods were investigated with regard to the estimation of distributed lags. The bulk of the results were estimated using the Almon interpolation method [7], i.e. the lag structure is assumed to lie on a polynomial whose order is to be specified, and where it is possible to tie front and end weights. A third order polynomial with front weight free and end weight tied is indicated by $(3, 0, T)$. If both weights were tied, it would be $(3, T, T)$. Error models were estimated using the Cochrane–Orcutt technique.

The second method was the generalized rational transfer function:

$$Y = \frac{A_1(L)X_1}{B_1(L)} + \frac{A_2(L)X_2}{B_2(L)} + \cdots + \frac{A_3(L)e}{B_3(L)}$$

where $A(L)/B(L)$ is a rational function and e is a disturbance term. The impulse response function implied by the rational function represents the distributed lag relationship between the dependent and the independent variables. However, this estimation method involves a hill-climbing search procedure over a non-linear likelihood function which is computationally expensive. Since the two methods implied broadly similar results, it was decided to concentrate the econometric effort on the cheaper estimation method.

The Determination of the 3-month Forward Rate [8]

Equation (9.12) is essentially a formulation of the 'modern theory' of forward exchange, i.e. the forward rate is determined by the relative weights of arbitrage and speculation (see Stoll 1968)). The model was estimated using quarterly data from 1958–1972. The expected exchange rate was represented by distributed lags on the various arguments considered above and especially equation (9.17). However, for brevity, we show a representative result only:

Table 9.1

$$F = 32 \cdot 4 + \underset{(0 \cdot 0548)}{0 \cdot 968} \; SUD_t + \sum_{i=1}^{10} a_i \Delta RES_{t-i} + \sum_{i=1}^{10} b_i RP_{t-i}$$

$$a(3, 0, T)$$
$$b(2, 0, T)$$
$$R^2 = 0 \cdot 93$$
$$\sigma = 2 \cdot 06$$
$$DF = 39$$
$$DW = 1 \cdot 66$$

a_t 0·000489   0·000341   0·000284   0·000293   0·000342
        (0·000257)   (0·000176)   (0·000168)   (0·000163)   (0·000159)

         0·000404   0·000454   0·000464   0·000409   0·000263
        (0·000175)   (0·000211)   (0·000239)   (0·000229)   (0·000157)

$\Sigma = 0{\cdot}00375$

b_t −12·44   −9·22   −6·45   −4·11   −2·21   −0·747   0·279   0·865
        (6·1)   (4·01)   (2·48)   (1·81)   (2·0)   (2·4)   (2·6)   (2·5)

         1·01   0·726 $\Sigma = -32{\cdot}3$
        (2·03)   (4·2)

where $SUD = RF - RD - S$

ΔRES = Reserve change (Data source: *OECD Main Economic Indicators*, $ million)

RP = ratio of West German export prices to weighted average of West German competitors' export prices (Data source: *OECD Main Economic Indicators*)

The expected spot rate is proxied by a moving average of the reserve change which represents the 'pressure' variable and by a moving average of relative export prices which represents the underlying 'expectations' variable. This result would therefore lend support to the rational expectations hypothesis of the determination of exchange rate expectations. Other specifications yielded results that were statistically significant. For example, lagged values of the current balance, world trade and industrial production generated plausible lag structures, too. However, the reported equation is of particular interest since its specification was derived on the basis of economic analysis rather than some arbitrary formulation.

A singularly robust feature of all the results was the coefficient on SUD which represents the weight of arbitrageurs in the determination of the forward rate relative to speculators. This weight was invariably about 97%, leaving very little for speculators to determine. None of the results allowed for any simultaneity which might be expected. A random increase in F would tend to lower SUD, in which case the results might contain positive simultaneous equations bias. Attempts to treat this using instrumental variables proved unsuccessful. The coefficient on SUD was reduced but no longer significant.

Private Short-term Capital Transactions

The dependent variable in the equations reported below is private short-term capital transactions plus the balance of unclassifiable transactions measured in DM million. These two items are aggregated on the grounds that the latter contain a large element of speculative capital movements and arbitrage capital. Indeed, better results were obtained on this basis than by disaggregating.

Table 9.2

$STC_t =$

1. $1075 + 685 \cdot 5 \ \Delta CD + \sum\limits_{i=1}^{18} a_i \Delta CB_{t-1}$

   $(2, 0, T)$
   $R^2 = 0 \cdot 599$
   $\sigma = 2453$
   $DF = 34$
   $DW = 1 \cdot 9$

   a_t

$-1 \cdot 012$	$-0 \cdot 7411$	$-0 \cdot 495$	$-0 \cdot 2747$	$-0 \cdot 07947$	$0 \cdot 0905$	$0 \cdot 235$
$(0 \cdot 281)$	$(0 \cdot 242)$	$(0 \cdot 213)$	$(0 \cdot 197)$	$(0 \cdot 19)$	$(0 \cdot 19)$	$(0 \cdot 194)$
$0 \cdot 355$	$0 \cdot 4488$	$0 \cdot 5177$	$0 \cdot 5613$	$0 \cdot 5796$	$0 \cdot 5727$	$0 \cdot 5404$
$(0 \cdot 199)$	$(0 \cdot 203)$	$(0 \cdot 204)$	$(0 \cdot 201)$	$(0 \cdot 194)$	$(0 \cdot 1823)$	$(0 \cdot 1655)$
$0 \cdot 4829$	$0 \cdot 4$	$0 \cdot 292$	$0 \cdot 1586$	$\sum = 2 \cdot 632$		
$(1 \cdot 435)$	$(0 \cdot 116)$	$(0 \cdot 083)$	$(0 \cdot 0443)$			

2. $\quad 260 \cdot 5 \quad -0 \cdot 10186 Z_t + 800 \cdot 37 \Delta CD_t + \sum\limits_{i=1}^{16} a_e \Delta RP_{t-1}$
   $\quad (205 \cdot 8) \quad (0 \cdot 06) \qquad (146)$
   $(2, 0, T)$
   $R^2 = 0 \cdot 434$
   $\sigma = 2655$
   $DF = 42$
   $DW = 1 \cdot 56$

   a_t

34790	24407	15119	$6924 \cdot 8$	$-174 \cdot 7$	$-6179 \cdot 7$
(16857)	(13574)	(11347)	(10268)	(10182)	(10693)
-11090	-14906	-17628	-19255	-19788	-19226
(11398)	(12015)	(12379)	(12396)	(12009)	(11186)
-17570	-14819	-10974	$-6034 \cdot 2$	$\sum = 76403 \cdot 8$	
$(9906 \cdot 5)$	(8156)	(5925)	(3208)		

Whereas the level of the expected spot rate is specified for the level of the forward rate, the change in the expected spot rate is logically specified as a determinant of capital flows. However, what limited success was achieved with the rational expectations hypothesis under fixed rates in the case of the forward rate equations was not repeated in the present context. Instead significant results were obtained by separately using the change in the current balance, relative export prices, etc. The initial negative weights on the ΔCB lag distribution can be interpreted as speculators discounting the J-curve.

More interesting is the significance of the change in the covered differential. In principle, and in line with equation (9.12) the changes in the uncovered differential and the cost of forward cover should have been specified separately to allow for the separate effects of spot speculation and arbitrage.

However, attempts to disaggregate the covered differential foundered. Whatever the specification, the coefficient on the change in the covered differential was fairly robust, indicating that a 1% improvement in the covered differential would lead to an inflow of about DM 700–800 million. This coefficient does not allow for any possible simultaneous equations bias which would bias downwards the result. These results compare with DM 800 million in Branson and Hill (1971) (pp. 34–5) and about DM 770 million in Porter (1972) (p. 406). However, Porter finds a two quarter effect of DM 2320 million.

An additional feature of the results is the importance of the trade credit variable Z in the second equation. In 1973 the West German current balance was DM 33 billion. A 0·04% improvement in the covered differential which is the effect on the covered differential of a 1% increase in the uncovered differential via the forward rate equation would attract inflows of about DM 150 million in the light of these results.

Private Long-term Capital Transactions

The main explanatory variable is the change in the long-term uncovered differential $\Delta LUD = \Delta(RDL - RFL)$, there being no forward cover for long-term capital positions. An associated problem is the treatment of exchange rate expectations in the longer term. The forecasting methodology suggested on p. 220 is more appropriate for shorter term projections given the dependence of the method of distributed lags, i.e. these lags run out with the extension of the projection horizon. Long-term investors can always hedge, if they so wish, on the short-term forward market and no doubt they in part influence the forward rate in the equations already discussed on pp. 222–3.

A surprising feature of all the various specifications was the relatively high response of private long-term capital transactions to changes in the long-term uncovered differential. For example, in the reported equation the long-run response is DM 9511 million:

Table 9.3

$$LTC = -313 + \sum_{i=0}^{9} a_i \Delta LUD_{t-i} + \sum_{i=0}^{9} b_i \Delta S_{t-1}$$

$$\Delta LUD\ (2, T, T)$$
$$\Delta S\ (3, 0, T)$$
$$R^2 = 0\cdot724$$
$$\sigma = 1302$$
$$DF = 46$$
$$DW = 1\cdot91 \qquad \rho = 0\cdot514$$
$$(0\cdot126)$$

a_t	432·4	778·3	1037·2	1211	1297·1	1297·1
	(112·2)	(201·9)	(269·2)	(314·1)	(336·5)	(336·5)
	1211	1037·7	778·3	432·4	$\Sigma = 9511$	
	(314·1)	(269·2)	(201·9)	(112·2)		
b_t	65·3	61·9	89·4	136	189·9	239·1	271·8
	(28·7)	(45·6)	(59·2)	(68)	(75·3)	(82·5)	(87·5)
	276·1	240·1	152	$\Sigma = 1721·6$		
	(86·6)	(75)	(47·8)			

In other words, while the short-run effect is less than was obtained for short-term capital flows, the long-run effect is many times greater.

For comparison we note that Branson and Hill (1971) (page 38) find that the effect on a 1% increase in German long-term rates is about DM 2700 million. If, however, the overseas interest rate falls by 1% point, the effect is DM 3000 million. Branson and Hill do not investigate lagged effects.

Conclusions

It was argued at the outset that the existence of exchange risk and risk aversion would tend to weaken the elasticities of international capital movements and so afford the domestic monetary system a degree of insulation from world monetary developments even when the exchange rate is fixed. The extent to which exchange risk might achieve this is essentially an empirical issue and it would appear that the case of West German exchange risk affords a very substantial degree of monetary insulation from capital account transactions. The domestic economy could still be affected, however, by current account transactions.

For example, let us consider the effects on the West German monetary system of a fall in world interest rates at the short end by 1%. The equations reported indicate that if world interest rates were to fall by 1%, the cost of forward cover is likely to rise against West Germany by about 0·95% generating a net improvement of the covered differential of only 0·5%. The equations reported for short-term capital suggest that such an improvement in the covered differential would only attract a short term capital inflow of about DM 37·5 million, which expressed as a proportion of the West German money supply is insignificantly small. Therefore, West German interest rates would scarcely be influenced by world interest rates even assuming the exchange rate to be fixed.

These results imply that the elasticity of supply of speculative forward cover is extremely small. Indeed if $\hat{a}_1$ is equal to about DM 750 million where the rise in the forward rate adds 1% to the covered differential, the slope $\hat{e}$ of the speculation schedule would be as little as DM 39·5 million. Thus even if the covered interest arbitrage schedule were infinitely elastic as many would consider it to be, the spot flow that would follow a 1% rise in the uncovered differential would be only about DM 40 million. However, these findings are not dissimilar to (unpublished) results I have obtained for the U.K., where $\hat{e}$ was £44 million, and for France where $\hat{e}$ was FF 45 million. In the case of Canada, $\hat{e}$ was CAN $ 150 million when the exchange rate was fixed. Thus the results for West Germany are consistent with those I have obtained for other countries.

More surprising is the low value for a_1—the slope of the covered interest arbitrage schedule which on *a priori* grounds may reasonably be expected to be large. Here too, however, the West German results are broadly similar to those obtained in comparable studies for other countries (see Hutton (1976) for example). It would seem therefore that there is a growing body of evidence that covered interest arbitrage schedules are less elastic than might be expected and that the speculative supply of forward cover is inelastic too. These two factors combine to produce a very high degree of monetary insulation.

There is no obvious reason why the response of the capital account to long-term interest rate movements should be any less sensitive to the response at the short end. However, bearing in mind that the results allow for exchange risk, we are in fact comparing results at the short end of DM 35 million with results at the long end of at least ten times this amount in the current quarter and two hundred and seventy times this amount after the full stock adjustment. I have found a similar result in the context of the French capital account, and others (see Leamer and Stern (1972) Table 4) have noted that the capital account may be more responsive to long-term interest rates than to short-term interest rates.

While data limitations make an empirical analysis of the determinants of exchange rate expectations notoriously difficult, the results reported lend some support to the rational expectations hypothesis. Unfortunately, this limited success did not carry over to the remaining two equations of the estimated model. Not surprisingly, however, the evidence confirms that the West German balance of payments has been considerably influenced by speculative factors over the estimation period.

Footnotes

* The views expressed in this paper in no way represent those of H.M. Treasury and are the Author's responsibility only.
1. See Courakis, pp. 30–1, and Neumann, p. 83, in this volume.
2. In their general equilibrium analysis, Argy & Porter assume that the forward rate reflects previous movements in the spot rate. Because of this their model loses much analytical interest. See Argy & Porter (1972).
3. All interest rate data, etc., are measured at end-quarters to correspond with a quarterly stock adjustment model.
4. Sources: *RD, Deutsche Bundesbank Monthly Report*; *RF, Bank of England Quarterly Bulletin*.

5. Source: *OECD Main Economic Indicators*.
6. However, it is comforting to note that J. P. Hutton (1976) found that simultaneity was not important in the U.K. context.
7. I wish to thank Honor Stamler who wrote this programme.
8. I would like to thank David Smith who bore the brunt of what was an arduous estimation task.

.   .   .   .   .

Monetary Independence under Fixed Exchange Rates: the Case of West Germany—a Comment

MARCUS H. MILLER

On the basis of his econometric investigations of West German capital movements from 1958 to 1972, Michael Beenstock comes to the surprising conclusion that 'exchange risk affords a very substantial degree of insulation' from such flows. In what follows I shall discuss in some detail what is meant by this, and how consistent is the support to this view provided by the estimates reported here.

The proposition that the West German economy is insulated from external monetary influences means, to judge from the conclusions, that variations in the uncovered short-term interest rate differential as between West Germany and the U.S. are not likely to trigger large capital flows. The reason given for this is that short-term capital flows, in so far as they respond to interest rate differentials, do so only after taking account of the cost of cover, and the evidence presented suggests first that the elasticity of the response of capital to the covered short-term differentials is not very high, and second that the cost of cover will, in any case, adjust to eliminate most of any change in the uncovered differential. It is to the second of these two factors, the sharply rising cost of covering forward arbitrage flows, that Michael Beenstock attaches most importance.

The evidence for these two features is contained in Tables 9.1 and 9.2. In Table 9.1 it is clear that the forward rate does appear to move almost one-for-one with uncovered interest differential. The coefficient estimate does not, indeed, appear to be significantly different from one. According to the modern theory of forward exchange being fitted to the data, this coefficient equals $a_1/(a_1 + e)$ where a_1 is the responsiveness of arbitrage flows to changes in the uncovered differential, and e is the response of speculative holdings with respect to expected profits. Now values of $a_1/(a_1 + e)$ which are close to one only imply a low value of e relative to a_1. To establish the absolute value of e we need to get more idea of the size of a_1.

Table 9.2 contains estimates of the value of a_1 of only 'around 700', i.e. a one point rise in the uncovered differential (at an annual rate) would induce only

DM 700 million of capital flows, all coming in the current quarter. And, as shown in the conclusion, a value of a_1 of 750 together with a value of $a_1/(a_1 + e)$ of 0·95 implies an estimate of e which is only 37·5.

This means that if the price of DM 3 months forward were to fall by a $\frac{1}{4}\%$ relative to the spot price expected to prevail in three months' time, speculators will only buy DM 37·5 million forward. Such a small response to the expected profits is interpreted as evidence of strong risk aversion, and it is this which is the main factor in providing insulation for the economy from short-term capital movements, as even infinite arbitrage elasticities could not generate much inflow when faced with such an inelastic supply of cover.

But when we turn to long-term capital movements the picture is quite different. No attempt is made to estimate an explicit cost of cover 'there being no forward cover for long-term capital positions'. The response of capital to the change in the *uncovered* long-term interest differential (for a given expected future spot price of the DM) is put at DM 432 million in one quarter, rising to a total of almost DM 10 billion over 10 quarters. So we appear to have the odd result that the actual market in the provision of cover is so risk averse as to virtually choke off all arbitrage flows, so that only DM 37·5 million comes in for a 1% rise in the short-term uncovered differential, while those arbitrageurs who come in uncovered (i.e., cover themselves) are sufficiently unaverse to risk as to sustain (in response to a similar change in an uncovered differential) stock adjustments which are around 270 times as large. The evidence from long-term capital flows is thus hardly consistent with the interpretation given above to the coefficients of Tables 9.1 and 9.2.

But we do not have to accept the suggested implications of the results of Tables 9.1 and 9.2. If one did believe that short-term capital was very mobile then one would expect the cost of cover to get rapidly pushed into line with uncovered differentials, and indeed it is commonplace for exchange dealers to argue that their first response to changes in interest differentials is to mark forward rates into line and then let positions be taken at these new rates. With arbitrage capital flowing with virtually infinite covered-interest elasticity, the determinants of capital flows would be the availability of cover at virtually zero covered differentials. Thus the size and timing of the response of speculators with respect to newly available profit opportunities would determine the size and timing of the flows of capital. The above picture suggests that one could accept the evidence from Table 9.1, that arbitrage pressure keeps forward discounts in line with interest differential, without accepting that this pressure is properly estimated by the arbitrage elasticity measured in Table 9.2.

It is interesting to note that the explicit arbitrage elasticity (and corresponding speculative elasticity) measured by the structural approach applied to short-term capital flows in Tables 9.1 and 9.2 is less reasonable than what is implied for these parameters, for the case of long-term capital flows, by the reduced form approach of Table 9.3. I would, indeed, argue that the structure of the capital flows equation does not seem well suited to measuring the response of highly mobile short-term capital moving at virtually zero un-covered differentials in response to the availability of cover at forward rates determined by uncovered interest differentials. The approach followed by Porter (1972) was not to go to a reduced form but to explain monthly short-term capital movements in terms of current *and lagged* values of the *partitioned* covered differential. Given the bias undoubtedly present in respect of the domestic interest rate and the cost of cover, Porter concluded that the Eurodollar coefficients are probably the best estimates of the true interest sensitivity of capital flows. The total inflows resulting from a once-for-all 1% fall in the Eurodollar rate (with other rates constant) are found to add to DM 5·3 billion after six months, an amount considerably higher than that revealed in previous estimates. The pattern of lagged response is that 25% of the effect is recorded concurrently, with 20%, 15%, 12%, 10%, 9% being recorded in succession for the next six months.

Such results, on West German data from 1963 to 1974 are much more consistent with what Beenstock has found in respect of long-term capital flows and suggest that his estimate of a low arbitrage elasticity at the short end is not as unshakable a finding as his report might seem to imply.

For these reasons, I do not find the empirical support presented for the proposition that risk aversion affords West Germany a high degree of mone-tary independence nearly so compelling as does the author in the challenging conclusions of his most interesting paper. Since I am not convinced by Been-stock's evidence, I stand by my prior belief that the West German economy suffered from increasingly severe difficulties in pursuing anti-inflationary monetary policy in a world of fixed exchange rates and rising inflation.

10

Dynamic Multipliers and the Trade Balance*

ULRICH SCHLIEPER AND PATRICK C. McMAHON

Brechling and Wolfe (1965) argued some time ago that the success of expansionary fiscal policy depends, among other things, on the speed with which aggregate demand is increased. The argument was put forward with special reference to the British stop-go cycle. In short, their argument is as follows: if demand is increased too quickly (so that output cannot be increased as rapidly) there will be a positive excess demand during the period of adjustment, and this is likely to have three effects.

(*a*) Excess demand will partly be switched to foreign suppliers, and consequently imports will increase more than the marginal propensity to import would indicate.

(*b*) Prices will increase and possibly amplify the switch to imports, and the loss in exports.

(*c*) The diversion from domestic to foreign suppliers may not be completely reversible once output has increased to catch up with increased demand.

The purpose of this paper is to construct a theoretical model which displays these features and to test this model on British and West German data. Before doing so it may be useful to put this kind of approach into some perspective. It is well known that in macro-economic models of the income expenditure type the balance of payments can be an effective constraint on economic expansion. This is due to the fact that exports are largely determined exogenously whereas imports increase with rising income.

In a general equilibrium framework, however, things are different since prices, wages, the rate of interest (and exchange rates) will change to restore the balance of payments equilibrium. Therefore, the income expenditure approach is based on the assumption that not all prices and quantities adjust rapidly enough to an exogenous change to restore general equilibrium.

The problem of quantity and price adjustments has gained some importance in the recent controversies over 'Keynesian economics' (e.g. Leijonhufvud (1973) and Grossman (1974)). In this paper we are concerned with the process of quantity adjustments. The argument of Brechling and Wolfe can be interpreted in the following way.

Neither quantity nor price adjustments work instantaneously. If the response of supply is slow relative to the increase in aggregate demand, then price increases are likely to be higher and some of the increase in demand will be lost to foreign competitors (temporarily and/or permanently).

Brechling and Wolfe seem to argue that it is the excessive speed of expansion in aggregate demand created by the Government which is responsible for these 'spillovers'. Of course, the price rises and losses of orders during the adjustment process are the result of the interaction of excess demand *and* supply response. It will be shown that for certain supply response functions the speed by which demand is increased does not influence spillovers at all.

We now construct a model of quantity adjustment in its simplest form.

Let aggregate demand for domestic production be

$$X = A + bY - \Gamma \tag{10.1}$$

where A stands for autonomous demand (including foreign demand), b is the marginal propensity to consume less the marginal propensity to import, Y stands for GDP, and Γ will be explained below. A Government sector can easily be accommodated in this model by redefining b and A. Aggregate supply is equal to Y, and change in production depends on excess demand:

$$\dot{Y} = g(X - Y) \tag{10.2}$$

As long as there is positive excess demand a part of this excess demand will be switched to foreign producers, resulting in a decrease of exports and increase of imports. These spillovers can be temporary or permanent. Temporary spillovers are denoted by $\alpha(X - Y)$ with $0 < \alpha < 1$. These are called temporary because they vanish when $X - Y = 0$. Permanent spillovers Γ will be linked to temporary spillovers, and we assume that the change in permanent spillovers is a portion of temporary spillovers:

$$\dot{\Gamma} = \alpha\beta(X - Y); 0 \leqslant \beta \leqslant 1$$

Thus, permanent spillovers are defined as

$$\Gamma(t) = \alpha\beta \int_0^t (X - Y) \, d\tau + \Gamma(0) \tag{10.3}$$

As to temporary spillovers we assume that these reflect only a temporary loss of orders. Customers prefer not to wait but place their orders temporarily with foreign suppliers. Producers assume that these temporarily frustrated buyers will return once goods can be delivered more promptly. Consequently, temporary spillovers do not immediately decrease the excess demand which producers take as a signal to expand production. Temporary spillovers do not diminish aggregate demand X immediately, but only with a lag in the form of permanent spillovers Γ. On the other hand, temporary spillovers do affect the trade balance as realized imports increase and/or realized exports decrease. If we define $A = D + Ex$ where D stands for domestic autonomous demand and Ex for (autonomous) exports, the balance of current account can be written as

$$B(t) = B(0) - q[Y(t) - Y(0)] - \alpha[X(t) - Y(t)]$$
$$- [\Gamma(t) - \Gamma(0)] + Ex(t) - Ex(0) \quad (10.4)$$

Assuming equilibrium (as defined in the income expenditure model) in $t = 0$, i.e.,

$$Y(0) = \frac{A(0) - \Gamma(0)}{1 - b}$$

and defining

$$y(t) \equiv Y(t) - Y(0)$$
$$\gamma(t) \equiv \Gamma(t) - \Gamma(0)$$
$$a(t) \equiv A(t) - A(0)$$
$$ex(t) \equiv Ex(t) - Ex(0)$$

we can rewrite (10.4) as

$$B(t) = B(0) - qy(t) - \alpha[a(t) - \gamma(t) - sy(t)] - \gamma(t) + ex(t) \quad (10.5)$$

where $s \equiv 1 - b$.

Now let $a(t) = \Delta A = \Delta D + \Delta Ex$. The variable $y(t)$ is determined by the differential equation

$$\dot{y} = g(\Delta A - sy - \gamma) \quad (10.6)$$

and can be solved by using $\gamma = \alpha\beta(\Delta A - sy - \gamma)$.

Hence, $\dot{\gamma} = \dfrac{\alpha\beta}{g}\dot{y}$ and $\gamma = \dfrac{\alpha\beta}{g}y$.

By substitution we obtain $\dot{y} = g\left[\Delta A - \left(s + \dfrac{\alpha\beta}{g}\right)y\right]$ which gives the solution

$$y(t) = \frac{g\Delta A}{gs + \alpha\beta}[1 - e^{-(gs+\alpha\beta)t}] \quad (10.7)$$

For $t \longrightarrow \infty$ we have

$$y(t) = \bar{y} = \frac{g\Delta A}{gs + \alpha\beta}$$

and the new equilibrium income $\bar{Y}$

$$\bar{Y} = Y(0) + \frac{g\Delta A}{gs + \alpha\beta}$$

which is smaller than the income as indicated by the simple multiplier as long as

$$\frac{\alpha\beta}{g} > 0$$

The balance on current account develops over time as follows:

$$B(t) = B(0) + (\alpha s - q)y(t) + (\alpha - 1)\gamma(t) - \alpha\Delta D + (1 - \alpha)\Delta Ex$$

As $\gamma(t) = \dfrac{\alpha\beta}{g}y(t)$ we get

$$B(t) = B(0) + \left[\alpha s - q - (1 - \alpha)\frac{\alpha\beta}{g}\right] y(t) - \alpha\Delta D + (1 - \alpha)\Delta Ex$$

Substituting for $y(t)$ we finally have

$$B(t) = B(0) - \left(q + \frac{\alpha\beta}{g}\right)\frac{g(\Delta D + \Delta Ex)}{sg + \alpha\beta}\,[1 - e^{-(sg + \alpha\beta)t}]$$
$$- \alpha\Delta D + \Delta Ex\, e^{-(sg + \alpha\beta)t}$$

For comparison we distinguish three cases ($\Delta A = \Delta D + \Delta Ex$):

(a) no spillovers: $\alpha = \beta = 0$

$$y(t) = \frac{\Delta A}{s}(1 - e^{-gst})$$

$$\bar{Y} = Y(0) + \frac{\Delta A}{s}$$

$$B(t) = B(0) - \frac{q}{s}\Delta A(1 - e^{-sgt}) + \Delta Ex$$

$$\bar{B} = B(0) - \frac{q}{s}\Delta A + \Delta Ex$$

(b) only temporary spillovers: $\alpha > 0$, $\beta = 0$
    $y(t)$, $\bar{Y}$, and $\bar{B}$ as in (a).

$$B(t) = B(0) - \frac{q}{s}\Delta A(1 - e^{-gst}) - \alpha\Delta A e^{-gst} + \Delta Ex$$

(c) temporary and permanent spillovers: $\alpha, \beta > 0$

$$y(t) = \frac{g\Delta A}{gs + \alpha\beta} [1 - e^{-(gs+\alpha\beta)t}]$$

$$\bar{Y} = Y(0) + \frac{g\Delta A}{gs + \alpha\beta}$$

$$B(t) = B(0) - \left(q + \frac{\alpha\beta}{g}\right)\frac{g\Delta A}{sg + \alpha\beta}[1 - e^{-(sg+\alpha\beta)t}] - \alpha\Delta A e^{-(sg+\alpha\beta)t} + \Delta Ex$$

$$\bar{B} = B(0) - \frac{gq + \alpha\beta}{gs + \alpha\beta}\Delta A + \Delta Ex$$

The different time paths are illustrated in the two diagrams below.

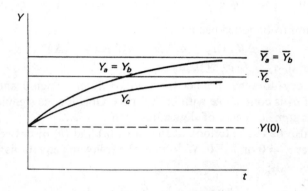

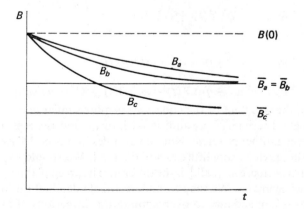

Figure 10.1.

We notice that the balance on current account shows also the effects of only temporary spillovers (case (b)). This may result in losses of foreign exchange reserves and may warrant a premature stop to the expansion policy. If the adjustment is fairly rapid we could use the equation

$$\bar{B} = B(0) - \frac{gq + \alpha\beta}{gs + \alpha\beta}\Delta D + \frac{g(s-q)}{gs + \alpha\beta}\Delta Ex \qquad (10.8)$$

as a basis for empirical testing. With annual data we could expect that $\bar{B}$ is approximately achieved within the unit period.

We test the equation

$$\Delta B = a_0 + a_1\Delta D + a_2\Delta Ex$$

where $a_1 < 0, a_2 > 0$, and $a_2 - a_1 = 1$.

If the adjustment is slow we should take the following equation as a basis:

$$B(t) = B(0) + \left[\alpha s - q - (1-\alpha)\frac{\alpha\beta}{g}\right]y(t) - \alpha\Delta D + (1-\alpha)\Delta Ex \qquad (10.9)$$

The equation to be tested becomes

$$\Delta B = a_0 + a_1\Delta D + a_2\Delta Ex + a_3\Delta Y$$

where $a_1 < 0, a_2 > 0, a_3 \gtreqless 0$, and $a_2 - a_1 = l$.

As the theory does not predict the sign of a_3 an insignificant parameter estimate of a_3 is compatible with both forms. Only if a_3 is significant can we take this as some evidence of slow adjustment.

It may also be useful to look at the cases (a) and (b) discussed above, i.e. where either $\alpha = 0$ or $\beta = 0$. We obtain the following equations:

Case (a) ($\alpha = 0$):

$$\Delta B(t) = -\frac{q}{s}\Delta D(t) + \frac{s-q}{s}\Delta Ex(t)$$

$$\Delta B(t) = -q\Delta Y(t) + \Delta Ex(t)$$

Case (b) ($\beta = 0$):

$$\Delta B(t) = -\frac{q}{s}\Delta D(t) + \frac{s-q}{s}\Delta Ex(t)$$

$$\Delta B(t) = (\alpha s - q)\Delta Y(t) - \alpha\Delta D(t) + (1-\alpha)\Delta Ex(t)$$

Here again, the structure of the equations is quite similar and does not allow for immediate discrimination; additional information is necessary.

There is yet another problem. Not all variables in the model are observable, especially those which constitute excess demand. We should expect that statistical results decrease in quality if the difference between planned demand and realized sales increases. We tend to underestimate demand during periods of positive excess demand and to overestimate this in periods of excess supply. This has an interesting consequence for the trade balance estimates.

ents α, β and g have different values in periods of excess
riods of excess supply there will be ratchet effects in
trade balance. Frequent fluctuations in autonomous
ss income and deteriorate the trade balance.

st to the hypothesis of Brechling and Wolfe the speed of
nomous demand (or the way ΔD is spread out over time)
n the results. This is due to the assumption that supply re-
ortional to excess demand. The timing of changes of autono-
is only important when the supply response function is non
en then the speed of supply response plays a crucial role.

main consequence for economic policy is that Government
should not be changed too frequently. Attempts to 'fine tune'
my by frequent swings in taxes and autonomous expenditure are
be counterproductive.

evident that there remains a lot to be done to improve this model,
regard it only as a first step. The following items should be included
analysis:

(a) On the supply side we would like to consider capacity constraints
d the labour market.

(b) The change of production should not only depend on excess demand
ut also on expected demand. This raises the difficult question of how expectations are being generated.

(c) The most important shortcoming of the model is perhaps that prices
have not been considered. Terms of trade, real wage rates, interest rates have
to be incorporated into the model.

The major difficulty in accommodating these variables in a dynamic disequilibrium model is that the system of differential or difference equations
becomes extremely difficult to analyse. Sometimes parameter and sometimes
even the structure of a differential equation changes when excess demands
change in sign. In such circumstances computer simulations are perhaps the
only way to analyse such models. For these simulations, however, one needs
at least an idea about the size of some parameters. Empirical estimates are
necessary.

This brings us to another difficulty of dynamic disequilibrium models.
Many of the variables contained in the model are not directly observable.
Excess demand, spillovers (Γ) etc. usually can only be observed in an indirect
way. So far we can only present results of some preliminary tests. They are not
meant to give parameter estimates (so far there are too many parameters
and too few equations to do this) but rather to see whether there is some
support for the model or none at all.

If exports get some
closer to the 'true'
hence the coeffi
cumstances. If du
than domestic dema
ficant than ΔEx.

So far we have mainly
generated by excess deman
supply and recession.

There is no reason to assum
ferent for these periods, but it n
different values. The following shal

(a) It is easier to reduce than to
of supply response g is larger in recession

(b) It is more difficult to regain marke
to lose them, and the corresponding spillove

These assumptions give rise to some ratche
cussed by Brechling and Wolfe (1965) and by S
vided some empirical evidence for ratchets in Brita

The main consequence of these assumptions is tha
expenditure creates a more rapid and a larger decrease
GDP generated by an increase in autonomous demand of th

How does this effect the trade balance? As income decr
amount we may expect that the trade balance improves more.
not hold can be ascertained by inserting α', β' and g' into equ

Let $\kappa = \dfrac{ab}{g}$ and $\kappa' = \dfrac{\alpha'\beta'}{g'}$.

We can derive the inequalities

$$\frac{s-q}{s+\kappa} < \frac{s-q'}{s+\kappa} \quad \text{and} \quad \frac{q+\kappa}{s+\kappa} > \frac{q+\kappa'}{s+\kappa'}$$

This means that over two phases of a positive and a negative change of autonomous demand of the same magnitude the model shows a net deterioration in the trade balance.

Some tentative conclusions and suggestions can be drawn from this model:

(a) If there are only temporary spillovers to foreign trade the new equilibrium is not effected by the time path of adjustment, only the trade balance is likely to run into higher deficits, and the loss of foreign exchange reserves is greater.

(b) Permanent spillovers also affect the new equilibrium as the income expenditure multiplier is reduced.

(c) If the coeffic
demand than in p
income and in th
demand will depr

(d) In contr
increase in auto
has no effect
sponse is prop
mous deman
linear. But e

(e) Th
expenditur
the econo
likely to

It is
and v
in th

an

The Data

Our study uses annual data covering the period 1954–1971. All series are in constant prices (1972 is the base year for Germany and 1970 is the base year for the U.K.). *Source*: *Economic Trends* (U.K. data) *Statistische Beihefte zu den Monatsberichten der Deutschen Bundesbank*, Reihe 4. (West German data).

Notation:

Y gross domestic product
A Government current expenditure + gross domestic capital formation + export of goods and services
Ex exports of goods and services
D Government current expenditure + gross domestic capital formation
B balance on current account
t time trend
Δ as a prefix indicates annual changes

Estimation Procedures

The estimation procedure we use is the Rth Order Least Squares RALS package. RALS is a programme developed by D.F. Hendry which enables one to obtain consistent estimates for an equation with autoregressive errors and lagged endogenous variables. In addition to providing the ordinary least squares OLS estimates RALS also estimates for first order up to rth order autocorrelation in the error term, where r is specified. The principle behind the method is very simple and can best be illustrated by an example. Consider

$$y_t = b_0 + b_1 y_{t-1} + u_t$$

where

$$u_t = \xi u_{t-1} + t$$
$$E(\varepsilon_t) = 0$$
$$E(\varepsilon_t^2) = \sigma^2$$
$$E(\varepsilon_t \varepsilon_{t-i}) = 0 \; i \neq 0$$

The application of OLS to the above structural equation will yield inconsistent estimates due to the presence of autocorrelation with a lagged endogenous variable, Y_{t-1}.

Consider now the following transformation

$$Y_t - \xi Y_{t-1} = b_0(1 - \xi) + b_1 Y_{t-1} - b_2 \xi Y_{t-2} + u_t + \xi u_{t-1}$$

and hence

$$Y_t = b_0(1 - \xi) + (b_1 + \xi)Y_{t-1} - b_1 \xi Y_{t-2} + \varepsilon_t$$

Notice that the error term of the transformed equation is non-autocorrelated so minimizing $\sum \varepsilon_t^2$ will give consistent estimates. But note that b_1 and ξ cannot be estimated directly by OLS since there is a non-linear restriction between the parameters.

The preceding example can be generalized to more variables and higher order autocorrelation—the programme handles up to a seventh order autoregressive structure. In addition likelihood ratios are constructed so that the order of autocorrelation may be tested by means of a χ^2 distribution. For large samples and autoregressive structure of low order the estimates will be effectively maximum likelihood estimates. All significance tests are at the 5% level unless otherwise stated.

Results

First we estimate the equations

$$\Delta Y = a_0 + a_1 \Delta A$$
$$Y = a_0 + a_1 \Delta A + a_2 t$$

for 'boom' and 'recession' periods separately.

To isolate the boom and recession periods the index of industrial production was plotted against time for Germany and the U.K. The years were classified as follows:

	U.K.		Germany
'boom'	'recession'	'boom'	'recession'
1955	1956	1955	1956
1959	1957	1959	1957
1960	1958	1960	1958
1963	1961	1964	1961
1964	1962	1965	1962
1968	1965	1968	1963
1969	1966	1969	1966
	1967		1967
	1970		1970
	1971		1971

The statistical results are presented in Table 10.1. Three conclusions can be drawn:

(a) The 'multiplier', i.e., the coefficient of ΔA is smaller in boom periods than in recession periods, and this order holds for both countries. This is consistent with the model.

(b) The model appears to work well for recession periods in both economies. Without the time trend the 'boom multiplier' in the U.K. is larger than in the recession. This runs contrary to our model. However, introducing the time trend (which is significant) corrects this.

(c) The model does not work well in boom periods in West Germany; the t-tests are insignificant and the R^2 are extremely low. We think that there are two possible reasons for this:

(i) There is only a small number of observations.

(ii) As the West German economy is very likely to operate at full capacity during these periods output is determined by capacity rather than by aggregate demand and supply response.

A more efficient approach for estimating the value of the multiplier would be to pool the data from both periods and to use dummy variables. Accordingly we estimate the following equation

$$Y = a_0 + a_1 Z_1 + b_1 \Delta A + b_2 Z_2$$

where $Z_2 = Z_1$

and $Z_1 = \begin{cases} 0 \text{ in each recession year} \\ 1 \text{ in each boom year} \end{cases}$

Thus the boom function is

$$\Delta Y = (a_0 + a_1) + (b_1 + b_2)\Delta A$$

Table 10.1. Estimated regression coefficients and t-tests. Dependent variable ΔY

	Constant	ΔA	t	R^2	ε_{t-1}	ε_{t-2}
Boom						
U.K.	887·184	0·75	—	0·221	0·925	−0·972
	(3·722)	(3·41)			(2·369)	(1·847)
	1120·835	0·441	−320·775	0·623	0·235	0·592
	(2·646)	(2·994)	(4·82)		(1·204)	(2·798)
Germany	20·83	0·218	—	0·082	—	—
	(2·357)	(0·731)				
	19·84	0·452	−0·543	0·104	—	—
	(1·989)	(0·61)	(0·351)			
Recession						
U.K.	359·236	0·578	—	0·736	−0·881	−0·699
	(5·605)	(6·257)			(2·212)	(1·618)
	396·828	0·939	−26·949	0·781	−0·798	−0·789
	(11·929)	(8·673)	(3·662)		(3·206)	(3·479)
Germany	8·608	0·259	—	0·459	—	—
	(2·933)	(2·766)	—			
	13·988	0·418	−0·911	0·646		
	(3·815)	(3·744)	(2·053)			

and the recession function is

$$\Delta Y = a_0 + b_1 \Delta A$$

We do not report these estimates here since they are similar to those presented in Table 10.1. However, there was a substantial improvement in efficiency obtained for the boom period in Germany. The t-value for the coefficient of ΔA nearly doubled, but it was still insignificant.

We also tested the equations

$$\Delta B = a_0 + a_1 \Delta D$$
$$\Delta B = a_0 + a_1 \Delta D + a_2 \Delta Ex$$
$$\Delta B = a_0 + a_1 \Delta D + a_2 \Delta Ex + a_3 \Delta Y$$

Table 10.2. *Estimated regression cofficients and t-tests. Dependent variable* ΔB

	Constant	ΔD	ΔEx	ΔY	R^2	ε_{t-1}	ε_{t-2}
U.K.	329·459	−0·749	—	—	0·562	—	
	(3·308)	(4·236)					
	269·848	−0·741	0·156	—	0·580	—	
	(2·11)	(4·122)	(0·761)				
	305·358	−0·626	0·214	−0·097	0·589		
	(2·042)	(2·126)	(0·889)	(0·503)			
Germany	11·749	−0·195			0·073	1·102	−0·674
	(6·725)	(1·391)				(4·385)	(2·236)
	9·723	−0·218	0·326		0·223	1·114	−0·662
	(4·666)	(1·61)	(1·659)			(4·23)	(2·566)
	9·126	−0·457	0·334	0·124	0·381	1·115	−0·639
	(4·043)	(1·67)	(1·623)	(1·087)		(3·803)	(2·151)

The statistical results are reported in Table 10.2, and we would like to draw attention to the following points:

(*a*) The constant terms are significant, and were therefore included, although the theoretical model does not contain such a constant term.

(*b*) It is interesting that ΔD is significant for the U.K. while ΔEx and ΔY are not. For West Germany, however, neither ΔD nor ΔY nor ΔEx are significant.

(*c*) The contribution of ΔEx and ΔY to R_2 for Germany is 0·15 and 0·158 respectively while in the U.K. the corresponding contributions only amount to 0·018 and 0·009.

Conclusions

Bearing in mind that the model is highly aggregated and as yet a rather crude one, we would like to interpret the statistical results as somewhat encouraging. So far there are certainly a number of other theories which can explain the statistical results as well, but we think it worthwhile to develop our model further and to test it on more disaggregated data. Thus, we hope to obtain more conclusive evidence on the validity of the model.

Footnote

* This paper benefited from helpful comments made during the discussion. We would like to express our special appreciation to Klaus Hennings and Rudiger Dornbusch.

Dynamic Multipliers and the Trade Balance—a Comment

KLAUS H. HENNINGS

It has long been realized that there are cyclical fluctuations in the average propensity to import in many if not most industrialized economies. One way in which this has been explained is to argue that if an economy experiences an upswing in economic activity a gap will develop between domestic demand and domestic supply which leads to increased imports to fill the gap. In their model Schlieper and McMahon combine this argument with the proposition, put forward by Brechling and Wolfe (1965), that such a switch from domestic to imported supply in a period of rapid expansion may result not only in a temporary but also in a permanent worsening of the balance of trade because some part of the demand switched abroad will be permanently lost to domestic suppliers. This adds an interesting twist to their model because it allows them to show that a disequilibrium situation, even if it is transient, results in a permanent change in a 'stock' variable. Once demand and supply are balanced again internal equilibrium is achieved, but there is no external equilibrium because the increased 'stock of lost opportunities' now requires a higher level of imports than before.

The model Schlieper and McMahon present is clearly a first shot at a much more complex analysis which would allow for effects and interactions excluded for the time being either explicitly or implicitly. I therefore conceive it as my task in these comments to point to those aspects of the model which in my opinion would repay further study. This means that I will have to be critical of some of the assumptions the authors make; let me say therefore at the outset that I found their work interesting and stimulating, and that I look forward to further developments of their model.

The model rests on a separation of all imports into three categories:

    (*a*) what one might call 'normal' imports, that is those which are determined by the level of output rather than the level of aggregate demand;

    (*b*) temporary spillovers which arise only if there is excess demand in the economy;

    (*c*) permanent spillovers, i.e., that part of temporary spillovers which are permanently lost to domestic suppliers.

On the basis of this division of all imports and the hypotheses about their determinants the authors obtain multiplier expressions for once-and-for-all changes in aggregate demand in which the 'normal' propensity to import (q in their model) is corrected for the effects of both temporary and permanent spillovers. The main analytical results can be written as follows, employing the same notation as Schlieper and McMahon:

$$\Delta Y(t) = \frac{1}{s + \alpha\beta/g}\left[1 - e^{-(gs+\alpha\beta)t}\right]\Delta A(t) \qquad \text{(C10.1)}$$

$$\Delta B(t) = \Delta Ex(t) - \left[q - \alpha s + (1 - \alpha)\frac{\alpha\beta}{g}\right]\Delta Y(t) + \alpha\Delta A(t) \qquad \text{(C10.2)}$$

Note that the Δ-operator here defines the difference between the level of a variable at time $t > 0$ and the equilibrium value of that variable just before an exogenous rise in demand at time $t = 0$. It will be seen that in the formulation Schlieper and McMahon have provided the propensity to import remains constant: all the change comes from a multiplier changing in time as the adjustment process goes on. This comes out clearly when one considers a case which the authors have excluded: the case in which the full gap between aggregate demand and supply is filled by imports (i.e. in which $\alpha = 1$). Then the balance of trade will deteriorate immediately by the full amount of the change in autonomous demand, and will improve over time as the expansion of domestic supply narrows the gap.

The first question to be raised therefore is why the authors restrict α to be less than unity. No reason is given, nor does there seem to be an obvious justification for that assumption. Indeed none of their results is changed qualitatively if it is not made. Moreover, making that assumption involves making further assumptions. For what happens to that part of domestic excess demand which is not channelled into imports? In a model formulated in real terms such unsatisfied excess demand will raise domestic prices, but this price rise must be assumed to be without effect on real variables for the model Schlieper and McMahon have constructed to hold. Alternatively, in a model formulated in nominal terms it must be assumed that excess demand not satisfied by imports, and thus remaining unsatisfied, does not lead to a decline in the level of excess demand. Concentrating on the case in which all excess demand is channelled into imports would not require these assumptions, and would also emphasize the fact that a full discussion of the case in which not all excess demand is channelled into imports must await the more complicated model with price and quantity adjustments the authors envisage.

Another question to be raised relates to the adjustment process itself. It is assumed that supply expands in response to excess demand, and that the temporary rise in imports does not affect it. This is acceptable as long as the temporary spillover imports are consumer goods. If they are imports of

producer goods, whether capital goods, raw materials, or intermediate products, aggregate supply should be able to expand more rapidly than if they
were not. No account is taken of this effect, mainly because the supply side
of the model remains virtually unspecified. This has some bearing on one of
the authors' conclusions, namely that the speed of increase in autonomous
demand has no effect on the final result of the adjustment process. If investment demand is part of that autonomous demand, and if part of it is spilled
over into imports of producer goods, then the gap between aggregate demand
and supply will be closed more rapidly the larger the proportion of producer
goods in temporary spillover imports. But it is the speed with which the gap
is closed which determines the amount of permanent spillovers. Hence these
will be the smaller the more producer goods are imported as temporary
spillover imports.

Another result by Schlieper and McMahon which calls for comment is
their recommendation that 'Government expenditure should not be changed
too frequently'. The source of excess demand in their model is a change in
autonomous investment, exports, and Government spending. Their recommendation follows only if investment and exports can be taken to be fairly
stable, so that all instability can be ascribed to Government expenditure. If
that is not the case, their recommendation may well exacerbate the problem.
As parts of private expenditure behave in their model in exactly the same way
as public expenditure no valid rule about either can be drawn from it which
does not also apply to the other.

In the empirical part of their paper Schlieper and McMahon try to estimate
the parameters of equations (C10.1) and (C.10.2) above from annual data
for the U.K. and for West Germany. It is obvious that this can be done only
on very stringent assumptions. The most important of these is that adjustment
is rapid so that the differences in their theoretical equations can be equated
to year-to-year changes in empirical data. This is a very strong assumption,
and one will not be surprised to find that the results the authors report show
that it cannot be made.

The equations estimated deviate from those discussed in the theoretical
part of their paper. That makes it difficult to draw conclusions about the
probable size of the hypothesized parameters from the estimated regressions,
as the authors propose to do. Thus equation (C10.1) is estimated with a constant term and a conventional time trend although the rapid adjustment
hypothesis would suggest that there should be neither. Admittedly Schlieper
and McMahon want to show only that the multiplier is larger in boom years
than in recession years. But is the coefficient they have estimated a multiplier?
I submit that it is not, and so little confirmation of their theory is to be had
from the fact that in their regression analyses the coefficients they estimate
show the expected magnitudes. Rather, it seems to me, one should conclude

that the rapid adjustment hypothesis is not justified. If it were, then $\Delta Y(t)/\Delta A(t)$ should be a constant, and this is clearly not the case. Yet if adjustment is not accomplished within a year, recourse must be had to estimation procedures which incorporate the adjustment process.

Similarly in the case of the balance of trade equation (C10.2). The inclusion of a constant could in this case perhaps be justified by the hypothesis that there was a 'fundamental disequilibrium' in the balance of trade at the beginning of the estimation period. But the one estimated equation which comes close to the theoretical formulation does not give very encouraging results, so that again one would suspect that the equation has been misspecified.

To end on a more constructive note. It is reasonable to argue that further progress along the lines Schlieper and McMahon have traced out is possible only by computer simulation. But it seems to me that little knowledge about probable parameter values can be gained from regression analyses of the kind the authors report. For one thing, the transformations which consistent estimation requires will prevent one from obtaining coefficients which can be equated to the parameters of their theoretical model. For another, the model as it stands can be seen as a re-interpretation of the familiar multiplier and import propensity formulae. Even if consistent estimation did not pose identification problems there would be no information which would permit one to isolate the various parameters which make up the (then correctly estimated) multiplier or import propensity. For that a complete model is required. Rather than attempt to gain information about the hypothesized parameters from what is, after all, the estimation of reduced forms, it seems more promising to simply assume probable ranges for them, and to experiment with them in computer simulations. That this is a worthwhile endeavour is without doubt, for the model Schlieper and McMahon have presented is of interest not only because it formulates rigorously some of the ideas which have played a role in the discussion of recent British economic policy issues, but also because it points to the importance of disequilibrium processes for the assessment of economic performance as well as for economic theory.

Bibliography

ALBACH, H., (1969) 'New Trends in the Economic Policy of the Federal Republic of Germany', *The German Economic Review*, 7, 1969

ALEXANDER, V., (1973) 'Neuere Entwicklungen auf dem Gebiet der Geldangebotstheorie', Diskussionsbeiträge des FB Wirtschaftswissenschaften, Universität Konstanz, No. 36, May, 1973, p. 64

ALMON, S., (1969) 'The Distributed Lag Between Capital Appropriations and Expenditures', *Econometrica*, 33, 1965, pp. 178–96

ANDERSEN, L. C., & JORDAN, J. L., (1968) 'The Monetary Base—Explanation and Analytical Use', *Federal Reserve Bank of St. Louis Review*, August, 1968, pp. 7–10

ANDERSEN, L. C., & JORDAN, J. L., (1968) 'Monetary and Fiscal Actions: A Test of Their Relative Importance in Economic Stabilization', *Federal Reserve Bank of St. Louis Review*, 50, 11, November, 1968, pp. 11–24

ANDERSEN, L. C., & JORDAN, J. L., (1969) 'Reply', *Federal Reserve Bank of St. Louis Review*, April, 1969, pp. 12–16

ANDO, A., & MODIGLIANI, F., (1975) 'Some Reflections on Describing Structures of Financial Sectors', in: *The Brookings Model: Perspective and Development*, North-Holland, Amsterdam

ARESTIS, P., FROWEN, S. F., & KARAKITSOS, E., (1977a) 'The Dynamic Impacts of Government Expenditure and the Monetary Base on Aggregate Income: The Case of Four O.E.C.D. Countries, 1965–1974', (forthcoming)

ARESTIS, P., FROWEN, S. F., & KARAKITSOS, E., (1977b) 'Die reale Geldmenge in einer Volkswirtschaftlichen Produktionsfunktion', *Ifo-Studien*, 22, no. 1/2, 1977

ARGY, V., & PORTER, M. G., (1972) 'The Forward Exchange Market and the Effects of Domestic and External Disturbances under Alternative Exchange Rate Systems', *IMF Staff Papers*, 19, 1972, pp. 503–32

ARTIS, M. J., & NOBAY, A. R., (1972) 'The Attempt to Reinstate Money', in: JOHNSON, H. G. (ed.), *Readings in British Monetary Economics*, Oxford University Press, 1972

AUFRICHT, H. (ed.), (1968) *Central Banking Legislation*, Volume II: Europe

BALL, R. J., EATON, J. R., & STEUER, M. D., (1966) 'The Relationship between

United Kingdom Export Performance in Manufactures and the Internal Pressure of Demand', *Economic Journal*, September, 1966, pp. 501–18

BASEVI, G., (1973) 'A Model for the Analysis of Official Intervention in the Foreign Exchange Market', in: CONOLLY, M. B., & SWOBODA, A. K., (ed.), *International Trade and Money*, Allen & Unwin, London, 1973, chapter 7

BAUMGARTEN, P., & WOLFGANG, J. M., (1971) 'On the Relationship Between the Economic Targets in the Federal Republic of Germany, 1951–69', *German Economic Review*, **9**, 1971

BECK, H., (1959) *Gesetz über die Deutsche Bundesbank vom Juli, 1957: Kommentar*, Mainz-Gosenheim, 1959

BEENSTOCK, M., & MINFORD, A. P. L., (1976) 'A Quarterly Econometric Model of World Trade and Prices 1955–71', in: PARKIN, M., & ZIS, G. (ed.), *Studies in Inflation—No. 6*, Manchester University Press, 1976

BERGEN, V., (1970) *Theoretische und empirische Untersuchungen zur längerfristigen Geldnachfrage in der Bundesrepublik Deutschland (1950–67)*, Mohr, Tübingen, 1970

BIEHL, D., *et al.*, (1973) 'On the Cyclical Effects of Budgetary Policy from 1960 to 1970 in the Federal Republic of Germany', *The German Economic Review*, **11**, 1973

B.I.S., 'Quantitative Credit Restrictions', 1971

B.I.S., 'The Money Supply: Economic Activity and Prices', 1972

BLACK, S. W., (1973) *International Money Markets* and *Flexible Exchange Rates*, Princeton Studies in International Finance, No. 32, 1973

BOCKELMANN, H., (1973) 'Monetary Policy in Germany', *The Banker*, February, 1973

BOCKELMANN, H., (1975) 'Charting Monetary Policy', in: MASERA, F., *et al.* (eds.), *Econometric Research in European Central Banks*, Banca d'Italia, 1975

BOCKELMANN, H., (1977) 'Current Problems of Monetary Policy in Germany', in: COURAKIS, A. S., (ed.), *Inflation, Depression and Economic Policy in the West: Lessons from the 1970's*, Basil Blackwell, Oxford, 1977

BOUGHTON, J. M., & NAYLOR, T. H., (1971) 'A Model of the United States Monetary Sector', in NAYLOR, T. H. (ed.), *Computer Simulation Experiments with Models of Economic Systems*, New York, 1971

BRAINARD, W. C., & TOBIN, J., (1968) 'Pitfalls in Financial Model Building', *American Economic Review*, Papers and Proceedings, **58**, 1968, pp. 99–122

BRANSON, W. H., & HILL, R. D., (1971) 'Capital Movements in the OECD Area', *OECD Economic Outlook, Occasional Studies*, December, 1971, pp. 34–5

BRECHLING, F. P., & WOLFE, J. N., (1965) 'The End of Stop-Go', *Lloyds Bank Review*, **75**, January, 1965, pp. 23–30

BRITTON, A. J. C., (1970) 'The Dynamic Stability of the Foreign Exchange Market', *Economic Journal*, March, 1970

BRUNNER, K., (1971) 'A Survey of Selected Issues in Monetary Theory', *Schweizerische Zeitschrift für Volkswirtschaft und Statistik*, 1971, pp. 1–146

BRUNNER, K. *et al.*, (1973) 'Fiscal and Monetary Policies in Moderate Inflation: Case Studies of Three Countries', *Journal of Money, Credit and Banking*, 5, No. 1. February, Part 2, 1973, pp. 313–53

BRUNNER, K., (1973a) 'A Diagrammatic Exposition of the Money Supply Process', *Schweizerische Zeitschrift für Volkswirtschaft und Statistik*, 109, No. 4, December, 1973, pp. 481–533

BRUNNER, K., (1973b) 'Money Supply Process and Monetary Policy in an Open Economy', in: CONOLLY, M. B., & SWOBODA, A. K., (ed.), *International Trade and Money*, Allen & Unwin, London, 1973, pp. 127–66

BRUNNER, K., & MELTZER, A. H., (1964) 'Some Further Investigations of Demand and Supply Functions for Money', *Journal of Finance*, 19, May, 1964, pp. 240–83

BRUNNER, K., & MELTZER, A. H., (1966) 'A Credit Market Theory of the Money Supply and an Explanation of Two Puzzles in U.S. Monetary Policy', *Essays in Honour of Marco Fanno*, Padova, 1966, pp. 151–76

BRUNNER, K., & MELTZER, A. H., (1967) 'The Meaning of Monetary Indicators', in: HORWICH, G., (ed.), *Monetary Process and Policy: A Symposium*, Homewood, Ill., 1967

BRUNNER, K., & MELTZER, A. M., (1968) 'Liquidity Traps for Money, Bank Credit, and Interest Rates', *J. Polit. Econ.*, Jan./Feb., 1968, pp. 1–37

BRUNNER, K., & MELTZER, A. M., (1971) 'The Uses of Money: Money in the Theory of an Exchange Economy', *Amer. Econ. Rev.*, Dec., 1971, pp. 784–805

BRUNNER, K., & NEUMANN, M. J. M., (1971) *'The Monetary Fiscal Approach to Inflation: A Multi-Country Study: The German Case'*, unpublished manuscript, 1971

BRUNNER, K., & NEUMANN, M. J. M., (1971) 'Analyse monetärer Hypothesen des Sachverständigenrats zur Begutachtung der gesamtwirtschaftlichen Entwicklung, *Kyklos*, Vol. XXIV, Fasc. 2, 1971, pp. 223–39

BRUNNER, K., & NEUMANN, M. J. M., (1972) 'Monetäre Analyse des Sachverständigengutachtens: Eine Antwort', *Kyklos*, Vol. XXV, Fasc. 1, 1972, pp. 128–32

BRUNNER, K., & NEUMANN, M. J. M., (1972) 'Monetäre Aspekte des Jahresgutachtens 1971/72 des Sachverständigenrats', *Weltwirtschaftliches Archiv*, 108, 1972, pp. 257–85

BURGER, A. E., (1971) *The Money Supply Process*, Belmont, California, 1971

CARLSON, J. A., & PARKIN, J. M., (1975) 'Inflation Expectations', *Economica*, 42, 1975, pp. 123–38

CLINTON, K., (1973) 'Pitfalls in Financial Model Building: Comment', *American Economic Review*, 63, 1973, pp. 1003–4

CORRIGAN, E. G., (1970) 'Budgetary Measures of Fiscal Performance—Comment', *Southern Economic Journal*, April, 1970, pp. 470–3

CORRIGAN, E. G., (1970) 'The Measurement and Importance of Fiscal Policy Changes', *Federal Reserve Bank of St. Louis Review*, June, 1970, pp. 133–45

COUNCIL OF EXPERTS ON ECONOMIC DEVELOPMENT, (1974) 'The German Bundesbank and Control of the Quantity of Central Bank Money', *The German Economic Review*, **12**, 1974

COURAKIS, A. S., (1970) 'The Definition of Money', Oxford Monetary Workshop Paper, May, 1970

COURAKIS, A. S., (1973a) 'Monetary Policy: Old Wisdom Behind a New Facade', *Economica*, February, 1973

COURAKIS, A. S., (1973a) 'Testing Theories of Discount House Portfolio Selection', *Review of Economic Studies*, October, 1975, pp. 643–8

COURAKIS, A. S., (1974) 'Clearing Bank Asset Choice Behaviour: A Mean Variance Treatment', *Oxford Bulletin of Economics and Statistics*, **36**, No. 3, 1974, pp. 173–201

COURAKIS, A. S., (1976a) 'Bank Behaviour: Theories and Evidence', forthcoming

COURAKIS, A. S., (1976b) 'Monetary Rules: A Note on the Bundesbank's Monetary Target', (mimeo) Brasenose College, July, 1976

COURAKIS, A. S., (1976c) 'Serial Correlation and the Bank of England's Demand For Money Function: An Exercise in Measurement Without Theory', *The Economic Journal*, (forthcoming)

CULBERTSON, J. M., (1968) *Macroeconomic Theory and Stabilization Policy*, New York, 1968

DEN DUNNEN, E., (1973) 'Monetary Policy in the Netherlands', in: HOLBIK, K., (ed), *Monetary Policy in Twelve Industrial Countries*, Federal Reserve Bank of Boston, 1973

DEUTSCHE BUNDESBANK, (1970) 'Longer-term Movement of the Money Stock', *Monthly Report of the Deutsche Bundesbank*, July, 1970, pp. 26–34

DHRYMES, P. J., (1970) *Econometrics: Statistical Foundations and Applications*, New York, 1970

DHRYMES, P. J., (1971) *Distributed Lags: Problems of Estimation and Formulation*, San Francisco, 1971

DURBIN, J., (1960) 'Estimation of Parameters in Time-Series Regression Models', *Journal of the Royal Statistical Society*, Series B (Methodological), **22**, 1960, pp. 139, *et seq.*

E. C. MONETARY COMMITTEE, (1962) *The Instruments of Monetary Policy in the Countries of the E.E.C.*, 1962

E. C. MONETARY COMMITTEE, (1966) *The Development of a European Capital Market*, 1966

E. C. MONETARY COMMITTEE, (1970) *Policy on the Bond Markets in the Countries of the E.E.C: Current Instruments and the use made of them from 1966 to 1969*, 1970

E. C. MONETARY COMMITTEE, (1972) *La Politique Monetaire dans les Pays de la Communaute Economique Europeene: Institutions et Instruments*, 1972

EHRLICHER, W., (1973) 'On the Reform of the Portfolio of Instruments of the German Bundesbank', *Kredit und Kapital, 3*, 1973

ESHAG, E., (1971) 'The Relative Efficacy of Monetary Policy in Selected Industrial and Less Developed Countries', *The Economic Journal*, 1971

FASE, M. M. G., & VAN NIEWKERK, M., (1975) 'Anticipated Inflation and Interest Rates: A Study of the Gibson Paradox for the Netherlands', in: MASERA, F., *et al.* (ed.), *Econometric Research in European Central Banks*, Banca d'Italia, 1975

FEIGE, E. L., (1964) *The Demand for Liquid Assets: A Temporal Cross-Section Analysis*, Prentice-Hall, Englewood Cliffs, 1964

FEIGE, E. L., (1967) 'Expectations and Adjustments in the Monetary Sector', *The American Economic Review, Papers and Proceedings, 57*, 1967, pp. 462 *et seq.*

FELDSTEIN, M. S., & ECKSTEIN, O., (1970) 'The Fundamental Determinants of the Interest Rate', *Review of Economics and Statistics, 52*, 1970, pp. 363–75

FELDSTEIN, M. S., & CHAMBERLAIN, G., (1973) 'Multimarket Expectations and the Rate of Interest', *Journal of Money, Credit and Banking, 5*, 1973, pp. 873–902

FISHER, G., & SHEPPARD, D., (1972) *Effects of Monetary Policy on the United States Economy: A Survey of Econometric Evidence*, Organisation for Economic Co-operation and Development, Occasional Studies, O.E.C.D., Paris, December, 1972

FISHER, I., (1896) *Appreciation and Interest*, New York, 1896

FISHER, I., (1930) *The Theory of Interest*, The Macmillan Co., New York, 1930

FRATIANNI, M., (1972) 'Bank Credit and Money Supply Processes in an Open Economy: A Model Applicable to Italy', *Metroeconomica*, 1972, pp. 24–69

FRIEDMAN, M., & MEISELMAN, D., (1964) 'The Relative Stability of Monetary Velocity and the Investment Multiplier in the United States, 1897–1958', in: *Research Study Two in Stabilization Policies*, prepared by E. C. Brown and others for the Commission on Money and Credit, Prentice Hall, Englewood Cliffs, 1964, pp. 165–269

FROWEN, S. F., & ARESTIS, P., (1976a) 'Some Investigations of the Demand and Supply Functions for Money in the Federal Republic of Germany, 1965 to 1974', *Weltwirtschaftliches Archiv, 112*, 1, 1976, pp. 136–64

FROWEN, S. F., & ARESTIS, P., (1976b) 'The Dynamic Impacts of Government Expenditure and the Monetary Base on Aggregate Income: The West German Case, 1965 to 1974', *Kredit und Kapital, 9*, No. 3, September, 1976, pp. 368–83

FROWEN, S. F., & KOURIS, G., (1977) 'The Existence of a World Demand for

Money Function: Preliminary Results', *Kredit und Kapital*, **10**, No. 1, March, 1977

GEBAUER, W., (1973) 'Die Determinanten des Zinsniveaus in der Bundesrepublik Deutschland: Ein Kommentar', *Kredit und Kapital*, **6**, 1973, pp. 187–202

GEBAUER, W., (1974) 'Money Supply and Money Demand in Germany', Carnegie-Mellon University, Pittsburgh, 1974, mimeo

GEBHARDT, F., (1966) 'Verteilung und Signifikanzschranken des 3. und 4. Stichprobenmomentes bei normalverteilten Variablen', *Biometrische Zeitschrift*, **8**, 1966, pp. 219–41

GERELLI, E., (1966) 'Intergovernmental Financial Relations: The Case of the German Federal Republic', *Weltwirtschaftliches Archiv*, 1966

GIBSON, W. E., (1970) 'Price Expectations Effects on Interest Rates', *Journal of Finance*, March, 1970, pp. 19–34

GIBSON, W. E., (1972) 'Interest Rates and Inflationary Expectations: New Evidence', *American Economic Review*, **62**, No. 5, December, 1972, pp. 854–65.

GIBSON, W. E., (1972) 'Demand and Supply Functions for Money in the United States: Theory and Measurement', *Econometrica*, **40**, 1972, pp. 361 *et seq.*

GOLDFELD, S. M., (1966) 'Commercial Bank Behaviour and Economic Activity', in: *A Structural Study of Monetary Policy in Postwar United States*, Amsterdam, 1966

GOLDFELD, S. M., (1969) 'An Extension of the Monetary Sector', in: DUESENBERRY, J. S., *et al.* (eds.), *The Brookings Model: Some Further Results*, Amsterdam, 1969, pp. 319–59

GOLDFELD, S. M., & JAFFEE, D. M., (1970) 'The Determinants of Deposit Rate Setting by Savings and Loan Associations', *Journal of Finance*, **25**, 1970, pp. 615–32

GOLDFELD, S. M., & QUANDT, R. E., (1968) 'Nonlinear Simultaneous Equations: Estimation and Prediction', *International Economic Review*, **9**, 1968, pp. 113–36

GOODHART, C. A. E., (1977) 'Problems of Monetary Management: The U.K. Experience', in: COURAKIS, A. S., (ed.), *Inflation, Depression and Economic Policy in the West: Lessons from the 1970's*, Basil Blackwell, Oxford, 1977

GOODHART, C. A. E., & CROCKETT, A. D., (1970) 'The Importance of Money', *Bank of England Quarterly Bulletin*, **10**, No. 2, June, 1970, pp. 159–98

GRAMLICH, E. M., & HULETT, D. T., (1972) 'The Demand for and Supply of Savings Deposits', in: GRAMLICH, E. M., & JAFFEE, D. M., (eds.), *Savings Deposits, Mortgages and Housing*, Lexington/Mass., 1972

GRAMLICH, E. M., & KALCHBRENNER, J. H., (1969) 'A Constrained Estimation Approach to the Demand for Liquid Assets', presented at the Federal Reserve Committee on Financial Analysis, Special Study Paper No. 3, December, 1969

GROSSMAN, H. I., (1974) 'Effective Demand Failures: A Comment', Unpublished discussion paper, Brown University, 1974

GUPTA, S. B., (1970) 'The Portfolio Balance Theory of the Expected Rate of Change in Prices', *Review of Economic Studies*, **37**, April, 1970, pp. 187–204

HAMBURGER, M. J., (1974) 'The Demand for Money in an Open Economy: Germany and the United Kingdom', *Journal of Monetary Economics*, **3**, No. 1, 1977, pp. 25–40

HANSEN, B., (1969) *Fiscal Policy in Seven Countries: 1955–65*, O.E.C.D., 1969

HEIN, (1964) 'Mainsprings of German Monetary Policy', *Economia Internazionale*, 1964

HELLIWELL, J. F., *et al.*, (1969) 'The Structure of RDX1', Bank of Canada Staff Research Studies No. 3, 1969

HENNINGS, K., (1971) *Some Features of the West German Financial System*, (unpublished manuscript), 1971

HERRING, R. J., & MARSTON, R. C., (1977) *National Monetary Policies and International Financial Markets*, North-Holland Publishing Co., Amsterdam

HODGMAN, D. R., (1974) 'The Effectiveness of Monetary Policy: A Comparative Analysis', Chapter 8 in: HODGMAN, D. R., *National Monetary Policies and International Monetary Co-operation*, Little Brown, Boston, 1974

HOFFMAN, D. H., (1971) 'German Banks as Financial Department Stores', *Federal Reserve Bank of St Louis Review*, November, 1971

HOWREY, E. P., & KELEJIAN, H. H., (1971) 'Simulation versus Analytical Solutions: The Case of Econometric Models', in: NAYLOR, T. H., (ed.), *Computer Simulation Experiments with Models of Economic Systems*, New York, 1971

HUDEC, C., (1975) 'Experience with the Econometric Model of the Deutsche Bundesbank', in: MASERA, F., *et al.*, (eds.), *Econometric Research in European Central Banks*, Banca d'Italia, 1975

HUTTON, J. P., (1976) 'U.K. Short-Term Capital Flows and the Foreign Exchange Market', *Review of Economic Studies*, 1976

IRMLER, H., (1972) 'The Deutsche Bundesbank's Concept of Monetary Theory and Monetary Policy', in: BRUNNER, K., (ed.), *Proceedings of the First Konstanzer Seminar on Monetary Theory and Monetary Policy*, Supplements to *Kredit und Kapital*, No. 1, 1972, pp. 137–64

ISSING, O., (1974) 'Foreign Assets and the Investment Income Balance of the Federal Republic of Germany in the years 1950–1970', *The German Economic Review*, **12**, 1974

KASPER, W., (1972) 'Stabilization Policies in a Dependent Economy: Some Lessons from the West German Experience of the 1960s', in: CLAASSEN, E., & SALIN, P. (eds.), *Stabilization Policies in Interdependent Economies*, North Holland, Amsterdam, 1972, pp. 270–95

KATH, D., (1973) 'Asset Reserves and Open Market Policy in Controversial Monetary Theory Conceptions', *Kredit und Kapital*, **6**, 1973

KERAN, M. W., (1969)'Monetary and Fiscal Influences on Economic Activity: The Historical Evidence', *Federal Reserve Bank of St. Louis Review*, November, 1969, pp. 5–27

KERAN, M. W., (1970) 'Monetary and Fiscal Influences on Economic Activity: The Foreign Experience', *Federal Reserve Bank of St. Louis Review*, **52**, no. 2, February, 1970, pp. 16–28

KERAN, M. W., (1970) 'Selecting a Monetary Indicator: Evidence from the U.S. and other Developed Countries', *Federal Reserve Bank of St. Louis Review*, September, 1970

KETTERER, H., (1971) 'Ein Indikator für die Stärke und Wirkungsrichtung monetärer Impulse', *Konjunkturpolitik*, **17**, 1971, pp. 349–62

KEYNES, J. M., (1931) *Treatise on Money*, Macmillan, 1931

KLAUS, J., & FALK, H. J., 'Monetary Policy and Overall Control', *The German Economic Review*, **8**, 1970

KLOEK, T., & MENNES, L. B. M., (1960) 'Simultaneous Equations Estimation Based on Principal Components of Predetermined Variables', *Econometrica*, **28**, 1960, pp. 45–61

KOCH, W., 'Steuerpolitik', (1959) *Handwörterbuch der Sozialwissenschaften*, **10**, Fischer, Stuttgart, Mohr, Tübingen, Vandenhoeck und Ruprecht, Göttingen, 1959, pp. 124–36

KÖHLER, C., (ed.), (1973) *Geldpolitik—kontrovers*, Bund-Verlag, Cologne, 1973

KÖNIG, H., (1968) 'Einkommenskreislaufgeschwindigkeit des Geldes und Zinssatzveränderungen: Eine ökonometrische Studie über die Geldnachfrage in der BRD', *Zeitschrift für die gesamte Staatswissenschaft*, **124**, 1968, pp. 70 *et seq.*

KÖNIG, H., GAAB W., & WOLTERS, J., (1973) *An Econometric Model for the Financial Sector of the Federal Republic of Germany, Part 1, Discussion Paper 38*, Institut für Volkswirtschaftslehre und Statistik der Universität Mannheim, 1973

KORTEWEG, P., (1973) 'The Supply and Controllability of an Open Economy: the Dutch Experience 1953–1971', Paper prepared for the Fourth Konstanzer Seminar on Monetary Theory and Policy, June, 1973

KOURI, P. J. K., & PORTER, M. G., (1974) 'International Capital Flows and Portfolio Equilibrium, *J. Polit. Econ.*, **82**, 1974, p. 455

KOYCK, L., (1954) *Distributed Lags and Investment Analysis*, Amsterdam, 1954

KULLMER, L., (1969) 'Problems of Financial Reform in the Federal Republic of Germany', *The German Economic Review*, **7**, 1969

LADENSON, M. L., (1971) 'Pitfalls in Financial Model Buildings: Some Extensions', *American Economic Review*, **61**, 1971, pp. 179–86

LADENSON, M. L., (1973) 'Pitfalls in Financial Model Building: Reply and Some Further Extensions', *American Economic Review*, **63**, 1973, pp. 1005–8

LAIDLER, D., & PARKIN, M., (1970) 'The Demand for Money in the United Kingdom, 1956–1967: Preliminary Estimates', *The Manchester School of Economic and Social Studies*, **38**, No. 3, September 1970, pp. 187 *et seq.*, reprinted with revisions in: JOHNSON, H. G., (ed.), *Readings in British Monetary Economics* and a Committee of the Money Study Group, 1972, pp. 181 *et seq.*

LÄUFER, N. K. A., (1975) 'Fiskalpolitik versus Geldpolitik: Zur Frage ihrer relativen Bedeutung: Eine empirische Untersuchung für die BRD', *Kredit und Kapital*, **8**, 1975, pp. 346–78

LEAMER, F. A., & STERN, R. M., (1972) 'Problems in the Theory and Empirical Estimation of International Capital Movements', in: MACHLUP, F., SALANT, W., & TARSHIS, L., (eds.) *International Mobility and Movement of Capital*, NBER, 1972

DE LEEUW, F., (1965) 'A Model of Financial Behaviour', in: DUESENBERRY, J. S., *et al.* (eds.), *The Brookings Quarterly Econometric Model of the United States*, Amsterdam, 1965, pp. 464–530

DEL EEUW, F., & GRAMLICH, E., (1968) 'The Federal Reserve–MIT Econometric Model', *Federal Reserve Bulletin*, **54**, January, 1968, pp. 11–40

DE LEEUW, F., & KALCHBRENNER, J., (1969) (Commentary), *Federal Reserve Bank of St. Louis Review*, April, 1969, pp. 6–11

LEIJONHUFVUD, A., (1973) 'Effective Demand Failures', *The Swedish Journal of Economics*, March, 1973, pp. 27–48

LOTZ, J., (1971) *Techniques of Measuring the Effects of Fiscal Policy*, O.E.C.D. Occasional Studies, July, 1971

LUTZ, F. A., (1970) 'Geldschaffung durch die Banken', *Weltwirtschaftliches Archiv*, **104**, 1970, pp. 2–19

MCCARTHY, M. D., (1972) 'Some Notes on the Generation of Pseudo-Structural Errors for Use in Stochastic Simulation Studies', in: HICKMAN, B. G., (ed.), *Econometric Models of Cyclical Behaviour, Studies in Income and Wealth*, **1**, No. 36, National Bureau of Economic Research, New York and London, 1972

MACESICH, G., (1972) 'Währungspolitik in den EWG-Ländern: Spielregeln oder Ermessensentscheidungen', *Weltwirtschaftliches Archiv*, 1972

MACESICH, G., & FALERO, F. L., (1969) 'Permanent Income Hypothesis, Interest Rates and the Demand for Money', *Weltwirtschaftliches Archiv*, 1969

MATTFELDT, H., (1973) *Das Geldmengenproblem: Empirische Untersuchungen in der Bundesrepublik*, Berlin, 1973

MIDLAND BANK, (1973) 'European Banking Systems: Balance Sheet Structures and Influences', *Midland Bank Review*, February, 1973

MILLS, R. H., (1968) 'The Regulation of Short-Term Capital Movements: Western European Techniques in the 1960's', Board of Governors of the Federal Reserve System, *Economic Studies*, No. 46, May, 1968

MILLS, R. H., (1972) 'The Regulation of Short-Term Capital Movements in Major Industrial Countries', *ibid*, No. 74, October, 1972

MINTZ, I., (1969) *Dating Postwar Business Cycles: Methods and Their Application to Western Germany*, 1950–67, NBER Occasional Paper 107, New York and London, Columbia University Press for NBER, 1969

MÜLLER, H., & WOLL, A., (1971) 'Zur Theorie der Geldnachfrage: Modell eines Prognoseeinkommens für die kurzfristige Geldnachfrage', *Zeitschrift für die gesamte Staatswissenschaft*, 1971

MUTH, J. F., (1961) 'Rational Expectations and the Theory of Price Movements', *Econometrica*, **29**, July, 1961

NEUMANN, M. J. M., (1972) 'Bank Liquidity and the Extended Monetary Base as Indicators of German Monetary Policy', in: BRUNNER, K., (ed.), *Proceedings of the First Konstanzer Seminar on Monetary Theory and Monetary Policy*, Supplements to *Kredit und Kapital*, No. 1, 1972

NEUMANN, M. J. M., (1973) 'Germany', in: BRUNNER, K., FRATIANNI, M., JORDAN, J. L., & NEUMANN, M. J. M., 'Fiscal and Monetary Policies in Moderate Inflation: Case Studies of Three Countries', *Journal of Money, Credit and Banking*, **5**, No. 1, February, Part 2, 1973, pp. 339–47

NEUMANN, M. J. M., (1977) 'Price Expectations and the Interest Rate in an Open Economy: Germany, 1960–72', *Journal of Money, Credit and Banking*, **9**, 1, part 2, February, 1977, pp. 206–27

NORTON, W. E., COHEN, A. M., & SWEENY, K. M., (1970) *A Model of the Monetary Sector*, Reserve Bank of Australia, Occasional Paper No. 3 D, 1970

OAKLAND, W. H., (1969) 'Budgetary Measures of Fiscal Performance', *Southern Economic Journal*, April, 1969, pp. 348–58

OECD Monetary Studies, (1973) *Monetary Policy in Germany*, December, 1973

OH, A. E., (1971) 'Magic Polygons in Economic Policy: A theoretical Analysis of Conflicts of Economic Targets', *The German Economic Review*, **9**, 1971

OPIE, R. G., (1963) 'Western Germany', in: SAYERS, R. S., (ed.), *Banking in Western Europe*, 1963

OU, C. C. F., (1972) 'Demand for Short-Term Foreign Assets by German Banks', *Journal of Finance*, 1972

PARKIN, J. M., (1970a) 'Discount House Portfolio and Debt Selection', *Review of Economic Studies*, **37**, 1970, pp. 469–97

PARKIN, J. M., (1970b) 'The Portfolio Behaviour of Commercial Banks', in HILTON, K., (ed.), *The Econometric Study of the United Kingdom*, Macmillan, 1970, pp. 229–51

POHL, R., (1972) 'Monetäre Analyse des Sachverständigengutachtens: Ein Kommentar zur Kritik von Brunner-Neumann an der Konzeption des Sachverständigenrats', *Kyklos*, XXV, Fasc. 1, 1972

PORTER, M. G., (1972) 'Capital Flows as an Offset to Monetary Policy: the German Experience', *IMF Staff Papers*, **19**, 1972, pp. 395–424

POWELL, A., (1969) 'Aitken Estimators as a Tool in Allocating Predetermined Aggregates', *Journal of the American Statistical Association*, **64**, 1969

PRICE, L. D. D., (1972) 'The Demand for Money in the United Kingdom: A Further Investigation', *Bank of England Quarterly Bulletin*, **12**, No. 1, March, 1972

PYLE, D. H., (1972) 'Observed Price Expectations and Interest Rates', *Review of Economics and Statistics*, **54**, No. 3, August, 1972, pp. 275–80

REVEL, J., (1973) *The British Financial System*, Macmillan, 1973

RICHTER, R., MCMAHON, P. C., & FRIEDMANN, W., *A Note on West German Money Supply Functions with Special Reference to the Bundesbank's Free Liquidity Concept*, (unpublished draft)

ROSKAMP, K. W., & LAUMAS, G. S., (1967) 'The Relative Importance of Autonomous Expenditures and Money in the West German Economy', *Weltwirtschaftliches Archiv*, **99**, 1967, pp. 127–37

ROSKAMP, K. W., & LAUMAS, G. S., (1970) 'The Demand for Monetary Assets in the West German Economy: Evidence from Short Run Data', *Zeitschrift für die gesamte Staatswissenschaft*, **126**, 1970, pp. 468–83

Sachverständigenrat zur Begutachtung der gesamtwirtschaftlichen Entwicklung *Jahresgutachten*

SARGENT, T. J., (1972) 'Anticipated Inflation and the Nominal Rate of Interest', *Quarterly Journal of Economics*, **86**, May, 1972, pp. 212–25

SARGENT, T. J., (1973) 'The Fundamental Determinants of the Interest Rate: A Comment', *Review of Economics and Statistics*, **55**, 1973, pp. 391–3

ST LOUIS (Federal Reserve Bank) 'Production, Prices, and Money in Four Industrial Countries', **54**, No. 9, September 1972, pp. 11–15

ST LOUIS (Federal Reserve Bank) 'Rates of Change of Economic Data for Ten Industrial Countries', **54**, No. 11, 1972

SCHILLER, K., (1967) 'Stability and Growth as Objectives of Economic Policy', *The German Economic Review*, **5**, 1967

SCHLESINGER, H., 'Neuere Erfahrungen der Geldpolitik in der Bundesrepublik Deutschland', *Kredit und Kapital*, **9**, No. 4, 1976, pp. 433–54

SCHLOENBACH, C., (1974) 'The Stabilization Programmes of the Federal Government in 1973', *The German Economic Review*, **12**, 1974

SCHMIDT, P., & WAUD, R. N., (1973) 'The Almon Lag Technique and the Monetary versus Fiscal Policy Debate', *J. Amer. Statistical Assoc.*, **68**, 1973, pp. 11–19.

S.C. ON NATIONALIZED INDUSTRIES *First Report on the Bank of England*, 1970

SIEBKE, J., (1972) 'An Analysis of the German Money Supply Process: The Multiplier Approach', in: BRUNNER, K., (ed.), *Proceedings of the First Konstanzer Seminar on Monetary Theory and Monetary Policy*, Supplements to *Kredit und Kapital*, No. 1, 1972, pp. 243–72, Duncker & Humblot, Berlin

SIEBKE, J., & WILLMS, M., (1970) 'Das Geldangebot in der Bundesrepublik Deutschland: eine empirische Analyse für die Periode von 1958 bis 1968', *Zeitschrift für die gesamte Staatswissenschaft*, **126**, 1970, pp. 55–74

SIEBKE, J., & WILLMS, M., (1972) 'Zinsniveau, Geldpolitik und Inflation', *Kredit und Kapital*, **5**, 1972, pp. 171–205

SIEBKE, J., & WILLMS, M., (1973) 'Die Determinanten des Zinsniveaus in der Bundesrepublik Deutschland. Bemerkungen zu einem Kommentar', *Kredit und Kapital*, **6**, 1973, pp. 203–19

SIEBKE, J., & WILLMS, M., (1974) *Theorie der Geldpolitik*, Heidelberger Taschenbücher, Springer-Verlag, **157**, Berlin, Heidelberg, New York, 1974

SILBER, W. L., (1970), *Portfolio Behaviour of Financial Institutions—An Empirical Study with Implications for Monetary Policy, Interest Rate Determination and Financial Model Building*, New York, 1970

SMYTH, D. J., (1968) 'Stop-go and United Kingdom Exports and Manufactures', *Bulletin of the Oxford University Institute of Economics and Statistics*, **30**, No. 1, February, 1968, pp. 25–36

SNYDER, W. W., (1970) 'Measuring the Effects of German Budget Policies', *Weltwirtschaftliches Archiv*, 1970

SPARKS, G. R., (1974) 'Econometric Estimation of Constrained Demand Functions for Assets', *Technical Report 2*, Bank of Canada, 1974

SPENCER, R. W., & YOHE, W. P., (1970) 'The "Crowding-out" of Private Expenditures by Fiscal Policy Actions', *Federal Reserve Bank of St. Louis Review*, **52**, No. 10, October, 1970, pp. 12–24

STOLL, H., (1968) 'An Empirical Study of the Forward Exchange Market under Fixed and Flexible Exchange Rate Systems', *Canadian Journal of Economics*, February, 1968

SURREY, M. J. C., (1974) 'Money and the Multiplier', *Oxford Bulletin of Economics and Statistics*, February, 1974, pp. 1–19

TEIGEN, R. L., (1964) 'Demand and Supply Functions for Money in the United States: Some Structural Estimates', *Econometrica*, **32**, No. 4, October, 1964, pp. 476–509

TOBIN, J., (1961) 'Money, Capital and Other Stores of Value', *American Economic Review*, **51**, 1961, Papers and Proceedings, pp. 26–37

TOBIN, J., (1963) 'Commercial Banks as Creators of Money', in *Banking and Monetary Studies*, CARSON, D., (ed.), Homewood, Ill., 1963, pp. 408–419

WADBROOK, (1972) *The German Balance of Payments*, 1972

WALLIS, K. F., (1972) 'Testing for Fourth Order Correlation in Quarterly Regression Equations', *Econometrica*, **40**, 1972, pp. 617–36

WAUD, R. N., (1974) 'Monetary and Fiscal Effects: a Reduced Form Examination of their Relative Importance', *Review of Economics and Statistics*, **56**, 1974, pp. 177–87

WEBER, G., (1966) 'Interest Rates on Mortgages and Dividend Rates on Savings and Loan Shares', *Journal of Finance*, **21**, 1966, pp. 515–21

VAN DER WERF, D., (1972) 'The Economy of the Federal Republic of Germany in Fifteen Equations', *The German Economic Review*, **10**, 1972

WESTPHAL, U., (1970) *Theoretische und empirische Untersuchungen zur Geldnachfrage und zum Geldangebot*, Mohr, Tübingen, 1970

WHITE, W. R., (1975) 'Some Econometric Models of Deposit Bank Portfolio Behaviour in the U.K., 1963–70', in RENTON, G. A., (ed.), *Modelling the Economy*, Heinemann, London, 1975, pp. 457–99

WHITEMAN, J., (1970) *The Theory and Policy of External Balance: A European Study*, B.Phil. Thesis, Oxford, 1974

WILLMS, M., (1970) 'Monetary Targets and Economic Stabilization Policy of the Deutsche Bundesbank', (unpublished manuscript), 1970

WILLMS, M., (1971) 'Controlling Money in an Open Economy: The German Case', *Federal Reserve Bank of St. Louis Review*, **53**, No. 4, 1971, pp. 10–27

WILLMS, M., (1972) 'An Evaluation of Monetary Indicators in Germany', in: *Proceedings of the First Konstanzer Seminar on Monetary Theory and Monetary Policy*, BRUNNER, K., (ed.), Supplements to *Kredit und Kapital*, No. 1, 1972, pp. 219–42

WOLL, A., (1969) 'Die Theorie der Geldnachfrage: Analytische Ansätze und statistische Ergebnisse für die Bundesrepublik Deutschland', *Zeitschrift für die gesamte Staatswissenschaft*, **125**, 1969, pp. 56 *et seq.*

WOLL, A., (1971) 'Monetary Aspects of a Stabilization Policy geared to Growth', *The German Economic Review*, **9**, 1971

YOHE, W. P., & KARNOSKY, D. S., (1969) 'Interest Rates and Price Level Changes, 1952–1969', *Federal Reserve Bank of St. Louis Review*, December, 1969, pp. 18–38

ZEITEL, Z., (1968) 'Government Loans as an Instrument of Financial and Economic Policy', *The German Economic Review*, **6**, 1968

Index